DREAMS AND VISIONS

**Recent Titles in
Contributions in American Studies
Series Editor: Robert H. Walker**

A New World Jerusalem: The Swedenborgian Experience in Community Construction
Mary Ann Meyers

Musical Nationalism: American Composers' Search for Identity
Alan Howard Levy

The Dilemmas of Individualism: Status, Liberty, and American Constitutional Law
Michael J. Phillips

Sons of Liberty: The Masculine Mind in Nineteenth-Century America
David G. Pugh

American Tough: The Tough-Guy Tradition and American Character
Rupert Wilkinson

Uncle Sam at Home: Civilian Mobilization, Wartime Federalism, and the Council of National Defense, 1917–1919
William J. Breen

The Bang and the Whimper: Apocalypse and Entropy in American Literature
Zbigniew Lewicki

The Disreputable Profession: The Actor in Society
Mendel Kohansky

The Formative Essays of Justice Holmes: The Making of an American Legal Philosophy
Frederic Rogers Kellogg

A "Capacity for Outrage": The Judicial Odyssey of J. Skelly Wright
Arthur Selwyn Miller

On Courts and Democracy: Selected Nonjudicial Writings of J. Skelly Wright
Arthur Selwyn Miller, editor

A Campaign of Ideas: The 1980 Anderson/Lucey Platform
Clifford W. Brown, Jr., and Robert J. Walker, compilers

DREAMS AND VISIONS

A STUDY OF AMERICAN UTOPIAS, 1865–1917

Charles J. Rooney, Jr.

Contributions in American Studies, Number 77

Greenwood Press
Westport, Connecticut
London, England

Library of Congress Cataloging in Publication Data

Rooney, Charles J.
  Dreams and visions.

  (Contributions in American studies, ISSN 0084-9227 ; no. 77)
  Bibliography: p.
  Includes index.
  1. American literature—19th century—History and criticism. 2. Utopias in literature. 3. American literature—20th century—History and criticism. 4. Utopias. I. Title. II. Series.
  PS217.U8R65   1985   321'.07   84-8932
  ISBN 0-313-23727-1 (lib. bdg.)

Copyright © 1985 by Charles J. Rooney, Jr.

All rights reserved. No portion of this book may be reproduced, by any process or technique, without the express written consent of the publisher.

Library of Congress Catalog Card Number: 84-8932
ISBN: 0-313-23727-1
ISSN: 0084-9227

First published in 1985

Greenwood Press
A division of Congressional Information Service, Inc.
88 Post Road West
Westport, Connecticut 06881

Printed in the United States of America

10 9 8 7 6 5 4 3 2 1

To my parents, Charles and Ruth
To my wife, Lee, and
To my children, Brian and Mark
—with gratitude

In the days to come—it is the Lord who speaks—
I will pour out my spirit on all mankind.
Their sons and daughters shall prophesy,
your young men shall see visions,
your old men shall dream dreams.

Acts 2:17

Contents

	Preface	ix
1.	Utopia and America	3
2.	Sources of Utopian Thought	19
3.	Specific Problems and Solutions	41
4.	Types of Utopias	93
5.	Utopian Values	141
6.	Conclusion	171
	Bibliography	*181*
	Index	*205*

Preface

The word *utopia* has become unpopular lately. The increasing cynicism of our time, with its dystopias, anti-utopias, science fiction, and the visionary extremes of a nightmarish Marxism—all have produced an antipathy to the dreamer and visionary. Yet, the nuclear age has produced a tentativeness about the future. More and more we are questioning the direction of history. We are in a period of historical change; and, when the old and new meet, history has shown revolution and war to be inevitable. We can no longer afford this alternative. Some kind of intelligent plan, a reasonable model, is needed for the advent of the twenty-first century. Such a plan, before it becomes a reality, is nothing less than a utopia—a mental picture of a "good place" to live and be. Even our process-oriented culture needs a model to evaluate its progress; a means always needs an end. Today, these mental pictures of the good life are no less important than those of the later half of the nineteenth century, for we need the encouragement of knowing that the seemingly idle dreams of that time have become, for the most part, an unassuming segment of our daily lives.

Even so, until twenty years ago, few people, including historians or literary scholars, were aware of the full extent of utopian writing. Edward Bellamy's *Looking Backward* seemed to be the sole reference point. By 1947, Vernon L. Parrington, Jr.'s, book had increased the list of writers to a couple of dozen, but the extent and range of these authors was not truly known until an odd and fortuitous event in 1961.

Late in that year, a group of students in Professor Robert H. Walker's graduate seminar in American social history at The George Washington University were investigating a partially completed bibliography of Lisle A. Rose, published in *American Literature*. Rose promised another installment, but it never appeared. A letter to his office produced a reply from his widow announcing his untimely death and offering the students an opportunity to look at Rose's notes. The next summer, Walker acquired these notes. After investigating several boxes of entries, the students realized the extent of Rose's work: he had checked every publishing source from 1865 to 1917 listing novels, romances, political tracts, essays, utopias, and religious works. In the utopian section alone there were 362 titles. It became clear that even if half of these turned out to be true utopian works, the standard generalizations about this movement had to be revised. A year of reading through these titles produced at least 100 utopian authors, three times any previously known number. From that point on, any evaluation of this movement would require an analysis of the contents of these works.

This book is a result of that investigation. Its aim is to reveal, in as close to their own words as possible, the attitudes and values of these utopian writers, the problems they were most concerned with, and the types of solutions they offered. Though there are many differences among these writers, parts of this study speak of the "utopian" or the "utopian writer" as if he or she spoke with one voice. In terms of their values and their intellectual heritage, they are surprisingly similar. The variety and individuality of their work are best seen in the types of societies they proposed as models for their own day: they range from the most individual to the most authoritarian. If their work is at all representative of the middle class to which most of them belonged, then the ideal societies they proposed tell a lot about the political, economic, and social expectations of the time. As Kenneth Roemer has suggested, these writers may not be totally representative of Victorian culture in America, but their attempt to cling to the traditional values of its older segments reveals the intensity of their struggle. This work hopes to add insight and depth to the growing body of literature about this fascinating and visionary group of men and women who had the courage to criticize the assumptions of their own time.

I would like to acknowledge my appreciation and thanks to those who supported me during the preparation of this manuscript with their encouragement and critical judgment. My particular thanks to Professor Robert H. Walker at The George Washington University, whose steady and supportive encouragement made the entire study possible. In addition, my thanks to Professors Gillert Alleman, Richard Alcock, and Louis Zocca at Rutgers University in Newark, N.J., for their guidance and affirmation; to Sister Mary Tarcilia, C.S.S.F., and Sister Theresa Mary Martin, C.S.S.F., at Felician College; to Mrs. Dorothy Feula, who so devotedly typed and retyped this manuscript, and finally, to the members of my family, my wife Lee, and my sons Brian and Mark, without whose encouragement it would not have been possible.

DREAMS AND VISIONS

1
Utopia and America

Despite the simple and readily observable characteristics that identify a utopia, any contemporary study of the subject must provide a working definition of that word, for the fact is that when, in the last half century, the word became synonymous with all forms of political idealism, it also underwent a constant redefinition.

This complication no doubt arose from the vigorous debate throughout the nineteenth century over the question of what would be the best way to organize society. Defenders of the status quo often hurled the epithet "utopian" at the many schemes devised to end the problems of industrialization and the growth of cities; but ironically, it was Friedrich Engels, often called a utopian himself, who chose to present this word to the public in its most derogatory sense. In an attempt to differentiate pure communist dialectic from other socialist ideologies, such as those put forth by Robert Owen, Claude-Henri St. Simon, and Charles Fourier, he called his own brand of socialism "scientific" while invidiously labeling theirs "utopian."[1] The distinction was hardly noticed at the time except by the most devoted party members. Nevertheless, in the next three decades the communist movement itself and the political reaction to it once again thrust the word *utopian* into public prominence. In addition, the rise of fascism alarmed thinkers everywhere, causing them to create a large body of literature that analyzed the impetus for the popularity of various political ideologies.

4   Dreams and Visions

One of these studies, Karl Mannheim's *Ideology and Utopia*, employed the word *utopia* to characterize all thinking that differed from that which supported the status quo.[2] This extended definition of the term was so widespread among later scholars that it became customary to distinguish between utopian thought and the more restricted meaning of the term as Thomas More conceived it.[3] Thus, in a recent journal, when Frank Manuel described his attitude toward the idea of utopia as both latitudinarian and ecumenical, he included the following types of writing in his definition:

"extraordinary voyages," moon-travelers' reports, fanciful descriptions of the lost islands, ideal constitutions, advice to princes on the most perfect governments, novels built around life in a utopian society; the works of men like Owen, Saint-Simon, and Fourier... and also Karl Marx... as well as a number of contemporary philosophers of history who have ventured to speculate about the future history of man.[4]

In addition to this broader definition of utopia, the recent development of derivative forms of utopia, such as the antiutopia, dystopia, or psychtopia—all of which have been inadequately defined—has made the definition of utopia a necessity.

Thus, for the purpose of this study, the word *utopia* applies to any fictional work that presents an alternative way of life from the status quo by describing an ideal society. The described way of life, society, or culture should be comprehensive—that is, refer to a cross-section of social, cultural, political, and economic functions—and the author must clearly prescribe this ideal society as a model for solving the problems of his or her own time.[5] These criteria separate those fictional works with utopian elements whose primary purpose is to entertain from those whose obvious intention is to provide a model of reform. True, intention is not always so clear-cut; nevertheless, the literary form of a work is as good an indication as we have. There will always be some disagreement about whether a particular work fulfills these criteria; even so, almost all scholars agree that the number of utopias written during the post–Civil War period in America constituted "the largest single body of utopian writing in modern times."[6] Neither before 1865 nor after 1920 did utopian fiction form so extensive a part of the literature of social protest in America. In fact only twenty-four fictional utopias were discovered in the 149 years beginning in 1715 and ending in 1864; whereas between 1865 and 1917, at least 120 utopias appeared.[7]

This absence of a tradition of utopian writing before 1865 in America was partly due to the Puritan antipathy to all things speculative. John Milton himself used the word in its pejorative sense in his famous tract "Areopagitica" when he wrote: "To sequester out of the world into Atlantic and Utopian politics, which can never be drawn into use, will not mend our condition."[8] Even earlier, on this side of the Atlantic, William Bradford expressed the same attitude in his history of Plymouth Colony when he deplored "the emptiness of the theory of Plato and other ancients" after the Plymouth experiment in communal living failed.[9] In other words, according to Bradford, a practice proved its worth after the test of experience, not from any preconceived notion of its ideal qualities. Furthermore, there was little need to propagandize the ideal. It was already incorporated in the Bible, an authority so absolute in its application to daily living that other sources were rarely consulted. Richard Niebuhr added another reason for the early American opposition to utopia:

Seventeenth century Protestants could not be utopians or idealists in the popular sense of the words, for they did not share the fundamental presuppositions of utopianism—the beliefs that human ills are due to bad institutions, that a fresh start with good institutions will result in a perfect commonwealth, and that human reason is sufficiently selfless to make the erection of a perfect society possible. They were for the most part thoroughly convinced that mankind had somehow been corrupted, they knew that the order of glory had not been established; they were pilgrims all who did not expect to be satisfied in the time of their pilgrimage.[10]

Another possible reason for the lack of literary utopias in the early days of the American republic also stemmed from colonial times. If the early colonists were truly endeavoring to create a "city in the wilderness," then the real problem of life would be to reshape that wilderness, whose opposition merely represented man's limited capacity to master nature. But this kind of problem did not require the creation of an ideal. It was only when long-established human institutions changed and presented difficulties that the demand for utopia arose. In fact, utopian scholars have asserted that utopias were usually written in times of great social and political upheaval.[11] Such widespread and extensive questioning of basic values did not take place in America before the Civil War, possibly excepting the period of the American Revolution and the social experiments, such as Brook Farm. It was only with the advent of industrialism and the vast migration to the cities that the traditional values of democracy, individualism, and progress came to be extensively challenged.

The utopians themselves attested to the chaos that threatened their times. It was Corwin Phelps's representative judgment that "in no period of our history have the signs of the times been more ominous or portentous of evil than at the present."[12] The writers of these utopias largely feared that their vision of a great middle class was being destroyed by the increasing disparity between rich and poor. They dreaded the establishment of an aristocracy. The self-perpetuating system of trusts mocked the values of individualism and equal opportunity. Labor unrest evoked fears of anarchy and class struggle with their attendant destruction of morality and progress. Religious and educational institutions, themselves guardians of these values, were charged with indifference to the poor and with slavish emulation of the rich. Thus, the very morality of society was viewed by the utopian as the plaything of an economic aristocracy.

These conditions in themselves did not automatically demand an outpouring of utopian romances, however. In fact, choosing the literary form of a utopia to represent these grievances seemed contrary to the general public's antipathy to any form of idealization. Disparaging remarks levied against the impracticality and un-businesslike qualities of utopia appeared often in magazines and the press. An anonymously written editorial in the newspaper the *Citizen* declared:

Abstract ideas are well enough in Utopia, but until we arrive at Utopia, and it is a long way off as yet, these men need to understand that in order to accomplish any practical good, they must submit to compromises, or waste their work and words.[13]

Even the utopians themselves showed their awareness of the pejorative connotations of their genre. The Reverend H. I. Stern, attempting to defend Bellamy, wrote in the *Nationalist*: "The vulgar, popular conception of the ideal is contemptuous and scornful. It is regarded as the opposite of the practical. A man who deals in ideals is a useless, visionary dreamer, a fool."[14] The clergy, perhaps sensing a criticism of their own work, excoriated this same attitude in their professional journals. Writing in the *Unitarian Review*, Nicholas P. Gilman spoke for the members of his faith. "I must confess my surprise," he said, "at the stupidity of mankind, which has chosen this adjective [utopian] especially to mark the fantastic, the chimerical, and the utterly impractical."[15]

In view of this public disaffection for idealism, it would seem likely that the popularity of utopias abroad might have provided the original idea to these writers. Aside from the traditional literature of Plato's *Republic* and More's *Utopia*, those most popular foreign utopias accessible to the American reader were: Edward Bulwer–Lytton's *The Coming Race* (1871); Samuel Butler's *Erewhon* (1872); William Morris's *News from Nowhere* (1890), written in reaction to Bellamy's work; Theodor Hertska's *Freeland* (1890); and, after the turn of the century, the utopias of H. G. Wells. Of all these books, only Butler's *Erewhon* had wide enough circulation in this country to have prompted imitation.[16] However, if Butler's work did have any influence, no utopian author in America later gave him credit for his inspiration.

Indirectly, European literature had much to do with American utopian writing. Aside from Henry George and the Populists, the basic designs of these utopias were largely derived from European sources. The influence of Charles Darwin and especially Herbert Spencer prevailed everywhere.[17] The utopians themselves alluded to Spencer more than to any other writer; in fact, three of them wrote entirely under the influence of that author.[18] The proposals of the socialist utopians, Owen, St. Simon, and Fourier, accounted for almost a fourth of the designs of these utopias, while other European thinkers, such as Karl Marx, John Stuart Mill, John Locke, and Leo Nikolai Tolstoi, were cited frequently.

An even more immediate source of European influence upon utopian writing in America during this period came from immigrants. Laurence Gronlund, who left Denmark in 1867, soared to fame and controversy in 1885 when he published his book entitled *The Cooperative Commonwealth*. William Dean Howells was known to have been deeply affected by it, and it was mentioned by several other writers.[19] No doubt, this work did much to account for the surprisingly large proportion of socialist utopias. Three other utopian writers, Albert Chavannes, John Macnie, and Solomon Schindler, were themselves immigrants from Europe. Both Macnie and Schindler befriended Bellamy; although Macnie, if the evidence for his relationship with Bellamy can be trusted, could not reconcile his Scotch-bred respect for law with what he called his friend's disrespect for authority.[20]

On the other hand, the utopian writer was not entirely oblivious of his own American intellectual heritage. In fact, after Darwin and Spencer, the most quoted historical figures were Benjamin Franklin, Thomas Jefferson, and Ralph Waldo Emerson. The natural-rights philosophy, derived essentially from Locke and long a part of the American tradition, provided the general outline of thought for a great number of utopian writers.[21] The Declaration of Independence was the most frequently cited political document. Communitarian experiments, both before and after the Civil War, were alluded to; and three utopian writers, Ralph Albertson, Alcander Longley, and Lewis Masquerier, were members of such communities. Ten other authors created utopias in direct imitation of those experiments. Even closer in influence to the utopians was Henry George, whose system of taxing the unearned increment on land values was enthusiastically adopted by many. In fact, the extensive nature of his reforms, proposed in 1879, already suggested the utopian form. Yet it was not until nine years later, when Edward Bellamy published *Looking Backward*, that the utopia became popular. Bellamy's phenomenal success served as the immediate stimulus for 95 percent of all the utopias written during this period. Though only seven utopians supported Bellamy's form of utopia, all but ten of the 119 utopias were written after 1888 (see figure 1). In fact, one-third of all these works were published during the next five years.

Whether or not the writers who published their utopias in the wake of Bellamy's success were merely trying to capitalize upon it for their own profit will never be entirely known. Some writers, however, were at least as interested in correcting what they considered to be the deleterious effect of *Looking Backward*. Paul Devinne was representative of this group when he said:

No, you will find a different world from that described by Bellamy. Bellamy was, to be sure, a clever and inventive man, and had the good of mankind at heart, but his plans would not have made us much happier.[22]

Others—disciples of Henry George or Herbert Spencer—were also anxious to demonstrate the superior wisdom of their partiality. Yet, even though the same number of utopians directly supported George as did Bellamy, none of the single-taxers wrote until after the publication of *Looking Backward*. Even the proud bias of the Nationalist movement itself probably caused a reaction in the form of other utopias. When Bellamy wrote in the *North American Review* that a "book of propaganda like *Looking Backward* produces an effect precisely in proportion as it is a bare anticipation in expression of what everybody was thinking and about to say," not everyone agreed.[23] Nevertheless, it took the popularity and success of Bellamy's initial effort to bring out their views.

No section of the country monopolized the output of utopian writing during this period. Three cities, Boston, New York, and Chicago, accounted for the publication of 60 percent of the works; however, these were the main publishing centers in the country. The most prolific publishing house was Charles H. Kerr & Company in Chicago; however, utopias appeared in

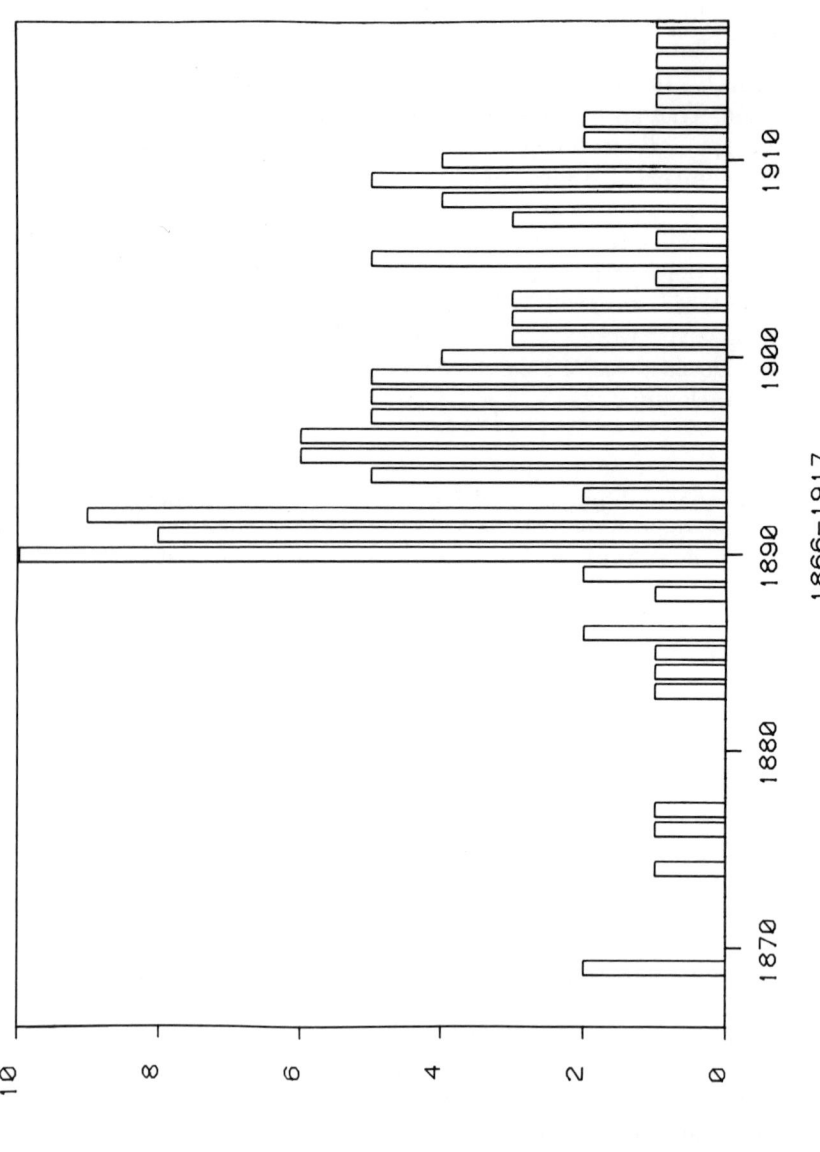

Figure 1
Annual Frequency of Utopias in America, 1866-1917.

other cities, including Washington, D.C., Atlanta, New Orleans, San Francisco, and Denver. Slightly more than 25 percent of these authors published their books at their own expense. The authors' backgrounds were surprisingly similar. Of the forty-eight authors for whom biographical information is available, all were engaged in professional, business, or public work. The most prominent field of endeavor was journalism, which accounted for more than ten writers. Other occupations, in the order of frequency, were teaching, politics and reform, business and invention, the ministry, medicine, and engineering. Thus, if these authors were representative, the utopian writer could be considered a well-established member of the middle class who usually performed work wherein he took responsibility for the public welfare.

Their range of talent, however, was far more extensive than indicated by their occupations. Fourteen writers (John Bachelder, Edward Bellamy, Byron Brooks, Ignatius Donnelly, John Fiske, King C. Gillette, Edward E. Hale, Edward House, William Dean Howells, Jack London, Alcander Longley, Lewis Masquerier, Solomon Schindler, and Thomas H. Tibbles) were considered important enough to be included in the *Dictionary of American Biography*. King C. Gillette was the organizer of the now famous Gillette Razor Company. Byron Brooks was a teacher in New York City when he invented the shift key on the typewriter. John Bachelder improved the Howe sewing machine. Walter Henry was professor of gynecology at the University of Nebraska as well as a supporter of YMCA work. Amos K. Fiske served as an editor for the *New York Times* and, later, the *Journal of Commerce*. William Bishop taught Romance languages at Yale and wrote a number of novels as well. Besides Bellamy, Howells, London, and Donnelly, the best-known figure among this group was Mortimer D. Leggett, Civil War general from Ohio, lawyer, educational reformer, and organizer of many industrial enterprises. David H. Wheeler was a professor of English at Northwestern University after serving as consul to Italy during the Civil War. Later he was president of Allegheny College. Solomon Schindler was a rabbi and radical reformer in Boston when he took up the cause of Bellamy's Nationalist movement. The clergy were also represented in Henry Pereira Mendes, a rabbi in New York City, the Reverend William Harris from Cleona, Pennsylvania, and the Reverend Thomas McGrady, a Catholic priest from Bellevue, Kentucky, who was a propagandist for the cause of socialism. George Morrison described his mechanical wonderland when he was close to retirement as head of the American Society of Civil Engineers, and Arthur Bird perpetuated his dream of America's manifest destiny after retiring as ambassador to Haiti. And finally, ten writers were women, but little is known about them.

The public-spirited character of these writers' occupations was carried over into their stated aims for writing their utopias. The prefaces and introductions of these works abounded with the language of reformers and prophets. "If I had my way," declared a character in William Bishop's utopia, "I would change some things in this world with a vengeance."[24] Each writer was convinced of his mission to establish the correct pattern of thought in the minds of his contemporaries. Richard Hatfield felt that "the ideal should precede the possible,"[25] and Henry Olerich was convinced that "thought is the only power that can move the world in the right direction."[26] After ten years of great popularity, Edward Bellamy defended his use of the utopian form by declaring: "If I could have been more useful to humanity as a fiction than as a reality, I ought not to have minded the inconvenience."[27]

Other utopians took on the role of seers, prophesying that "the last decade of the nineteenth century may well be called the seedtime of the twentieth."[28] Alonzo Van Deusen felt compelled to declare: "History clearly shows that all the great changes which have thus far taken place in the world, resulting in human progress, have been foreshadowed and set in motion by what were first termed utopian or ideal follies."[29] John Veiby intended to "give the floating population an aim"; he poetically announced that the purpose of utopia was to "stir the stagnant waters...converting them into a purifying stream."[30] Later Veiby elaborated. "As earth needs an atmosphere in order to sustain life," he said, "the republic needs a heaven reflecting its ideal, a heaven fostering social reforms wherein individuals imbued by its spirit shall flourish and in turn support it."[31] This missionary zeal, however, was most clearly reflected in the closing lines of Milan Edson's *Solaris Farm*: "May its purposes haunt the minds of its readers like the memories of some prophetic dream, which may not be obliterated, which cannot be forgotten."[32]

The utopian's hopes for reaching the widest possible audience, both educated and uneducated, seemed to foster his indifference to the problems of artistic creation. Apparently he catered to the common belief that art was the concern of a small minority of the population. Edgar Chambless announced in his preface that he was "a round peg in a square hole at book writing."[33] His book illustrated the point admirably. Conscious of his limitations, Warren S. Rehm prepared the reader by disavowing any literary intent. Rather, he hoped to "tell in simple words what we hope will interest you."[34] In preference to a concern for the art of writing, these authors spent much energy on their prefaces and introductions, trying to convince the reader of the truth of their stories. Richard Chapman asserted that "the subject dealt with is life in all of its radical details from the cradle to the grave."[35] Henry Olerich carefully informed, but probably confused, the reader when he wrote that his history was "a romance in which every event is a reality."[36]

Because the utopian had only immediate problems in mind when he wrote, and because he intended to speak only to his contemporaries, the movement declined with the passing of years and the return of prosperity. After 1900, only a few utopias were written each year, and by World War I, interest had practically disappeared. Walter Lippmann, much interested in ideal programs himself, tried to explain why the utopia no longer served as an inspiration to reformers:

Anyone who has been sentenced as I was once to study ten or fifteen descriptions of a perfect society knows why the fashion has passed. They read like the epilogue of Little Eva in heaven spread out into a five act play. They are the happy endings of a drama the author was unable to write. They give the result which is obvious and shirk the process which is difficult.[37]

Ever since World War I, utopias have not been popular in America. The reading public had apparently become too sophisticated to accept a sympathetic presentation of the ideal. In fact, with the rise of fascism and communism in Europe, Americans had been unusually suspicious of any ideology, political or otherwise. Stuart Chase demonstrated this attitude when, in 1928, he derisively spoke of utopia. He wrote: "To seek to describe with clearness and precision the specific target at which programs for ushering in the good life should aim can be an adventure tinged with absurdity."[38] The publication of Aldous Huxley's *Brave New World* in 1932 and George Orwell's *1984* in 1949 added to the popular disdain for utopian writing and made the dystopia a far more acceptable kind of writing. Neither did World War II help make utopian fiction popular again. When Lewis Mumford lost his son in that war, his embitterment turned upon the utopianism he had written so well of in the 1920s. In 1946 he declared:

This belief in an absolute good is the fabrication of people who have no understanding of the human personality, of the process of human society, of the inevitable relative and mutual quality of all human effort. For the kingdom of absolutes is not of this world; human life knows only partial or momentary fulfillments.[39]

As a conclusion, Mumford could only lament that the "spirit of utopianism has not yet been exorcised."[40]

Thus, the traditional form of utopian writing seemed inimical to the spirit of America and its literature except during a brief but prolific appearance in the late nineteenth century. Though the utopian writer drew upon a rich heritage of intellectual sources for both America and Europe, his immediate impetus for writing stemmed from Bellamy's sudden and enormous success. Also, there can be little doubt that if the very basic values of these writers had not been challenged by conditions arising from the advance of industrialism and the burgeoning population in the cities, few utopias would have been written. Surely, Bellamy's *Looking Backward* touched off the spark that lit the whole movement; yet few could deny that the fire was fed by the inner dissatisfaction of men and women who took responsibility for the public as well as their private destiny.

NOTES

1. Friedrich Engels, *Socialism, Utopian and Scientific*, trans. Edward Aveling (New York: New York Labor News Co., 1901), p. 17.
2. Karl Mannheim, *Ideology and Utopia*, trans. and introduction by Louis Wirth and Edward Shils (New York: Harcourt, Brace & Co., 1936).
3. For an extensive summary and critique of modern scholarship on utopia from a social scientist's point of view, see Fredrik L. Polak, *The Image of the Future*, trans. Elsie Boulding, 2 vols. (New York: Oceana Publications, 1961).
4. Frank Manuel, "Toward a Psychological History of Utopias," *Daedalus* XCIV (Spring 1965), pp. 293–94.
5. This definition closely corresponds to that of Kenneth Roemer: "a literary utopia is a fairly detailed description of an imaginary community, society, or world—a 'fiction' that encourages readers to experience vicariously a culture that represents a prescriptive, normative alternative to their own culture." See his essay, "Defining America as Utopia," in *America As Utopia*, ed. Kenneth Roemer (New York: Burt Franklin & Co., 1981), p. 3.
6. Alfred Kazin, *On Native Grounds* (New York: Doubleday & Co., 1956), p. viii.
7. For a study of early American utopias, see Joel Nydahl, "Early Fictional Futures: Utopia, 1798–1864," in Roemer, *America As Utopia*, pp. 254–91).
8. John Milton, "Areopagitica," in *The Student's Milton*, ed. Frank Patterson (New York: F. S. Crofts & Co., 1930), pp. 740–41.
9. William Bradford, *The History of Plymouth Colony*, ed. George F. Willison (Roslyn, N.Y.: Walter J. Black, 1948), p. 151.
10. H. Richard Niebuhr, *The Kingdom of God in America* (New York: Harper & Bros., 1937), p. 49.
11. See Charles M. Andrews, ed., *Ideal Empires and Republics* (London: M. Walter Dunne, 1901), p. vi; J. K. Fuz, *Welfare Economics in English Utopias* (The Hague: Martimus Nyhoff, 1952), pp. 4–5.
12. Corwin Phelps, *An Ideal Republic: or, A Way Out of the Fog* (Chicago: W. L. Reynolds, 1896), preface.
13. "Life and Education," *Citizen* 1 (December 1895), p. 223.
14. Herman I. Stern, "Who Are the Utopians?" *Nationalist* 3 (October 1890), p. 166.
15. Nicholas P. Gilman, "The Way to Utopia," *Unitarian Review* 34 (July 1890), p. 56.
16. Elizabeth Sadler, "One Book's Influence: Edward Bellamy's *Look-*

ing Backward," New England Quarterly, XVII (December 1944), p. 541.

17. "It would hardly be too much to say that the bulk of American 'thought' in this period, measured solely by the weight of printed paper, was not thought at all, but only a recapitulation of Spencer" (Perry Miller, introduction to *American Thought, Civil War to World War I*, ed. Perry Miller [New York; Rinehart & Co., 1954], p. xxiii).

18. Albert Chavannes, Henry Olerich, and Henry Call.

19. For information on this point, see George Arms, "The Literary Background of Howell's Social Criticism," *American Literature* 14 (November 1942), pp. 260–76.

20. Glen Negley and J. Max Patrick, *The Quest for Utopia* (New York: Henry Schuman, 1952), p. 51.

21. Two provocative studies relating the natural-rights philosophy with reform writing during the progressive era are Louis Hartz, *The Liberal Tradition in America* (New York: Harcourt, Brace & Co., 1955), chap. 9, "Progressives and Socialists"; and Robert G. McCloskey, *American Conservatism in the Age of Enterprise: 1865–1910* (Cambridge: Harvard University Press, 1951).

22. Paul Devinne, *The Day of Prosperity: A Vision of the Century to Come* (G. W. Dillingham & Co., 1902), p. 61.

23. Edward Bellamy, "The Progress of Nationalism in the United States," *North American Review* 154 (May 1892), p. 746.

24. William Bishop, *The Garden of Eden, U.S.A.* (Chicago: Charles H. Kerr & Co., 1895), p. 24.

25. Richard Hatfield, *Geyserland: Empiricisms in Social Reform* (Washington, D.C.: The Author, 1908), p. 61.

26. Henry Olerich, *A Cityless and Countryless World: An Outline of Practical Co-Operative Individualism* (Holstein, Iowa: Gilmore and Olerich, Publishers, 1893), p. 39.

27. Edward Bellamy, *Equality* (New York: D. Appleton & Co., 1897), p. 2.

28. Byron Brooks, *Earth Revisited* (Boston: Arena Publishing Co., 1893), p. 40.

29. [Alonzo Van Deusen], *Rational Communism: The Present and Future Republic of North America* (New York: Social Science Publishing Co., 1885), p. 14.

30. John Veiby, *The Utopian Way* (South Bend, Ind., 1917), p. 10.

31. Ibid, p. 23.

32. Milan Edson, *Solaris Farm* (Washington, D.C.: The Author, 1900), p. 447.

33. Edgar Chambless, *Roadtown* (New York: Roadtown Press, 1910), preface.

34. Warren S. Rehm, *The Practical City* (Lancaster, Pa.: Lancaster Country Magazine, 1898), p. 11.

35. Richard Chapman, *The Vision of the Future* (New York: Cosmopolitan Press, 1916), p. 117.

36. Olerich, *A Cityless and Countryless World*, p. 20.

37. Walter Lippmann, "The White Passion," *New Republic* 8 (October 23, 1916), p. 293.

38. Stuart Chase, "A Very Private Utopia," *Nation* 126 (May 1928), p. 560.

39. Lewis Mumford, *Values for Survival* (New York: Harcourt, Brace & Co., 1946), p. 70.

40. Ibid., p. 74.

2

Sources of Utopian Thought

The crisis that precipitated this large body of utopian writing began as an intellectual one, for the utopian writer found that he could no longer comfortably rest on the suppositions formed in the time of his early manhood. He believed in Christianity, but his figure of the kindly and gentle Christ had no place in the acquisitive, self-seeking days of America's industrial advancement. He believed in the dignity of man; but he came to realize that if man were to survive, he would have to merge his individuality with that of the group, the organization, or the state.

By the same token, the Darwinists held out great hope for the improvement of humankind's always tenuous lot, yet they saw the doctrine of the "survival of the fittist" turned into a justification of ambition, greed, and ruthless exploitation. The socialists held out their hands to the great, helpless masses, promising them sustenance and a living wage, but also promising them conformity and the suppression of personal freedom. Thus, Edward Bellamy summed up this impossible choice of values in terms of a historical anachronism. "Ideas are born of previous ideas and are long outgrowing the characteristics and limitations impressed upon them by circumstances under which they came into existence."[1]

But explanations did not remove the anguish of reevaluating old beliefs. The utopian novel was calculated to relieve some of the distress, for it allowed a person to see on paper what he wished to embrace in his daily living. Thus, the writer could more clearly comprehend his own values; he could draw the blueprint for their application to the new conditions of society, and possibly he could find support for his ideas if he brought them into public view.

The utopian novel, however, was not intended to be a logical treatise, weighted down with the apparatus of 2000 years of intellectual history. Rather, it was an attempt to recreate life in simple and mundane terms. Such practical questions as what a person should earn, how he should eat, and how he should spend his leisure time occupied the minds of these authors. Nevertheless, they occasionally alluded to some end, some purpose that lent meaning to all these other questions. In their unphilosophical way, the utopian writers cited parts and pieces of their intellectual heritage to which they attached great significance. Often, they simply assumed that everyone believed in the old moral values, the theory of evolution, or the principles of Enlightenment, and in a number of cases, the beliefs they held without even knowing their source. Haphazard as the processes of their thinking may have been, these writers were bound to reveal their basic assumptions about the meaning of life, and it is these assumptions that constitute the subject matter of this chapter.

ENLIGHTENMENT

As a political entity, America was born during the eighteenth century. It was natural, therefore, that the enlightenment ideas of progress, the perfectibility of man, and the conquest of nature would have a dominant influence on the thinking of later generations. The utopian writer was no exception. He alluded constantly to natural law, order, and common sense. The characters of his ideal society possessed the virtues of detached objectivity and dispassionate judgment. In matters of controversy, this utopian character could sit down with his adversary knowing that his appeal would be to the same essential human nature he himself possessed. He believed reason would prevail.

Hence, the paramount concern of the enlightened utopian was order. The highest principle of perfection consisted in bending unnatural human activity toward some worthwhile goal. M. D. Leggett wrote:

> The world was filled with great activity and enterprise, but very largely it was the enterprise of greed—greed for riches were generally sought by preying upon each other, rather than by efforts to seize the laws of nature and organize them for the advantage of mankind, in converting idle and raw material to beneficient use.[2]

In general, the utopian writer continuously sought to match these "laws of nature" with his own purpose—"to establish a better order of things."[3] He envisioned society in the form of "a well ordered machine which moved without friction,"[4] and he was not embarrassed to borrow a phrase or two from the progenitors of his thought; "all worked together in harmony, like the machinery of a well regulated clock."[5] To the enlightened utopian, "order was heaven's first law"; and to create his heaven on earth, it was to become man's first law also.[6]

If order was the first necessity, the second was freedom from the past. The utopian felt that order was only attainable after the centuries of "invented supersitions and sentimental abuses that marred the welfare of the masses of humanity" had been supplanted with clear, rational thought.[7] "The past is useless," claimed George Phelps.[8] The older an idea, declared F. J. Worley, "the greater the probability it is the product of ignorant and superstitious minds in an undeveloped state and in an enlightened age."[9]

Reason and nature became substitutes for tradition in the enlightened utopian society. Worley replaced the "unenlightened" past with "trained reasoning power."[10] Perhaps the best description of the process of true judgment came from William Fishbough's proposal for better laws:

> If the wisdom of the assembled body should decide that the proposed "laws" are in accordance with national justice to all parties—in other words, in accordance with the *laws of nature*—they may be enacted.... It is the legitimate work of the human legislature only to discover them, define them and prescribe them as common rules of action.[11]

Apparently, then, for this type utopian truth was embodied in the laws of nature, and correct reasoning was the process of matching those laws with the laws and acts of man.

There was little need to define the "laws of nature," because the utopian writer thought they were obvious to all. "With us,...all natural laws are so well understood and so faithfully obeyed that there are no accidents....Everything is governed by law."[12] Chance and fate had little place in the utopia of these writers. If the laws were readily understood by all who had reason, they would be universally applicable. From this it was a short step to universal peace and harmony. The perfect harmony, however, was not always a by-product of this universal law. Often, its application undermined those things done from custom and tradition. When an inquiring visitor asked the representative of Devinne's utopian state when people ate, he replied, "All may eat at whatever hour of the day or night best suits them." When he was further asked if any maximum was fixed for the number of meals, the spokesman for this ideal land cited natural law. "Not by us is any limitation set, but by nature. When a man is no longer hungry, he usually ceases eating."[13] In education, the laws of nature were once again cited: "It was unwise to segregate the sexes during school. To do so was unnatural and contrary to the laws of Nature."[14] Byron Welcome cited man's "natural right to the use of land,"[15] and J. P. Armour felt that since death was decreed by natural law, it was not to be feared.[16]

The idea of natural law did not provide a solution to the problem of evil, however. The only recourse the enlightened utopian had when dealing with this phenomenon was to ignore it. Henry Allen roundly condemned those who conjectured that the "vice of mankind must always endure."[17] The enlightenment-minded utopian had to assume that man was innately good because his whole theory of state rested upon the principle of every man pursuing his own self-interest. If that interest were deemed anything but innately good, the society that these writers proposed would fail. Thomas Kirwin felt compelled to assert the principle of man's natural goodness as the basis of his state. "People are naturally inclined to do right," he said, "if left to themselves. The masses need no regulation. This was long ago proved a fallacy."[18]

Those few utopians who seriously considered the problem of evil happily took comfort in alluding to Emerson's law of compensation. "There is somehow a great compensating law in nature providing for the welfare of all its creatures."[19] They felt that man himself had little to do with the nature of things. "All life is but an expression of truths or forces that are inherent in nature, and are not our own creations."[20] If the presence of evil was recognized at all, it was not considered permanent: "We do not regard evil as being a necessary manifestation of life other than its use to prove that a compensatory punishment follows the violation of natural law."[21] Thus, they concluded that if man obeyed his reason and the natural law, evil was not a concern.

Thus, when the problem of human nature was solved by definition, the chief work remaining for these utopians was to discover the secrets of nature and utilize them to man's advantage. Science was the means to this end. For Cosimo Noto, a medical doctor by profession, scientific conclusions served as "infallible standards of right and wrong thinking."[22] Noto built his ideal land on the foundation of "scientific exactness, exactness of measurement, exactness of time, exactness of degree."[23] M. D. Leggett extolled the method of scientific investigation as "more honest," because it "approached questions without preconceived theories and notions."[24] When speaking of science, Mary Lane came close to worshipping it: "Oh daughter of the dark ages...turn to the benevolent and ever willing Science. She is the goddess who led us out of ignorance and superstition."[25]

Those who postulated the importance of Christian love opposed this line of reasoning. William Simpson, a man who started out as a businessman in California but who ended up a recluse admiring nature, felt it necessary to caution the wilder claimants for science. "At each of these scientific discoveries, we feel ourselves getting nearer to the Deity. A triumph of science with us is a triumph of religion."[26] Simpson thought that too great a love for the promise of science caused people to ignore a significant fact of life—death. To the people who took death into account, "the end comes placidly... in the belief that as we came from the Deity, so in the last we go back to Him."[27] Finally, J. P. Armour felt the need to reconcile religion and science. "The precepts of religion," he declared, "are such as to harmonize with all observable phenomena."[28] In the ideal world, he concluded, worship would be directed toward the "beneficent, eternal energies which pervade the universe."[29]

In short, the eighteenth-century ideals, though pervasive, were not entirely acceptable to the authors of these utopias. They valued the standard of natural law and an optimistic faith in man and the future so long as these did not oppose the expression of Christian love. Most utopians, however, did not consider this opposition a real possibility. Rather, they diligently sought every opportunity to garner support for their ideal societies through constant allusion to progress, reason, order, and science.

CHRISTIANITY

Like every other historically established institution in the late nineteenth century, Christianity was torn between its own long-established image and the anti-traditional spirit of reform engendered by the Enlightenment. The utopian was well aware of his Puritan origins and, for the most part, chose to speak in the traditional language of the Christian Church; however, he was also aware of the anachronistic tenor of his position. His problem was to retain the moral fervor that characterized the religion of his forefathers while, at the same time, to speak of that religion in terms that were acceptable to his contemporaries. Science, especially the theory of evolution, was already chipping away at the universal honor accorded the ancient faith. The utopian himself was disenchanted with the enormous dissipation of moral energy on interdenominational squabbling and doctrinal controversies. Disheartened, much like his counterpart in the Social Gospel movement, he sought to create a new religion in his utopia, hoping to imbue it with the zeal of the early Christians and, at the same time, to disassociate it from two thousand years of religious history.

On the matter of Christian doctrine, the utopian showed little interest. When speaking of religion, few even bothered to assert the existence of God or the divinity of Christ, and it could not be assumed that their failure to mention the traditional dogmas of faith indicated their concurrence. The defensive tone of those few who did comment on God's existence indicated the decline of that doctrine's popularity. George Phelps, an Ohio lawyer, boldly stated that "man is made in the image of his creator," but he found it necessary to add that everyone "may as well confess it before the world one time as another."[30] Similarly, James Cowen complained of those who alluded to Jesus Christ as a "good man":

In spite of your unbelief... there is a God whose steps are heard throughout the universe, whose hand upholds all worlds, and who looks with loving eyes upon all created beings, even those who have the intelligence but not the heart to acknowledge him.[31]

What Cowen denounced among his contemporaries, however, was confirmed by his fellow utopians. Mrs. J.M.D. Bartlett gave expression to the more common attitude:

We teach no so called system of theology. Since atheists, infidels, deists, and trinitarians all meet upon the common ground that the civilized world has never beheld a grander epitome of what is called "living" than that afforded by Jesus of Nazareth, we are content to forgo modern complications of creeds and isms and establish ourselves the fundamental truths taught by Jesus and, better yet, practiced by him.[32]

And so, to like-minded utopians, such as Alfred Hutchinson, Sunday was still a day of rest and devotion; but, unlike the "old Puritanical Laws which taught that one should remain indoors with solemn face the whole of the Sabbath day," it was to be spent out of doors, walking in the country, worshiping nature, God's creation.[33] By the same token, Col. Edward House, the morally oriented adviser to President Woodrow Wilson, scorned his fellow men for not recognizing "the full splendor of Christ's love, the grandeur of His life and doctrine"; but he admitted these things meant little to the "selfish and ignorant world."[34]

The main interest of the utopian lay in the practical application of Christian ethics. He disavowed any resemblance to the religious Puritan of old and was very careful not to cause dissention by any allusions to dogma or doctrine. It was enough for each man "to worship God according to the dictates of his own conscience."[35] The only exception to this rule was Henry Frisbie's requirement of church membership for all citizens in his ideal republic.[36] Otherwise, the utopian preferred the least controversial and most widely appealing form he could find for his religious institutions. When the inhabitants of Costello Holford's utopia were presented with the problem of choosing a minister, they preferred a man whose "theology was of a somewhat mild type, rather inclining to a doctrine of love than delighting to deal damnation to heretics, as was the fashion and the passion of the times in theology."[37]

Despite this undoctrinaire approach to religion, the utopian spoke constantly of the golden rule, the Christian law of love, and the Sermon on the Mount. The appeal of these doctrines rested on their ability to eliminate hatred, selfishness, and war. However, they were not obeyed because God commanded them, but because they served a practical and useful purpose—supporting social order. Love was considered a panacea, a cure-all for the ills of humankind. Furthermore, it was infectious. As Ralph Albertson, an early Christian socialist and member of the Georgia Commonwealth Community, stated:

We may devise reforms as cunning and convincing as Fourier or Bellamy or Cabet, and still men will reject them and refuse to pattern their institutions after them. But whenever love is proved by indisputable sacrifice, it wins its way into heart and life.[38]

Christian service, supported by Christian humility, was the motto of Henry Dowding's utopia. The practical effect of eliminating contention and social hatred was obvious. "He that would be the greatest among you, let him be your servant."[39]

Thus, the utopian selected those elements of his Christian heritage that bolstered his hopes for the material progress of mankind. In the process he suppressed all reference to the doctrine of man's fall and eternal punishment. A representative of Alcanoan Grigsby's Altrurian state declared, "The great mass of our people would not understand your allusion to fallen human nature."[40] Milan Edson was even more emphatic. "The soul," he declared, "cannot be totally depraved, but it can be debased through the body."[41] Even more optimistic was Charles Caryl's interpretation of the phrase, "Thy kingdom come, Thy will be done, on earth as it is in heaven." "It means," he said, "that everyone will be happy, pure, and good, and have everything delightful here on earth as it is in heaven."[42]

Thus, love, humility, service, the golden rule, and the Sermon on the Mount constituted the major portion of the body of Christian belief held by these writers. The utopian was primarily interested in ethics because of his conviction that the organized churches already wasted too much of their energy fighting over matters of dogma but ignored the more immediate and pressing problems of their faithful. The utopians assumed that the only true religious dogma was to create a heaven on earth, and therefore, faith in the unseen was unnecessary. The law of love would solve most of the human problems of life, leaving time and energy to conquer the last great problem of these ideal worlds—to perpetuate life itself.

EVOLUTION

Because the utopian writer was fundamentally optimistic, at least about the future, it was natural that he would seize upon the doctrine of evolution as another proof that progress was inevitable. If Thomas Huxley or Herbert Spencer could be believed, then science lent an air of respectability to what were once human hopes. Evolution guaranteed a hierarchy of perfection, or at least, steady improvement. Even though some unfortunates would succumb to the fate of the unfit, society as a whole could only benefit. There were differences of opinion as to whether the processes of nature could be simulated in human society. Many utopians, nevertheless, could agree to the proposition, "All things have ever been under the domination of evolution and they ever will be."[43]

Allusions to the doctrines of evolution abounded in the utopian novels. On awakening after two hundred years of sleep, a utopian character first asked, "Tell me, what has evolution done for you?"[44] In Henry Allen's industrial-cooperative society, when a character feared the violence connected with the overthrow of the plutocracy, his fears were calmed by the knowledge of where his fellow citizens stood in the evolutionary scale. He was told, "It will be a peaceful revolution...as you have many millions who have evoluted to a fit capacity to direct it."[45] Albert Merrill had no doubt that "all our acts are the result of environment, and of that alone."[46] In fact, the word "evolution" was used so widely that David Wheeler was forced to complain:

[It] has become a substitute for the less definite terms, *growth* and *progress*. The newer word is sadly overworked; we evolve everything these days. From a system of philosophy to a new mousetrap, the favorite description of the becoming of a thing is that it evolved.[47]

Because of the doctrine of evolution, the utopian was forced to see more than the individual at the center of his world. No longer did he view success or failure wholly in terms of human will or character. R. A. Dague, who believed that man was basically good, asserted that "our lives are largely what they are from heredity and environment." He felt that "there were thousands of noble men and women who would have preferred to do what was right, had they not been influenced by those conditions."[48] In the same manner, Henry Olerich extended his advice to the clergyman who, in his view, was all too ready to fix moral blame on people.

I will tell you, Reverend Dudley; we must always bear in mind that a man's conduct, as a whole, always nearly, if not exactly, corresponds to the social and industrial system under which he voluntarily lives. We must take into account the conditions and his culture.[49]

Thus, by making society morally responsible for each person's condition, the utopian hoped to remove the onus of guilt from individuals who failed to raise themselves on the ladder of success.

The utopian who asserted that "the development of the human race is due to the conditions on the surface of the earth" logically concluded that by manipulating those conditions he could improve man's lot.[50] Dague asserted that "the time to begin educating children is before they are born."[51] However, many utopian writers never accepted this dictum. Still greatly imbued with the doctrines of individualism and laissez faire, they were reluctant to entrust any agency other than themselves with the direction of their fate and fortune. They accepted evolution, but for them it was a fierce struggle for survival in which the most capable received the greatest reward. Like Herbert Spencer himself, who coined the phrase "survival of the fittest," some utopian writers were willing to conclude that "the strong are more useful to a nation than the weak."[52]

The typical utopian who advocated Spencerian evolution recognized competition as the law of life. The lowly were downtrodden because they were unfit. "The rank and file have no physical endowments of voice, beauty, or phenomenal skill."[53] This condition could not be changed; for, "an altruism which seeks to repeal the natural law of selection through competition can do infinite harm to the object of its pity," claimed David Wheeler.[54] This inviolable law provided all the incentive necessary to promote the good of society. It ruthlessly demanded the elimination of failures, including people in this category. The motivation of "working for the public good without reward is too weak an incentive for mankind," declared George Schuette.[55]

Not all utopian writers, however, thought unregulated competition was the sole means of progress. In fact, the majority could be classed as "reform Darwinists," who interpreted the process of nature as a cooperative one in which survival was dependent on the strong helping the weak. As Byron Brooks declared: "Society is not constructed like a cake in longitudinal layers, with the frosting on top; but like a tower, the strong supporting the weak."[56] G. W. Woodridge opposed the idea that natural selection allowed the best people to survive. "War, religious persecution, and the devastations of nature have destroyed the intellectually and morally best."[57] Another tenet of Spencerian evolution—that all men faced the same struggle for survival equally—was attacked by Henry Call. "Surely," he wrote, "it cannot for a moment be pretended that either the speculator cornering the market or the trust, still more effectively controlling it, are engaged in any struggle for existence like that of the common laborer."[58] Thus, in the eyes of many writers it was clear that the struggle for survival was not the same for all, and that the best people did not always survive.

There were further reservations about the law of the survival of the fittest. It not only made men seem little more than a highly automated animal, but also "put not only the necessities of life, but liberty and life itself up as a gambling stake to be won and lost in a manner well fitted to finally end civilization."[59] Rather, the utopian who took this position looked forward to seeing the world evolve to a state wherein "no conscious life is taken to support another life; no blood is let for our refreshment, and no minutest creature is pursued and slain to appease the appetite of its strongest neighbor."[60] The Christian law of love ameliorated the harsher aspects of the "conservative Darwinist" thesis.

The idea of evolution, though acceptable in part to both conservative and reform-minded utopians, was opposed by those few who saw that it was an attack upon the Bible. It was possible for even the mild believer to react against such an extreme claim as that of Cosimo Noto: "There can be no greater mistake of the human mind than one which leads us to believe that the bible is a direct revelation of God."[61] For the most part, the reaction was moderate though M. D. Leggett readily admitted that "modern science has made great progress in discovering no law of inorganic matter that could evolve the organic."[62] The conservative, Edward House, had a similar reservation. He agreed that the evolutionists "went far in the right direction [but] in trying to go to the very fountainhead of life, they came to a door they could not open."[63] Thus, a small minority of utopians rejected the part of the doctrine of evolution that opposed the idea of God's creation or the divine inspiration of the Bible, but their language indicated an acceptance of the overall idea of utopia as part of the prevailing thought of the day.

Because of this fact, most writers attempted to reconcile the opposition of science and religion. Fortunately, the doctrine of God's immanent will came to be interpreted by social-minded, religious leaders as a sign that God had a clear hand in the development of human destiny. Hence, the heavenly powers assured man's evolution to a millennial state. Henry F. Allen, a perennial reformer, gave credence to this view when he said, "All manifestations of the spiritual and physical are subject to fixed laws of evolution, and we comprehend truths in direct ratio with our moral progress."[64]

The orthodox utopian writers, therefore, allowed their optimistic belief in progress, especially when supported by certain tenets of their faith, to override what they came to regard as a minor theological objection. They were willing to look askance at a strict interpretation of the Bible just as, long ago, they were willing to forget about the doctrine of man's innate depravity. They looked forward to "ennobling ends, not to selfish purposes."[65] Like Herbert Spencer, some utopians supported the idea that "the higher civilization evolves, the less law is needed."[66] Law was a sign of man's weakness, and as man evolved into a stronger being, so too, his need for law would lessen.

Thus, the utopian accepted the doctrine of evolution as one of the dominant theories of his time. Although Spencer, in preference to Darwin or Huxley, was the source of their belief, the greater proportion of utopians did not accept Spencer's idea of the survival of the fittest. Rather, they perceived within the doctrine of evolution the inherent need for human cooperation and the necessity for the strong helping the weak. Evolution was regarded only in its most general sense of a steadily improving life on earth as time went on.

SOCIALISM

At this time in America, there was no clear-cut distinction among the various forms of socialism. The word seemd to cover a wide variety of ideas: anarchism, "communitarianism" (to employ Arthur Bestor's suggested substitute for the word *communism* in its nineteenth-century sense), utopian socialism, Populism, Nationalism, and "scientific" or Marxian socialism.

The only attribute they had in common was the radical character imputed to them by the general public, and for this reason, few utopians were willing to apply the label "socialist" to their ideal schemes.

Nevertheless, two writers, Cosimo Noto and Richard Hatfield, clearly identified themselves as Marxists. Two others, James Alexander and John Bachelder, favorably cited Marx and Engels. At least seven others called themselves socialists, and another ten could be considered socialists by virtue of the political organization of their utopias. Thus, about twenty, or one-fifth of the utopian writers of this period, could be called socialists in the most general sense. Though their ideals stemmed from many different sources, these utopians agreed to the general proposition that there should be some centralized control over labor and capital to bring about a more equitable distribution of wealth.

Within these limits, however, there were many differences of opinion. Richard Hatfield most nearly represented the Marxian ideal when he asked for a "complete organization of the people by the people for the people's best interests." The motto of his state was, "From each according to his ability, to each according to his need."[67] On the other hand, Daniel Bond derived his notion of socialism from Populism. He defined it as the "privilege of marketing such products as you are willing to trust to your government, and permitting the hungry and naked to feed themselves through government warehouses."[68]

The reconciliation of individualism with socialism caused many other differences of opinion within this group. Edgar Chambless fully believed that "the lamb of socialism shall lie down with the leopard of individuality."[69] Perhaps the use of biblical language indicated that Chambless was relying upon some miraculous power to effect this incongruous union. The socialism in his ideal state, however, was quite permissive. It was one in which "people can be together when they wished, and alone when they wished."[70] Conversely, Henry Frisbie viewed individualism as the antithesis of everything he stood for. As a follower of Eugene Debs, he condemned individualism as the source of a modern Tower of Babel. In biblical phraseology, he intoned: "By competition from tongues they were confounded, and labor without government failed utterly."[71] In fact, he even required all Christians to be socialists, for he said, "Ye cannot be one except ye be the other."[72]

One definition of socialism that would probably be acceptable to this entire group was offered by the anonymous author of *Man or Dollar, Which?*:

> To those who understand and are not frightened by the bugbear of a mere name, socialism means, and means nothing else, a theory of social relations among men by which there may be secured a more just and equitable distribution of opportunity, labor, and the products of labor.[73]

Certainly, all could agree that socialism did not mean anarchy. "They are as different as black and white, and convey exactly opposite meanings," claimed William S. Child. The fallacy, he said, of aligning socialism with anarchy stemmed from the "plutocracy and the hireling press."[74] Neither did the socialist utopian accept a definition of socialism that declared that "all persons should have just what they produce, or its equivalent, and no more."[75] This, said C. S. Griffin, was the doctrine of "semi-socialists," who falsely believed all men were born equal in ability as well as in nature. This thinking was recognized as the basis of the idea of competition—the very idea the socialist utopian opposed.

Though the socialist utopian was an outspoken critic of laissez-faire capitalism, he met a wall of opposition when he tried to undermine its foundation, namely, the entrenched idea of individual freedom. One utopian, who was attracted to socialism because it fostered "common justice" among men, excluded from his ideal state any part of socialism that meant that "men shall range themselves under military discipline as the employees of the state."[76] Albert Merrill, a disciple of Herbert Spencer, vehemently denounced socialism, which, he said, "if given full power, would force a country into one evil while trying to save it from another."[77] The evil cited by Merrill was the same for Alfred Hutchinson, that of making the individual "a mere puppet in the hands of government."[78] For this reason, too, Zebina Forbush declared, "I have never been a friend to political socialism as a factor in building up the cooperative Commonwealth."[79]

The individualist opposed socialism because he believed the purpose of government to be a negative one. Government's true function was "to direct or restrain the acts of individuals of whom, for whom and by whom the government was created."[80] The thing to be avoided was paternalism. Edward House fully believed that socialism would completely stifle human motivation:

> If we had pure socialism, we could never get the highest endeavor out of anyone, for it would seem not worthwhile to do more than the average. The race would then go backward instead of lifting itself higher by the insistent desire to excel and to reap the rich reward that comes with success.[81]

Even if the individualist sympathized with the socialist argument, as did David Wheeler, he inevitably concluded that it was unworkable, because the socialist "left human nature out of his system."[82]

The socialist utopians themselves recognized that their system might have shortcomings when dealing with human motivation. Clark Persinger, editor of the socialist publication *The Rebel* and a professor at the University of Nebraska, declared that "old time communism... rejected altogether the principle of competition and removed from life all ambition and much interest; modern socialism has wisely recognized this and is attempting to utilize the competitive idea." Though he did not say how this would be accomplished, he was careful to announce that this competition would be "beneficial instead of injurious to the social well-being of the people."[83] Ralph Albertson, a participant in the Georgia Commonwealth community, felt that the mechanism of altruism would remove the stifling quality of socialism. "A socialist cannot be a self-seeker," he asserted.[84]

Yet, it seemed that the individualist utopian had the last say. The problem of allowing maximum freedom to individuals in a highly organized state was not thoroughly explored by the socialist utopian. He either relied on each person's spirit of self-sacrifice or thought that the justice of redistributing the product of labor on a more equitable basis would allay any objections. Nevertheless, in one mildly socialistic utopia by Albert Chavannes, there was a character who probably spoke for the majority of the people of the time when he said, "I want some time to be my own master and have more breathing room."[85]

Thus, the majority of utopians were not willing to submit to what they regarded as the constrictive air of a socialist state. In the intellectual atmosphere of the time, imbued, as it was, with notions of progress, equality, individualism, and laissez-faire economics, it was natural for most people to think in terms of individuals. Socialism did not simply offer an alternative political structure; it suggested a basic change in the way one regarded society. It asked that an individual evaluate everything in terms of his relationship to others rather than by regarding his own interests as ends in themselves. Such a radical change could hardly be expected without long and elaborate preparation; however, significantly, 20 percent (40 percent including the nationalist and populist utopians) of the utopian writers made this basic alteration in their thinking.

In conclusion, the utopian writer fully demonstrated his awareness of the major intellectual systems of his time, but he found something objectionable in each of them. His optimistic hopes for the future made him susceptible to the enlightenment values of human perfectibility, progress, and universal natural law. In the same manner, the idea of evolution and Christian millennianism appealed to him. However, when the utopian saw that the detachment required for the scientific method precluded his commitment to the Christian law of love, he demurred. Similarly, when his commitment to the spirit of Christianity required his belief in the depravity of man and a spirit of otherworldliness, he objected. Likewise, the utopian who espoused the cause of socialism was careful to point out his concern for individual differences. And finally, when it came to supporting the doctrine of evolution, the utopian did his best to avoid the mention of strife, struggle, and natural selection; instead, he emphasized cooperation.

In the most important intellectual dilemma for the utopian—how to reconcile individual freedom with the need for survival—he faced similar difficulties. A clear majority, supporting the Christian emphasis on human will and responsibility as well as the enlightenment doctrine of man's innate goodness, were on the side of the individual. However, most writers took exception to the idea of making self-interest the sole basis of the economic order. By the same token, when the laissez-faire implications of the theory of evolution were painted in their extreme form of incessant biological warfare, the majority of writers preferred the evils of an excessively organized central authority. Significantly, in a time when being a socialist was tantamount to being an outcast, fully one-fifth of these writers chose to call their ideal societies socialistic. And even though Bellamy and the populist utopians went to great lengths to avoid that label, their systems were also excoriated for their resemblance to that idea. Still, these writers clearly saw that for the future an individual-centered state would be unworkable, even though they regretted the loss of individualism.

NOTES

1. Edward Bellamy, *Equality* (New York: D. Appleton & Co., 1897), p. 18.
2. Mortimer D. Leggett, *A Dream of a Modest Prophet* (Philadelphia: J. B. Lippincott & Co., 1890), p. 39.
3. J. P. Armour, *Edenindia* (New York: G. W. Dillingham Co., 1905), p. 34.
4. Solomon Schindler, *Young West* (Boston: Arena Publishing Co., 1894), p. 267.
5. [Henry F. Allen], *The Key of Industrial Co-operative Government* (St. Louis: The Author, 1886), p. 47.
6. Ephraim Peterson, *An Ideal City For An Ideal People* (Independence, Mo.: The Author, 1905), p. 19.
7. Armour, *Edenindia*, p. 99.
8. George H. Phelps, *The New Columbia; or, The Re-United States* (Findlay, OH: New Columbia Publishing Co., 1909), p. 1.
9. [F. U. Worley], *Three Thousand Dollars a Year: Moving Forward; or, How We Got There* (Washington, D.C.: J. P. Wright, 1890), p. 94.
10. Ibid., p. 93.
11. William Fishbough, *America and the World* (New York: Continental Publishing Co., 1898), p. 310.
12. James Cowen, *Daybreak: A Romance of an Old World* (New York: George H. Richmond & Co., 1896), p. 64.

Sources of Utopian Thought   37

13. Paul Devinne, *The Day of Prosperity: A Vision of the Century to Come* (New York: G. W. Dillingham & Co., 1902), p. 123.
14. Alfred Hutchinson, *The Limit of Wealth* (New York: Macmillan Co., 1907), p. 122.
15. Byron Welcome, *From Earth's Center: A Polar Gateway Message* (Chicago: Charles H. Kerr & Co., 1894), p. 125.
16. Armour, *Edenindia*, p. 188.
17. [Allen], *The Key*, p. 2.
18. Thomas Kirwin, *Reciprocity in the Thirtieth Century: The Coming Cooperative Age* (New York: Cochrane Publishing Co., 1909), p. 76.
19. D. L. Stump, *From World to World* (Asbury, Mo.: World to World Publishing Co., 1896), p. 59.
20. [Allen], *The Key*, p. 71.
21. Ibid., p. 7.
22. Cosimo Noto, *The Ideal City* (New York, n.p., 1904), p. 76.
23. Ibid., p. 197.
24. Leggett, *A Dream*, p. 43.
25. [Mary Lane], *Mizora, A Prophesy* (New York: G. W. Dillingham & Co., 1889), p. 132.
26. William Simpson, *The Man From Mars* (San Francisco: Bacon & Co., 1891), p. 54.
27. Ibid., p. 96.
28. Armour, *Edenindia*, p. 74.
29. Ibid., p. 136.
30. Phelps, *The New Columbia*, p. 30.
31. Cowen, *Daybreak*, p. 173.
32. J.M.D. Bartlett, *A New Aristocracy* (n.p.: Bartlett Publishing Co., 1891), p. 29.
33. Hutchinson, *The Limit of Wealth*, p. 259.
34. [Edward M. House], *Philip Dru, Administrator: A Story of Tomorrow, 1920–1935* (New York: B. W. Huebach, 1912), p. 13.
35. Charles W. Caryl, *New Era* (Denver: The New Era Union, 1897), p. 151.
36. Henry S. Frisbie, *Prophet of the Kingdom* (Washington, D.C.: The Neale Publishing Co., 1901), p. 168.
37. Costello Holford, *Aristopia* (Boston: Arena Publishing Co., 1895), pp. 82–83.
38. Ralph Albertson, *The Social Incarnation* (Commonwealth, Ga.: Christian Commonwealth, 1899) pp. 12–13.
39. Henry W. Dowding, *The Man From Mars; or, Service For Service's Sake* (New York: Cochrane Publishing Co., 1910), p. 7.

38   Dreams and Visions

40. Alcanoan Grigsby, *Nequa; or, The Problem of the Ages* (Topeka, Kans.: Equity Publishing Co., 1900), p. 74.
41. Milan G. Edson, *Solaris Farm, A Story of the Twentieth Century* (Washington, D.C.: The Author, 1900), p. 382.
42. Caryl, *New Era*, p. 90.
43. James B. Alexander, *The Lunarian Professor* (Minneapolis: n.p., 1909), p. vi.
44. Winnifred H. Cooley, "A Dream of the Twenty-First Century," *The Arena* 28 (November 1902), p. 512.
45. [Allen], *The Key*, p. 49.
46. Albert A. Merrill, *The Great Awakening* (Boston: George Book Publishing Co., 1899), p. 114.
47. David H. Wheeler, *Our Industrial Utopia and Its Unhappy Citizens* (Chicago: A. C. McClurg & Co., 1895), p. 10.
48. Robert A. Dague, *Henry Ashton* (Alameda, Calif.: The Author, 1903), p. 230.
49. Henry Olerich, *A Cityless and Countryless World: An Outline of Practical Co-Operative Individualism* (Holstein, Iowa: Gilmore & Olerich, 1893), p. 215.
50. Welcome, *From Earth's Center*, p. 136.
51. Dague, *Henry Ashton*, p. 206.
52. H. George Schuette, *Athonia: or, The Original Four Hundred* (Manitowoc, Wisc.: Lakeside Co., 1911), p. 439.
53. John Bachelder, *A.D. 2050* (San Francisco: Bancroft Co., 1890), p. 186.
54. Wheeler, *Our Industrial Utopia*, p. 304.
55. Schuette, *Athonia*, p. 439.
56. Byron Brooks, *Earth Revisited* (Boston: Arena Publishing Co., 1893), p. 64.
57. C. W. Woodridge, *Perfecting the Earth* (Cleveland: Utopia Publishing Co., 1902), p. 226.
58. Henry L. Call, *The Coming Revolution* (Boston: Arena Publishing Co., 1895), p. 47.
59. C. S. Griffin, *Nationalism* (Boston: The Author, 1889), pp. 3–4.
60. Cowen, *Daybreak*, p. 131.
61. Noto, *The Ideal City*, p. 72.
62. Leggett, *A Dream*, p. 50.
63. [House], *Philip Dru*, p. 31.
64. [Allen], *The Key*, p. 80.
65. William A. Taylor, *Intermere* (Columbus, Ohio: Twentieth Century Publishing Co., 1901), p. 41.
66. John I. Brant, *The New Regime: A.D. 2202* (New York: Cochrane Publishing Co., 1909), p. 121.

Sources of Utopian Thought 39

67. Richard Hatfield, *Geyserland: Empiricisms in Social Reform* (Washington, D.C.: The Author, 1908), p. 84.

68. Daniel Bond, *Uncle Sam in Business* (Chicago: Charles H. Kerr & Co., 1899), p. 35.

69. Edgar Chambless, *Roadtown* (New York: Roadtown Press, 1910), p. 117.

70. Ibid.

71. Frisbie, *Prophet of the Kingdom*, p. 30.

72. Ibid., p. 152.

73. [Anon.], *Man or Dollar, Which?* By a Newspaperman. (Chicago: Charles H. Kerr & Co., 1898), p. 66.

74. [William S. Child], *The Legal Revolution of 1902* (Chicago: Charles H. Kerr & Co., 1898), p. 66.

75. Griffin, *Nationalism*, p. 50.

76. Call, *The Coming Revolution*, p. 218.

77. Merrill, *The Great Awakening*, p. 208.

78. Hutchinson, *The Limit of Wealth*, p. 208.

79. Zebina Forbush, *The Co-Opolitan* (Chicago: Charles H. Kerr & Co., 1898), p. 86.

80. Hutchinson, *The Limit of Wealth*, p. 208.

81. [House], *Philip Dru*, p. 46.

82. Wheeler, *Our Industrial Utopia*, p. 252.

83. Clark E. Persinger, *Letters from New America; or, An Attempt At Practical Socialism* (Chicago: Charles H. Kerr & Co., 1900), p. 5.

84. Albertson, *The Social Incarnation*, p. 27.

85. Albert Chavannes, *The Future Commonwealth; or, What Samuel Balcom Saw in Socioland* (New York: True Nationalist Publishing Co., 1892), p. 74.

3
Specific Problems and Solutions

The authors of these utopias registered their protest against their contemporary society in a comprehensive manner. The most popular and frequent protest was against the imbalance of wealth; however, few failed to realize the pervasive nature of this disorder. According to these authors, the spirit of greed and commercialism that was so necessary for the functioning of the industrial machine had spread to politics, labor, education, religion, and even into the very atmosphere itself.

The utopians, however, were not revolutionaries; they denounced violence because they feared it might bring irreparable damage to the fabric of society. In fact, many would readily admit that there was much that had value in the old order. Although they condemned the competitive ruthlessness of the industrial order, they admired its efficiency and production. Although they excoriated the corruption of politicians and the indifference of the electorate, they saw no alternative but to place more power in their hands, albeit with certain checks. Although they bemoaned the loneliness of country life and the squalor of the city, they knew they could not survive without the healthful living of the one or the conviviality of the other. The problem, then, was to improve the present social order without destroying it. Each phase of living—economics, politics, labor, education, religion, environment—was examined with an eye toward retaining the good and purging the bad. The sum of the goods constituted utopia, and the sum of the bads defined very clearly what the utopian saw unfit in his own day (see table 1).

WEALTH

The problem most frequently discussed by the utopian author of this era was that of the distribution of wealth. Wealth provided the key to decent living; by it, the utopian judged the relevance of his beliefs in equality and the theory of progress. He would often ask himself if his commitment to these values had any meaning at a time when most of his fellow citizens were struggling to put bread on the table. He presumed that "all ought to share alike if each one does his best, each having the same right to God's world and to the blessings it contains."[1] Yet, the labor strikes, depressions, and political unrest indicated this was not so. The utopian felt that the prophets of the gospel of wealth preached the doctrines of greed and selfishness and suspected, moreover, that the idea of stewardship was not going to meet the demands of the time. Most of all, the utopian was frightened by the extremes of wealth and poverty, side by side. He knew that in a society based on self-interest, once all power was in the hands of the few, his faith in the boundless opportunities to rise to success would be pointless. The word *plutocracy* occurred frequently in the utopian novels; the most hated symbol of the status quo was the *monopoly*. The prevalence of these words in the novels revealed their authors' fear of being permanently fixed to one social and economic level. In short, the utopian feared he was being deprived of his chance to succeed. The greater proportion of utopian writers saw the bedrock of their faith in democracy threatened by the elimination of the equality of opportunity.

For this reason, an overwhelming majority of writers concentrated on the evils resulting from the pursuit of money. Money was called the "curse of mankind," and its acquisition was compared to some barbaric venture in which "this hunting for dollars and things in this age is just as exciting a game as hunting for bear could have been in the days of savagery."[2] One writer objected to the "crushing, elbowing, and treading on each other's heels in the attempt to get money."[3] Another

Table 1
Number of Explicit Statements of Specific Problems and Solutions.
(Based on 106 works.)

Problems	Number	Solutions	Number
Economic			
1. Greed and selfishness	76	State control of wealth	59
		Property tax	14
		Income tax	13
		Inheritance tax	5
		Total	91
2. Degrading charity	47	Equal opportunity	39
		Social security	22
		Total	61
3. Division of classes	42	Class equality	51
4. Monopolies	59	State production	39
		State distribution	35
		Common property	27
		Total	101
5. Scarcity of capital	45	Fiat money	15
		Low interest	11
		Free silver	10
		Total	36
TOTAL	269	TOTAL	340

Problems	Number	Solutions	Number
Labor			
1. Long hours	69	Shorter hours	69
2. Inefficient middlemen	54	Efficient production	44
		Invention	37
		Automated factories	26
		Electricity	15
		Total	122
3. Low pay	39	Minimum subsistence	50
		Equal pay	22
		Labor checks	17
		Total	89
4. Job security	33	Guaranteed work	34
		Eliminate child labor	12
		Limit immigration	4
		Total	50
TOTAL	195	TOTAL	330

Problems	Number	Solutions	Number
Political			
1. Corrupt public officials	55	Civil service	10
		Recall	7
		Total	17
2. Voting corruption	31	Secret ballot	21
		Educate electorate	11
		Voting restrictions (work, property, sex, intelligence)	11
		Total	43
3. Corrupt press	28	Free press and speech	25
4. Inadequate legislation	17	Referendum	11
		Initiative	11
		Total	22
5. Corrupt legal system	31	Eliminate legal apparatus	49
TOTAL	162	TOTAL	156

Problems	Number	Solutions	Number
Environmental			
1. Slums, poor living conditions	56	City planning	53
2. Air pollution	20	Air conditioning	5
		Electricity to replace coal, fuel	5
		Total	10
3. Overpopulation	13	Birth control	14
4. Sickness and poor health	35	Organized or required physical exercise	26
		Health education	21
		Cremation	20
		State health program	16
		Pure food law	15
		Vegetarian diet	9
		Total	107
TOTAL	124	TOTAL	184
Social			
1. Intemperance	29	Temperance	25
2. Inequality of women	29	Equality of women	36
3. Overburdened housewife	19	Living and eating in co-ops	25

Problems	Number	Solutions	Number
Social			
4. Poor marriage relations	15	Marriage for love	20
		Divorce	12
		Free love	4
		Total	36
5. Women denied vote	11	Woman suffrage	19
TOTAL	103	TOTAL	141
Educational			
1. Poor education	59	Free education	38
		Mandatory education	33
		Total	71
2. Poor upbringing	28	Community or state upbringing	21
TOTAL	87	TOTAL	92
Religious			
1. Failure of formal religion	28	Belief in man's self-sufficiency	25
		Belief in science	15
		Religious tolerance	14
		Universal religion	9
		Total	63

simply stated that the inordinate love of money was the most gigantic evil of the time.[4] In Paul Devinne's utopia, money was abandoned as a means of exchange. When a visitor to this ideal land asked why this was so, he in turn was asked, "Have you forgotten what part money played [in the previous era]?"[5] The implication was clear.

The utopian writer considered an unchecked appetite for wealth one of the chief obstacles to progress. In Bessie Rogers's utopia, where the children "are born good," success depended on relinquishing "the idea that money was the goal of all things."[6] William Taylor denounced "the animal instinct and barbarous appetite which reaches after the gaud and tinsel of excessive wealth" because it held human progress in check.[7] The very fact that men were greedy implied the presence of poverty in their lives. "Greed is the offspring of need," claimed C W. Woodridge, "scarcity is the breath of its life. A world in which need and greed reign supreme is a hell in which all manner of evils find their congenital habitat."[8]

The evils Woodridge alluded to were described in detail by his fellow utopians. Bradford Peck cited the constant tension of nerves and the perpetual care and worry that arose from the "piracy of individuals, striving as they ever did to rob one another."[9] The underdog in this struggle had few hopes, claimed Henry Call, for the struggle was not only hard, but uncertain and precarious. "Theirs is a contest in which many fail."[10] Indeed, not only did many fail, but, added Henry Frisbie, some "win the race by tripping down their fellow man."[11] Bryon Brooks's conclusion seemed to epitomize the judgment of these writers: "Formerly war was business; now business is war."[12]

The utopian writer often associated the methods of business with a breakdown in the moral sanctions of society. The language of war and ruthless plunder was employed; but most of all, horror was expressed at the lack of conscience and moral concern. In Frank Rosewater's utopia, a representative of the capitalistic 1890s declared his credo: "We make and unmake values, do works of bribery, execute revenges, carry forgery to the very documents of state, steal purses, rob houses, betray men and women—do all things that yield revenue."[13] The absence of any sanction to guide human action appeared in the motto that one utopian ascribed to his era: "What we need, we take freely."[14] A character in Alonzo Van Deusen's utopia complained of losing the simple moral dictum that he was taught in his youth when he first entered the business world:

[I found] that telling the *whole* truth in a business transaction was what is termed in common business parlance being "green and unsophisticated." I learned, too, that the sure indication of a weak mind, according to public sentiment, was the harboring of any compunction of conscience about living in luxury and enjoying a superabundance of material blessings while our fellow human beings, either from natural disqualifications or adverse circumstances, were forced to eke out a miserable existence in destitution and wretchedness. In a word, I learned that the current standard of good conduct was for each to look out for himself, regardless of the rights and happiness of others, save only to keep within the letter of the law.[15]

This moral indictment was complete when the objects of these business practices—wealth and leisure—were compared to the Christian purpose of life. Byron Brooks's biblical allusion—"for a man's life consists not in the abundance of the things he possesses"—questioned the whole aim of capitalistic endeavor; and though few utopians were willing to go this far, they frequently opposed the worst aspects of business enterprise with the traditional otherworldly attitude of religion.[16]

The accusation of greed naturally fell upon the most representative members of the capitalistic system: businessmen, financiers, and millionaires. They were blamed for ignoring the human element in their quest for profits. "Fools!" charged Jack London. "As if the meaning of life were profits."[17] Even more vitriolic was William S. Child's description of the rich:

...cannibals, who feasted upon human flesh and quenched their thirst with the blood of inoffensive people—for were they not maintaining a system that daily brought murder and starvation to thousands, and that made all mankind their slaves, that they might live in profligacy and untold luxury.[18]

R. A. Dague, a socialist reformer, tried to excuse the wealthy as being "not personally bad men"; he compared them to slaveholders before the Civil War whose greed prevented them from seeing the evils of the system.[19] Some, like Frank Rosewater, tried to lessen the stigma of guilt attached to this group by emphasizing their fear of the "threatening evils of the unknown future" while they remained "deaf to the curses of those they trample underfoot."[20]

It seemed that the wealthy man could do little to please the utopian author. On the one hand, the millionaire was accused of not using his wealth for the good of the people.[21] On the other hand, the millionaire was condemned for his paternalistic attitude when he did give to charity. The very necessity for charity incensed the utopian writer. "Every able-bodied man is entitled to a living, and a good living—not as a matter of charity.... Charity! Charity!" declaimed William Child. "It has no place in our vocabulary."[22] The word *charity* denoted inferiority, helplessness, and permanent class structure—all viewed with great disfavor by the utopian. Edward House expressed the more common attitude toward charity: "The strong will help the weak, the rich will help the poor, and it will not be called charity, but it will be called justice."[23] Merely changing the name of this activity, however, did not satisfy some utopians. They preferred to remove the cause of the problem, for "where distributive justice prevails, there will be no office for charity to perform."[24]

The very existence of the millionaire served as another cause for the disenchantment of these authors. By far the most indignant commentary was directed toward the great disparity between rich and poor, the disturbing fact that "there are now a few rich and many—very many—extremely poor."[25] Henry Call claimed that fewer than thirty thousand men already owned half the entire wealth of the country.[26] Edward Bellamy observed that the confusions of our political system would disappear when the outside observer "grasps the vital point that the rule of the rich, the supremacy of capital and its interests, as against those of the people at large, was the central principle of our system."[27] But the utopian was less interested in removing confusion than he was in initiating reform, and he considered the task impossible when the opulence of the rich was seen side by side with the rags of the poor.[28]

The utopian also feared class rebellion. Several utopias, most notably Ignatius Donnelly's *Caesar's Column*, depicted a bloody and violent conflict between the oppressors and the oppressed. The psychology of these oppressed was described by the anonymous author of *Man or Dollar, Which?*:

More and more every year men had begun to think this way: "There is evidently an abundance in this country, if not in the whole world, for all. Why is it that some have so much and the others so little or none at all? Where is the justice, where is the expediency of permitting a few to so monopolize the privileges, thus bestowing unnecessary wealth upon a small number and grinding the great many down to poverty?"[29]

This same kind of thinking led to what the more conservative Edward House called "sullen and rebellious discontent."[30] When the time came for the laboring man to give over the entire product of his efforts to the monopolizers of wealth, then, the utopian asserted, "there is no hope for mankind."[31] Rebellion seemed the most likely course of action.

Because the workingman relied on his ability to improve his status, nothing crushed his hope more completely than the monopoly. The utopian authors were conscious of the fact that it was a rare workingman who was willing to spend "the whole of his day and a portion of his night in monotonous endeavor, away from his home and family, without hope of betterment to give him courage and endurance."[32] Monopoly, by its very nature, perpetuated itself and became impregnable to change. The rich would always be rich; the poor would always be poor. For this reason, one writer asserted, "there was nothing that the masses feared and hated so much as monopolies."[33] The injustice of being forever placed in one economic class struck Albert Merrill, who asked, "Why in God's name should a lazy man's son be made to suffer for the father's fault?"[34] William Simpson reconciled himself to this conclusion by alluding to it as one of the "depressing effects of your monopolistic condition."[35]

The utopian writer viewed the menace of monopoly with alarm when he saw the tentacles of that monster extend into every sphere of life. The disciples of Henry George exposed the dangers of the land monopoly, which was described as "one of the most effective means by which the few and idle rich oppress the many toiling poor."[36] Most of the complaints about inequality rested on the insufficient money supply. Henry Call admitted that the problem is "not so much that men have to work, but it is the constant grind to earn every dollar they can, which makes the struggle for existence so intense."[37] Many a utopian thought the failure of the money mechanism accounted for the incongruity of a wealthy nation with so many poor. Frank Rosewater cynically noted that in the year 1893 "we had a Columbian Fair...but the panic was an outside exhibit to show the world our skill in finance."[38] The scarcity of capital, however, was considered by most to be an effect of the more basic problem of an economic system based on self-interest.

Because the existence of monopolies mocked the ideal of equal opportunity, several utopians became cynical when they alluded to this value. "Ay, all in equal degree. How glib such platitudes fell from the lips of the politicians," claimed C. A. Steere.[39] To him the word became "a byword and a jest."[40] William S. Child wryly added to this commentary: "You no doubt think you will draw the prize and become a millionaire. You have got a thousand better chances of dying in the poorhouse."[41]

Hence, the very necessity for poorhouses and charity demonstrated to the utopian that his contemporary society had failed. Because equality was the most universally honored value, these authors found it impossible to reconcile the existence of monopolies and millionaires with the astounding increase of poverty and squalor. It was clear that a large middle class, symptomatic of the prevalence of equality, was in fact disappearing. Because he felt he represented the values of that class, the utopian writer attacked the forces of dissolution. He called on the sanctions of religion to excoriate those who viewed wealth as an end it itself. Selfishness and greed were the greatest evils because they justified the dominance of the few and precluded the advancement of the many. The mere possession of wealth was not denounced by a majority of these writers; however, they demanded a concomitant sense of responsibility toward others who were less affluent. Furthermore, the utopians showed an increasing annoyance with the paternalism of the wealthy class and, by various devices, sought to preclude the existence of such a class in their ideal world.

The most popular solution to this problem was the control of wealth by law. Various taxes—property, income, and inheritance—were advocated. Alfred Hutchinson proposed an income limit of $5,000 for each member of a family. The government would collect the surplus to inaugurate public work projects. Many advocated state banks with low interest rates, the printing of fiat money, and the use of silver as a basis for currency. A number of works contained plans for state distribution of produce, to eliminate control of the distribution of goods by the money men or monopolistic industries. A few advocated nationalization of all industry.

On a more philosophical plane, the utopian relied heavily on the ability of his ideal society to inculcate the values of altruism and equal opportunity. "Equal opportunity is liberty, and free will, and good will," wrote Henry Frisbie, who felt that if people only agreed to this proposition, "all can have life, leisure, pleasure, health."[42] The utopians agreed that a better society would be one in which "the commercial type of man... is seldom seen; where money is merely a commodity."[43] It would be a society far removed from the time of "semi-barbarism" when people "had not yet learned to deal justly with each other."[44] Rather, it would be a place in which the motive of love or unselfishness would be the ideal power among men.[45] Utopia was conceived of as a place in which "nothing is done for the business profit of any person, persons, or class, but everything for the common interest of all."[46]

Thus, by relying on the Christian virtues of thrift and love, and by removing laws based on privilege and self-interest, the utopian hoped to realize his ideal of equality. Whether he meant a total equality of possessions or merely the equality of opportunity depended upon the radicalness of his view. In either case, however, a real application of the doctrine of equality to daily living would allow everyone a chance to enjoy the fruits of his labor.

LABOR

One of the highest values of the utopians, second to that of equality, was a belief in the value of work. Sheer effort could subdue any problem, they believed. However, it took little effort for the utopian to observe that many labored from morning till night without earning enough to survive. In a land of unlimited wealth, this phenomenon struck the utopian as particularly incongruous; to some it seemed a matter for outrageous protest. Not only must a man survive, they asserted, but the more important work of developing his "higher faculties" and his total needs as a human being could not be ignored. Failure in this regard robbed men of their dignity and self-respect; and if a man could not respect himself, he could not be counted on to respect others. Order rested on the respect men had for one another. A society that did not have the benefit of this sanction would inevitably come to a state of chaos—the very thing most feared by the utopian. Ultimately, William Taylor claimed, it was a problem of justice.

Where there is labor and no justice, the strong enjoy, the weak suffer and endure, opulence flourishes for the few, pain and poverty affect the many. Where there is neither labor nor justice, where might makes right, barbarism in its worst form curses the land.[47]

Next to greed and selfishness, the most persistent problem cited in these works was the lack of leisure time for the laboring man. Elaborate descriptions of the daily toil, dreary homecoming, and untimely death, which alone brought relief, filled the pages of these books. Albert Merrill protested that in his time "the masses who had to toil from morning to night in dark rooms, know nothing of nature, its beauties and charms. When one worked hard for ten hours a day, one is in no condition to think of anything."[48] Women were no less affected, according to Edward House: "After a deadly day's work, many of them found stimulants of various kinds, the cheapest means of bringing comfort to their weary bodies and hope-lost souls, and then the next step was the beginning of the end."[49] Crime, depravity, and alcoholism were frequently attributed to long hours and poor working conditions. This obvious relationship did much to change the utopian's older belief that such failures were due to a personal lack of character.

Nevertheless, the utopian did not propose relief for the workingman through these organized bodies that expressed an interest in his plight: the churches, the government, and the labor movement. The majority of utopians were suspicious of the extensive governmental control over labor such as Edward Bellamy advocated. Besides, the verbiage of politicians concerning the workingman came to nought in the eyes of the utopian observer.

> They [politicians] professed great concern for the welfare of the workingman... but manifested absolute indifference to bringing about a condition under which workingmen could find employment and secure a reasonable number of dollars.[50]

As for relief work done by churches and other interested organizations, the response ws unanimous. "It is not charity that workingmen want, but help that really changes the conditions and enables the weaker and less fortunate to obtain a more equal chance in life."[51] Charity was shunned at all costs; it only made permanent what all hoped and regarded as a temporary lapse in an otherwise opportunity-laden time.

Even though the four-, six-, or eight-hour day was their goal, few utopians supported the labor-union movement, which already advocated the shorter workweek. In the utopian mind, labor unions were synonymous with strikes, and strikes with violence, which all denounced. Even more antipathetic to the utopian, however, was organized labor's constant reference to a "class" of workingmen who appeared in an adversarial role to their employers. Because the utopian was committed to the idea of self-help, he refused to accept this division between employer and employee. James Cowen and many others considered this opposition unreasonable, because "the interests of the two classes were identical."[52]

In fact, quite frequently the employer was portrayed as the one whose efforts were defeated by strikes. He was variously described as a man seeking to produce better goods for less money, trying to raise the standard of living, and trying to organize a complex structure of production and distribution. When he happened to fire a few workers for the sake of efficiency, according to Alfred Hutchinson, the strike that resulted "was all wrong and injured the cause of labor."[53] Byron Brooks discredited the labor movement by describing it as an attempt to substitute one type of despotism for another. He predicted the movement's demise for, he said, "they could not procure for the idle and incompetent the returns of the skillful and industrious."[54]

For the utopian writer, the implied standard for judging the value of labor was productivity and efficiency. Any group that added the value of security was suspected of tampering with the basic goals of free enterprise. The laboring man was regarded by a majority of these writers as a subordinate element in the economic system. If he committed himself fully to the values of that system and worked hard, he could rightfully expect a just wage and some time to enjoy the fruits of his labor. But this could be accomplished only on an individual basis.

The utopian writer employed the very criteria of the economic system—efficiency and productivity—to criticize the failure of that system with regard to labor. He could not believe, for instance, that it was necessary for some to work ten or twelve hours a day, six days a week. Apparently, the utopian reasoned, some had to work hard because others worked not at all. According to Charles W. Caryl, "if the present unproductive people were put to work, in ten years they would be able to duplicate all the present cities, towns, villages, farms, factories, railroads and all other forms of wealth existing today."[55] R. A. Dague believed with Benjamin Franklin, whom he quoted, that "if every man did his share of the labor of the world, four hours work daily would be all that need be required of anyone."[56] All agreed that the problem was not the lack of manpower or resources, but the inefficient utilization of both that accounted for the excessive burden on the labor force. If the economic system were properly organized, claimed Edward House, "there would be none who were not sufficiently clothed and fed."[57]

The most frequently cited inefficiency was the existence of

what was called the "parasite—the useless middleman."[58] More than half the authors denounced this drain on the fruits of the genuine laborer. Among the unproductive, Jack London listed salesmen, advertising agents, real estate agents, and the large group of people living on inherited income.[59] Some, like William Stanley Child, objected to the myriad of little retail shops and establishments scattered all over the land.[60] John Veiby required the middleman in his utopia simply to order goods and sell them without a profit.[61] Alonzo Van Deusen objected not only to vast hosts of clerks seen in the "numberless petty little stores" but also to life, health, and fire insurance companies with their "lofty air and long turn of attendants."[62]

Coinciding with the complaint against unproductive labor was the denunciation of wasted human abilities. Edward Bellamy and many others devised elaborate schemes to provide a diverse training for young people, so that they could choose occupations best suited to their talents. In fact, the New Model City of Charles Caryl was built solely "to utilize the enormous amount of genius, skill and resources in our country, which is now going to waste or doing no practical good."[63] This waste was manifested not only in a misapplication of talent but also in the expensive employment of human ability in dull, repetitive, and unskilled work. Laborsaving machinery was mentioned often. The utopian rarely considered that automation would create the problem of unemployment; rather, he envisioned saving men from the drudgery of one kind of job so that they could perform more complicated and beneficial tasks in another.

But inefficiency was not the only consideration in advocating laborsaving machinery. The demeaning nature of work that could be replaced by a machine was emphasized by Mary Lane, who commented that "no people can rise to universal culture as long as they depend upon hand labor to produce any of the necessities of life."[64]

The institution of laborsaving machinery, then, served these writers as a partial solution for the problem of labor and inefficiency. Although few thought of it as a panacea for these problems, some, like William Fishbough, described its advantages in glowing terms.

Labor-saving machinery...will then be employed to an extent unknown before, in increasing the product of labor, in curtailing the hours of toil, and in creating wealth capital which, according to the very laws of nature, must either directly or indirectly end in the remuneration and enrichment of the laboring classes.[65]

James Cowen looked forward to his perfected society wherein "all work is done. No fleshly limb is strained, no conscious life is burdened, by any of the labor of our complex society."[66] Thus, a note of optimism often accompanied the utopian's discussion of the problems of labor; he viewed the problem as basically a technical one, and he thought that the application of man's inventive genius would obliterate its presence.

A majority of utopian writers, therefore, applied the criterion of efficiency to the problems of the laboring man. These authors preferred to speak in terms of science and the ingenuity of the human mind rather than in terms of human relations. They relied on the effective organization of manpower, talent, and machinery to relieve the personal problems of drudgery, fatigue, lack of time, and low wages. With an all-consuming faith in the power of work, they spoke of the proper utilization of resources rather than of class struggle or group exploitation. The labor-union movement was opposed almost unanimously, because it tended to deny the ideology of the businessman and to fix permanently the laboring man as a separate and opposed entity. As one writer stated, workingmen who belonged to unions ignored "the opportunity to become their own employers."[67] The problems of labor were not discussed as the problem of the laborer, but as the problem of production. It was thought that the usual methods of improving production would help the workingman because he was conceived of as a unit of production.

In few other areas did the utopian so clearly demonstrate his acceptance of the ideology of the capitalistic economic system. It seemed that his real complaint against free enterprise was that it failed to live up to its own principles of efficiency and full production; and because of this laxity, free enterprise punished the laborer who made it work.

POLITICS

Because the utopian believed that the government was the ultimate protector of the rights of the people, he held the lawmaker and politician responsible for the failures of his time. The principle of democracy was rarely questioned; in fact, it was the lack of consideration for the will of the majority that was cited as the chief problem. Edward House expressed the feeling of most utopian authors when he said, "Our present government is perhaps less responsive to the will of the people than that of almost any of the civilized nations.... It is nearly impossible for the desires of our people to find expression into law."[68] These writers felt that the law catered only to the powers of special privilege. The man without an organization or interest behind him stood alone confronting bewildering legalities and indifference to his personal rights. The utopian vigorously denounced the failure of the political system to foster equality of opportunity and equal justice before the law.

The range of attitudes of these authors toward the purpose of government coincided with the amount of authority they gave the governments of their ideal societies. About one-third preferred to diminish the government or do away with it entirely; they mainly opposed the *idea* of governmental authority. The other two-thirds thought the government should take a stronger hand in solving the problems of the people; the degree of participation and power exercised depended on the utopian's judgment of the urgency of the problem. Although heavily committed to the ideology of individualism and laissez faire, these writers looked to the central government as an independent organization that could counterbalance the preponderance of power in the hands of a wealthy elite. In fact, the government seemed to be the only organization large enough to control this group; and though few suffered illusions about the government's incorruptibility, it was still believed capable of protecting the interests of the people as a whole.

Even those who subscribed to the doctrines of laissez faire revealed the self-defeating nature of their argument. Henry Olerich, an admirer of Herbert Spencer, represented their case when he wrote:

Our government is largely invasive and despotic, and principally run by politicians who are grossly ignorant of the psychological principles of human nature.... Paternalism stunts individuality and monopoly prevents the masses from becoming prosperous.[69]

Behind this statement was a commitment to the exalted dignity of human nature; however, the impossibility of this position was hinted at by Olerich himself when he admitted that he could not understand "why each person does not desire to own himself or herself only."[70] The necessity for government completely escaped him, yet the helplessness of men in dealing with the overbearing powers on the state and economy was readily apparent.

A more consistent and popular solution provided for the extension of the negative and limited powers of the general government. William Simpson believed that anyone with a concern for the "general welfare [would] have come to regard the obligations of government as something much beyond the traditional definition of governmental powers: a defense against invasion from without and protection of person and property within."[71]

Other utopians defined the role of government in their day more brutally. Albert Merrill accused it of hypocritcally encouraged the criminal with barbaric laws enacted for private interests while, at the same time, trying to reduce criminality by punishment.[72] In a similar vein, F. U. Worley wrote:

Too long had the government played the part of an unnatural parent to the people giving them stones, serpents, and scorpions, while bestowing with a liberal hand the bread, the fish, and the eggs upon the corporations.[73]

Few wrote with greater bitterness than Charles W. Caryl when he said: "Capitalism is the same here as elsewhere. It grinds the face of the poor. The very fact that political equality exists appears to make economic despotism harsher."[74]

The common theme of these complaints demonstrated the utopian's disenchantment with a government that advocated equality while actively helping special interests. The utopian writer directed his attack against government officials who compromised their democratic principles for the sake of personal gain. Amazed indignation at public indifference to political corruption filled these works. T. H. Tibbles described how "with us, money-making has become a sort of national game, at which every man essays to play, and in which statesmen do not hesitate to take a hand."[75] Another writer incredulously recorded that "politicians...thoroughly believed that it was perfectly legitimate to operate city, state, and country affairs for the purpose of enriching themselves."[76] All too often, the tendency was to condemn categorically the whole political system. "Americans are a bunch of uncivilized grafters.... We had a republic that proved to be a government of grafters," wrote Jacob Horner.[77] The utopian writer felt himself alone in believing that it was a "serious matter when the people no longer can trust officers of their choice."[78]

If seeking public office as a path to riches seemed deplorable to these writers, then the process of attaining that office ought to be condemned as well. The failure of democracy rested with "the average American citizen [who] refused to pay attention to civic affairs."[79] People either allowed their votes to be bought or were unduly influenced by newspapers. "In politics," a utopian character observed, "a voter of your century never used his own brains. He always borrowed those of his pet newspaper."[80] Samuel Crocker expressed it more harshly: "Public sentiment was molded by the capitalistic press and all fell into line as before."[81]

Quite frequently, the will of the well-intentioned voter was defeated anyway. The utopian denounced ingeniously changed election laws and the practice of gerrymandering. No less an experienced political observer than Edward House declared that at conventions the delegates "think they have something to do with the naming of the nominees and the making of platforms. But the astute boss has planned all that in advance."[82] The general conviction of these writers was that "the cunning always found a way to defeat the public will."[83] With this in mind, James Cowen was not surprised to discover that "a large class of mean and venial citizens...would sell their votes to the highest bidders."[84] The most popular solution to this problem was the universal, private ballot. John Bachelder's comment that persons in his utopia should go to the polls "quietly and as unmolested as to church" represented the general feeling.[85] The only other remedies that made sense to the utopian were to prevent the disinterested citizen from voting and to educate the electorate to vote for honest men.

It went without saying that if the legislators were corrupt, so, too, were both the laws they created and the interpreters of those laws. A surprising number of writers—about half—advocated the total elimination of the existing legal system. Many utopians believed that the complexity of the system prevented the execution of simple justice. One complained that "the laws are so complicated that no one can understand their meaning."[86] The proverbial delay in legal procedure was cited.

Each state kept an expensive legislature at work grinding out laws, and each state had hundreds of courts that were kept so busy with the adjustments of those laws that when a man got into trouble, he sometimes had to wait for months, or even years, before the court could adjust his troubles for him.[87]

Furthermore, the expense of litigation angered many. Many pointed out that it was often better to suffer an injustice than to go to court. Moreover, even if a person did overcome all the obstacles to having his day in court, he could not expect justice; as Zebina Forbush maintained, there were powerful groups who could "obtain an interpretation of the Constitution when they wish it...to suit their purposes."[88] In sum, the utopian lamented the entire manner in which the law operated because he felt that people were only a "secondary consideration to the organization which had become the principal thing."[89]

Thus, the utopian's attitude toward the law and government revealed a yearning for a simple and elemental way of life. To him there was only one law, namely, do good and avoid evil. The problem of what constituted the "good" did not seem troublesome. It was defined to Paul Devinne's satisfaction as "every one of our thoughts, words, and deeds which injures neither ourselves nor any one of our fellow-men."[90] This utilitarian principle precluded the need for most of the political activity that perplexed the utopian, especially that in the area of law—

a profession he defined as "concomitant only with warring factions and elements of ignorance."[91] The very existence of law was antithetical to the perfected state in which the "spirit of service" was to prevail, and there was little doubt in the utopian's mind that those few needed services could be provided without the help of the vast and cumbersome legal system.

To lead an ideal existence, then, the utopian desired to reduce life to its most basic simplicity, to diminish the powers of government, and to eliminate the whole legal apparatus; however, most utopians realized that this was impossible. The complexity of both the organization and the power of the state, though regrettable, seemed inevitable. Justice and equality could only be attained through the power of government and law, but the utopian insisted on certain assurances—an educated electorate, civil service, the referendum, and a simplified legal system—so that corruption would be kept to a minimum.

ENVIRONMENT

When the utopian observed the large-scale social chaos and poverty of his time, he concluded that the oft-cited reason for its presence—individual moral weakness—was inadequate. So many could not willfully consign themselves to so much suffering. Some larger force undoubtedly controlled the fate of these people. Some writers called this force society, others labeled it environment. In either case, the utopian believed that only large-scale planning and organization would remedy the matter. The limitations of individuals were obvious. As Alfred Hutchinson observed, when a man has "poverty staring him in the face...he does not take that broad view of life; his ideas...are shaped by the food he eats and the clothes he wears."[92] "Who knows," asked another writer, "how large a part the mystery of birth and heredity play in one's life?"[93] To most utopian writers it had become apparent that man was not the sole master of his own fate, at least not in late nineteenth-century America.

What influenced the utopian most in his alienation from the prevalent social conditions was the squalor of city life. He associated it with the worst aspects of commercialism and human depravity. One writer treated the city as a "modern temple to the shrine of the God Mammon and monument to the folly of all men."[94] He hoped that God would wreak his vengeance upon the buyers and sellers in the marketplace just as he had done two thousand years before. This tone of moral indignation derived from the feeling of many utopians that the city was an unnatural place in which to live; they concluded that what was unnatural was also immoral. As early as 1869, Edward Everett Hale used this criterion when he condemned the slums of Boston and New York where, he said,

> you will find as many children as you choose who never saw the sea on the beach, never pitched shells from sand, never planted seed in ground, never watched birds nest on a tree, never crunched moss with foot, never sailed ship on stream, never hunted butterfly over grass, never rested under shady tree, never waded across mountain brook, never picked berry from bough, never enjoyed one of the little pleasures which are the daily food of children.[95]

George Phelps, who believed that the voice of the people was the voice of God, called the congestion in large cities violations of natural law. To him, however, violations of the natural law were engendered by the "spririt of cupidity, the spirit of commercialism and speculation, the get-something-for-nothing principle"—all of which abounded in the city.[96]

The utopian believed that because the city was unnatural, it blunted the sensibilities of its inhabitants. When the hero of William Simpson's utopia was ordered to the country for a rest by his doctor, he suddenly realized that he "had scarcely looked upon the sky and heavens, except between the margins of opposite house-tops, and viewed from infancy, without emotion, the rising and setting of the sun from a horizon of chimneys and steeples."[97] The city itself was presented in all its most unappealing aspects:

> ...the hideous elevated railroad trestles, the rough, cursing drivers, the ownerless dogs, the fat, sleepy policeman...the low wretchedly built, unwholesome houses with the thousand little shops, cigar saloons, brothels and the low dives, the posters, placards, bulletins, and sheriff's notices disfiguring the whole, the telephone, telegraph, and

Specific Problems and Solutions   65

electric wires, dangerous to life and the gallows-like poles reaching to the roofs...the pushing, jolting, human crowd...made up of dirty laborers, rapacious beggars, richly dressed idlers, fantastically arrayed ladies, pale, poorly clad factory and shop girls, insistent fakers, roaring half-naked newsboys and bootblacks.[98]

Some writers exasperatingly omitted the specifics; they merely referred to the "barbarously filthy and slavish lives" of the city dweller. Others, such as Ignatius Donnelly, were awed by the effects of this scene. "What struck me most," he said, "was their [city dwellers'] silence. They seemed to me merely automatic, in the hands of some ruthless and unrelenting destiny."[99] Though each writer sought to describe the failures of city life in his own way, the conclusion was almost unanimous. "All civilizations are false which do not civilize the lowest units of any social order."[100]

Although cities were condemned because of their inaccessibility to the beauties of nature, many writers were unwilling to grant their highest praise to life on the farm. In fact, one of the reasons for the overcrowding of the cities was the "dull and drab" character of farm life.[101] Bradford Peck recounted how many, torn between their love of the soil and their ambition to get ahead, reluctantly came to the city but could never reconcile themselves to it. Nevertheless, "the brighter boys," he said, "rushed to the great cities."[102] The unintelligent and ambitious were left to the "lonesome and unremunerative farm life."[103] Others, claimed Milan Edson, were able to perceive that the "encroachments of land monopoly...and the expense of the latest and best machinery" were insurmountable obstacles to the marginal farmer.[104] If a man wished to get ahead during a time when big business ruled, then the city offered more opportunities.

Thus, the utopian who recognized the limitations of farm life, and yet was repulsed by the squalor of the city, sought a solution that would combine the advantages of both. He well recognized that the advice of fifty years before—"Go West, young man"—was inapplicable; he had no romantic illusions concerning the attraction of the frontier. "The great gates to the West have just been closed," wrote William Stanley Child in

1898, "and they are closed tightly and are impassable. The opportunities are gone there."[105] Yet, in his ideal society, the utopian was unwilling to forgo the heady elixir of country air or the self-reliant spirit fed by the subdual of God's wilderness. The most obvious solution, therefore, was to plan the environment of each city in order to contain as much of the country as possible. Trees, lavish gardens, and parks were most prominent in the ideal city. Electricity replaced the burning of coal, wood, or oil for fuel. Buildings were air-conditioned. Glass domes and windows provided light everywhere. Factories were often isolated in the countryside. To decrease the growing numbers of people, a few utopian theorists advocated birth control and restrictions on immigration. Some allowed only living quarters in their cities. Several made physical fitness programs mandatory for both city dweller and farmer. At least three utopias—Henry Olerich's *A Cityless and Countryless World*, Warren S. Rhem's *Practical City*, and Edgar Chambless's *Roadtown*—were written chiefly to offer a solution to the problem of city living. The most elaborate scheme of all was Chambless's plan to house all the inhabitants of America in one two-story building stretching from New York to San Francisco. This would prevent overcrowding at any place, relieve the loneliness of farm life, and allow virtually everyone to take advantage of the nearby countryside. A few writers, like William Bishop and Milan Edson, ignored the problem by limiting the membership in their ideal communities, which were always established in the virgin countryside.

Two by-products of the unnatural life of the city were crime and ill health. Utopians who attempted to deal with these problems at all regarded them as environmental, has having been artificially created by society. If the problem resided wholly within the individual, it offered no systematic solution, except, of course, to change human nature itself. However, with his optimistic faith in human nature and his great sympathy for the downtrodden, the utopian thought that by creating economic equality and by fostering humane living conditions in cities, crime and sickness would disappear.

Henry W. Dowding had a simple and representative solution to the crime problem. "Crime," he said, "most frequently results from poverty."[106] The conclusion was obvious: the elimination of poverty would bring about the elimination of crime. Some chose to think that the great difference between rich and poor was itself responsible for much crime. This was especially true in the city, "where a single room would constitute the sole and only abiding place for a whole family... while half a block away might dwell a man whose wealth could not be counted... surrounded by every luxury the human intellect could devise."[107] Others, mindful of the self-efficiency of even the poor farmer, attributed the crime of the cities to the absolute need for money there as a medium of exchange. In this vein Lena Fry asked, "Are they responsible... when their labor is at a discount or no work is to be had at all?"[108]

When the problem was posed in this manner, the solution was apparent. Eliminate the degrees of wealth, get work for all, increase incomes at the bottom of the social scale, lower those at the top—and the slums with their crime would disappear. This belief rested on the doctrine that crime was engendered by human want, and nothing else.

The utopian also asserted that the city took more than its share of life through sickness and disease. Mary Lane maintained: "Go into the squalid portion of any large city, where Poverty and Disease go hand in hand, and one will have little difficulty meeting ill-fed, ill-clothed urchins."[109] Ignatius Donnelly, with his flair for satiric exaggeration, tried to show how city life stifled a concern for one's health and even life.:

Would you believe it, my dear brother, in this city they actually facilitate suicide. In all the public parks they have handsome houses. If a man has decided to die, he goes there. A doctor explains to him the different poisons, and he selects the kind he prefers. The truth is, that, in this over-crowded city a man is a drug, and I think many end their lives out of a sense of their own insignificance.[110]

For the utopian, the solutions to the problem of health were preventive rather than curative. The medical profession, like the legal profession, was largely mistrusted. Physicians were described as "ignorant young men... licensed to prey upon a more or less helpless people."[111] Even when the utopian was willing to grant the physician his knowledge, he denounced his exorbitant fees. The Reverend W. S. Harris asked a pointed question: "Have we not noted the laboring husband bending at his toil for eight or ten hours to pay the physician who calls for a few minutes?"[112]

Thus, in Albert Howard's ideal society, people were either taught to obey the laws of nature or learned to cure themselves with "psychic ether."[113] The oft-prescribed law of moderation was advocated by many. In Henry Dowding's perfected society the ideal man knew, if he knew nothing else, the meaning of the word *sufficient*. The frugality necessary for survival led another utopian writer to quote John D. Rockefeller admiringly: "It is not the high cost of living so much as the high living that is the reason the average man finds his purse empty in the middle of the week, and the Saturday payday far in the distance."[114] James Cowen advocated "that a man should take the day for labor and the night for rest, according to the indication of nature."[115]

Besides moderation, the only other prevention against sickness that the utopian advocated was cleanliness. In Paul Devinne's utopia, a character announced: "We consider cleanliness of the body in the same light as the purity of the soul. We cannot imagine one without the other."[116] Cosimo Noto, a doctor, marveled at the "resisting powers of the cells of the human body," especially when that body often had to compete with filth and vermin for life. He could only imagine how healthy humans would be if they "could live in an uncontaminated environment, according to the laws of health."[117] In the same vein, Solomon Schindler required every person in his new society to be taught that "unclear matter...is one of the most persistent enemies of humanity."[118]

Though most writers were unwilling to go beyond educating the populace in matters of health, a few did establish state health programs. These utopias were usually of the autocratic type in which the maintenance of health was one of many factors of daily living under the control of a central authority. In general, the utopian did not wish to be coercive in this matter, or in any matter dealing with personal life. Paradoxically, as he attempted to enhance the private lives of citizens, the utopian sought public means that required greater organization and control over individuals.

SOCIAL

Almost every issue discussed in the utopian works had its social implications. Among the problems were temperance and the role of women in society; although both were popular reform topics of the day, however, they received surprisingly little commentary in the utopian novel. The problem of temperance, in particular, was examined by no more than one-fourth of these writers. The subject of women's role in society received more extensive treatment; but here, more attention was paid to relieving the physical burdens of the ordinary housewife than to furthering her policial or social independence. Significantly, none of the female utopian writers advocated either suffrage or equal rights for women.

Little space in utopian novels was given to protesting against the evils of alcoholism. Most utopians assumed these evils were well known, and in their idealistic communities they simply either banned drink or enforced some kind of temperance or limit on the consumption of alcohol. They expressed much more interest in the methods of the liquor trade. One writer considered the liquor business a natural outgrowth of the competitive system, where, he said, "there is such an insane struggle to get money, saloons sprang up like mushrooms."[119] One ingenious solution made liquor available at little or no cost so that its evil character, and hence enticement, would be removed.[120] An even more radical suggestion was to allow the county government to run the liquor trade. "If the county wants to go into any kind of business, the liquor business is the business where success is assured."[121] Another writer advocated having women own the saloons and manage the business. After all, said John Veiby, "it was woman's function from time immemorial to prepare and serve the drinks."[122] Under this plan, women would be able to keep their eyes not only on the wayward males but also on the profits, which they would bring back into the home, thus eliminating the chief objection to unlimited alcohol consumption. This cavalier attitude, assumed by many writers who dealt with the problem, indicated that they thought it either unsolvable or insignificant.

Despite the romanticized heroines who appeared in the plots of most of the utopian works, these writers tried to understand the problems ordinary women faced daily. They sympathized with women whom they saw exploited in the home with endless housework, burdened by ceaseless childbearing, or driven into the streets because of lack of money. Some writers deplore the necessity for women to marry rich old men to avoid total destitution. Henry Dowding traced the source of these problems to a much more basic disorder, namely, the common inclination to regard women as inferior beings. He said:

The position of women on any planet...results from certain ideas as to her previous history, which, as you know, in the tradition of the Garden of Eden, gives her second place in the creation of the human family...from which various deductions are made, such as the Creator's intentions, inferiority of mind, physical weakness and a score of other foolish conclusions.[123]

To compensate for this attitude toward women as inferior, many authors gave them a superior place in their utopias. Alcanoan Grigsby considered women "more sympathetic than men"; consequently, he put them in charge of all humanitarian work in his ideal society.[124] In Ignatius Donnelly's *The Golden Bottle*, the hero modestly refused to rule the world himself; rather, he placed his wife on the throne as a fit object of universal adoration. T. H. Tibbles preferred to speak his mind directly. "I do not know in what esteem you may hold women in your country," he wrote, "but here, we think them the apex of creation."[125] Women were definitely superior to men in Dowding's ideal society with regard to natural refinement, intuition, patience, endurance, insensibility to pain, and in many other areas.[126] In William Bishop's utopia, women were considered competent enough to fill half the positions in the army.

However, a more complicated view of the problem was taken by a number of utopians. They believed that rather than a categorical answer concerning the inferiority or superiority of woman, what was imperative was an examination of her role as a person living in a society dominated by the opposite sex. There was an obvious need to differentiate between the tasks alloted to men and to women, but this did not necessitate inequities in sharing the common burden. The utopian writer felt that a woman should no longer be regarded merely as an incubator for her husband's children but "as one of the people with all the rights to learn, live, and do, that hithertofore has been regarded as man's right only."[127] William Bishop, who did allow women to vote, was more interested in the woman of his utopia "having an individuality separate and apart from the man she loves, and yet quite willing that the two be merged into one dual personality made up of two equal parts."[128] To Bishop, this did not mean having a wife become "a toy wife to be simply kissed and fondled... or a housewife to keep one well fed and good-natured"—a position he felt was fostered by the example of the "sentimental, lovesick heroines of the everyday novel."[129] Truly, many writers tried to overcome the tendency to overidealize women, a practice that the utopian saw leading to the belittlement of women in their actual lives. What the utopian required was a change in the prevailing attitude toward women, so that they could retain their femininity while, at the same time, they could enjoy the freedom permitted men.

However, it was obvious that if the men were not free, neither could the women be free. Many of the utopians appealed to the sympathies of their readers by vividly describing the burdens that fell on women because of the failures of the economic system. How could women assume a proper and dignified place in society, asked Paul Devinne, when half-grown girls were ruined mentally and physically by working in mills and were consequently made unfit for happy marriage and the joy of family life? When the whole burden of housekeeping, educating the children, and sometimes taking care of the husband fell on their shoulders? "True enough," he added, "rich women could get help, but these were comparatively few."[130] Mary Lane complained about the increasing number of women who "toiled early and late, in sorrow and privation."[131]

Because of these conditions, the utopian writer understandably took measures to prevent such a degraded life for women in his ideal society. Besides correcting the economic inequities, he enabled women to have access to "fresh air, free movement, suitable food, little worry, and plenty of sleep." In fact, Paul Devinne proudly went on to state, "You may look in vain for the pale, weak-nerved girls and women of a hundred years ago."[132]

In addition to the problems of inequality and the burdens of family life, a small number of writers took up the controversial problem of divorce. Those writers who dealt with marital questions in any way usually agreed that some marriages were bound to fail from the start. The chief reason for marital failure, according to the utopian, was the absence of love. Marriages contracted hastily or out of desperation for economic security once again reflected the instability engendered by a capitalistic society. It was assumed by these authors that economic and social equality would remove the need for this kind of marriage. For this reason, too, the most common solution was the simple requirement that all marry for love and for love alone.

Other solutions minimized the importance of marriage altogether. At least twelve authors mentioned divorce as an acceptable practice in their ideal community. Some reasoned that just as men and women were permitted to rectify errors made in other human activities, so, too, they should be allowed to correct an error made with regard to the choice of a mate. One author believed that "to make divorce respectable would help us to realize that marriage is only an episode in human life, that it is not the aim and end of all existence."[133] By extending this line of thought, the practice of free love, permitted by a few, could easily be justified. At the other extreme, the Reverend W. S. Harris offered a solution that would entirely remove the necessity for physical love. He defined intercourse between the sexes as "one of refined telepathy, soul-connected by thought transmission, a thousand-fold more charming than the low plane of intercourse in the flesh life."[134] Needless to say, this solution was unique to the utopia of Reverend Harris.

The more typical utopian recognized that the order of his ideal society rested on the preservation of the sanctity of marriage. Divorce and free love were mentioned by a very small minority; most utopians felt that the problems between men and women should be solved before marriage and in the society as a whole. If women were allowed to acquire an "air of frankness and independence," the utopian asserted, the social problems associated with the family, the raising of children, and even immoderate drinking would disappear—contingent, of course, on the prior disappearance of the inequalities bred by the economic system.[135]

Although suffrage for women was a political problem, the utopian usually considered the question of allowing women to vote a social one. All the utopians who advocated suffrage for women also advocated the equality of women. It was felt that if given a chance, women would prove as capable as men. Byron Welcome replied to the objection that women knew so little about politics by asserting that men, too, knew little before they were allowed to vote.[136] However, at least one-third of those advocating the equality of women did not allow women to vote in their utopias. Walter O. Henry asserted that "it was not a question of superiority or inferiority, but of doing work according to nature's laws."[137] Walter Henry and John Veiby both thought women were unfit by their very nature to engage in political activity.[138] If nothing was thought to be unfeminine by some, however, R. A. Dague hoped that voting and political activity would channel the energy of women away from their frivolous concerns for fashion and their appearance.[139] His socialist state did not allow any distinction between the sexes. Generally, though, more than three-quarters of these writers believed a woman's place to be in the home. The conservative attitude of the utopian toward marriage and social custom applied even more so to the question of suffrage for women.

In short, from the amount of space in these novels devoted to social problems, the utopian clearly considered them subordinate to political and economic ones. In fact, some felt that the restoration of economic equality would of itself remove the cause of excessive drinking and the exploitation of women. Others more daringly advocated an equal treatment for women in allowing them to share the burden of work and its rewards as well as the possibility of divorce. However, this small minority was overshadowed by most utopians who conservatively advocated women's place to be in the home and not contending with men in business or politics.

EDUCATION

The utopian critic fully realized the importance of education is his ideal society. Ninety percent of these utopias required or provided free education for their young citizens. There were a number of reasons why the utopian made education so readily available. First, the very dignity of man required it. Education was the process whereby men came to know their true value and nature; if left to chance, it could be expected that some men would not acquire the sense of discipline that the utopian thought necessary to suppress man's lower nature and develop his higher one. Few disagreed with Alonzo Van Deusen's conclusion:

In truth, long in advance of the time of which I speak, the conviction had become universal that the power and privilege to acquire and utilize knowledge were the most precious boon that had been bestowed upon man.[140]

Also, education was considered a necessary step in the evolutionary progress of American society toward the eventual achievement of its ideal—equality. The illiteracy of the masses was an obstacle in that path. As one writer claimed:

So long as learning was inaccessible to the masses, and they did not or could not know their rights, they were helpless and content, and lived and died as they were, tools and toilers, while those in power lived in luxury, ease, and splendor.[141]

Not only did the ignorance of the masses prevent them from improving their lot but, according to the utopian, it also made any attempt to change society impossible. In Albert Merrill's view, "any change, to be beneficial, must come from an increase of knowledge among the masses, since without this, any change is apt to create instability."[142] Thus, the conservative utopian, attributing a fickle and sometimes savage nature to the uneducated, felt the futility of his attempt to reform an unappreciative and possibly unwilling lower class. Since he did not wish to exclude any class or group from his utopia, and since the success of his ideal society rested on the intelligent and orderly conduct of its citizens, the utopian had little choice but to "consider the proposition unjust, that learning should only be bestowed in accordance with the occupation or station in life."[143]

Despite unanimity on the need for education, there was little agreement on the kind of education all should have. These writers were divided into two groups: those who thought education should deal with the practical problems of living in the world, and those who thought it should inculcate values of morality and independence that would enable the student to mold his life according to the highest ideals.

In the former group were utopians who believed that "education should fit a man for his environment."[144] They felt that the old classical curriculum, especially the "dead languages," had no place in the modern world. According to Fayette Giles, "Neither theology, history, literature, nor art, not the dead languages, nor Christian evidence can avail much."[145] The only subject worth studying, in their opinion, was science. To others in this group, science provided a key to an understanding of nature, and hence, nature's laws. These utopians, most of whom subscribed wholeheartedly to the values of the Enlightenment, defined the educated man as "one who possesses information which enables him to live in harmony with the laws of nature."[146] Like the Enlightenment distrust for the past, their criterion was mainly negative; their intent was to expunge the "prudishness and religionistic modesty of our forefathers" from the educational system as well as from the minds of people. In its place was the motto "All bathe in a natural state."[147]

However, these writers were a minority. The greater proportion of utopians placed their faith in the traditional subjects, especially those conveying moral virtue. A character in Byron Brooks's utopia, looking back to the 1890s, claimed, "Schools failed in the old days to give moral training."[148] Similarly, sectarian schools were praised because they

> were the only institutions in the land where the youth of both sexes could take to the best advantage those necessary lessons in self-restraint, self-reliance, self-control, and self-respect, with due regard for the rights of others.[149]

By the same token, vocational training was denounced. "People are educated for themselves, not for their livelihood," declared one utopian.[150] In reference to his own time, another complained, "The children of that age...were not permitted to select studies for which their innermost soul was yearning."[151] It was implied that their "innermost soul" did not yearn for the study of a trade or even for the knowledge necessary to become a corporation president.

The nature of these complaints revealed this group's stern belief in the moral value of education. They laid the same charge against education that they did against formal religion: both failed to inculcate the high-minded rectitude necessary to overcome the spirit of greed and commercialism. Education was accused of fostering that very limited and narrow outlook of the times. William Taylor claimed it never went beyond the point of discovery: "They stop short of the possibilities. They lose these possibilities in material and commercial utilization."[152] Furthermore, the schools were condemned not only for adopting the values of the commercial society by selling their knowledge to the few, but for reinforcing these values in their method of teaching. "The disciplinary system of education...crushed out individuality and molded all children in the industrial-political virtue of being bossed," claimed Edgar Chambless.[153]

The pervasiveness of anti-Christian values in contemporary society so embittered one writer that he lamented ever changing them through education. The disparity between the simple goodness taught in the schools and the hard reality of the "outside world" was too wide to be bridged. Paul Devinne described the problem:

At school, his [the student's] view of the outside world was rosy-hued, and the future was a dream. The good people of the outside world, he thought, would certainly help him. But on his entrance into this outer world, he began to realize that, instead of having to deal with helpful, kind-hearted people, he had to face, for the most part, a set of selfish and uncharitable enemies. His self-reliance, his faith, his religions—all shattered and wrecked, he wandered through the world a prey to disaster.[154]

Yet this was not the last word on this subject by the utopian. Though some sought to change the nature of education so that it might readily fit the world, the majority hoped the nature of the world would change to fit the ideals taught by education. Few took the trouble to outline what should be taught in the schools, but those who did constantly emphasized the moral virtues, especially concern for others. The fact that a good deal of the subject matter taught in the schools was inapplicable to daily living only served as one more proof to the utopian that the need for reform was evident.

RELIGION

Few utopian writers failed to realize that the ills of the era and the public morality were related. Religion was the guardian of that morality; it had obviously failed. A great number of writers laid the charge at the doors of the church and its clergy; a few others traced the source of social ills to the doctrines themselves. One voice proclaimed that the "sorrows of our decade are the result of abundance poured out upon a people imperfectly moralized," implying that institutionalized religion had not prepared its adherents for the abundance of industrialized capitalism.[155] Cosimo Noto added a further element to this reasoning when he blamed the churches for actually hindering the material development of society because they "hypnotized the mass of the people and made them believe what are really nothing but obscurities."[156]

Because he was a product of eighteenth-century thought as well as the anti-papal tradition of Protestantism, the utopian writer often associated institutionalized religion with the worst aspects of medieval history. While speaking of the Inquisition and the Crusades, Edward House declared: "In the name of Christ they committed atrocities that would put to blush the most benighted savages."[157] Albert Merrill, echoing the words of Charles M. Sheldon's "What Would Jesus Do?" movement, asked, "What would Christ have said if He had known the torture and the suffering in His name?"[158] There was great fear that history might return to an all-powerful single-church-dominated society. Some writers required a variety of religious sects in their ideal republic at all times. John Veiby prophesied that if one became dominant, "our Republic is doomed." It would be plunged into the "horrors of that night" that characterized society in the Middle Ages. Veiby would have tolerated incessant warfare between religious sects rather than allow one to remain without opposition.[159]

For the most part, however, sectarianism was denounced as much as a state-supported church. The Reverend W. S. Harris, whose experience was more direct than most people's, labeled interdenominational squabbles "humiliating." He declared:

If an effort is made to anticipate some form of sin that has taken sudacious root in the soil of our moral life, one reform element or denomination fights with the other until the hoe is so broken that there is nothing left wherewith to dig out the miserable roots of an obnoxious weed. Thus do we spend energies opposing one another instead of fighting the Devil.[160]

For the same reason, Henry Dowding boasted that in his Martian republic, "it is a common saying that there are no Sects...on Mars." A representative of this ideal society proudly claimed that his society "had not been handicapped by precedents contained in a thousand years of history."[161] To Dowding, this meant church history. The simplest solution to the problem—that is, the complete removal of institutionalized religion—occurred to several utopian writers. A representative of Albert Howard's future republic declared: "With respect to our religions, we are now happily able to say that visible religion is a thing of the Past."[162]

In ways quite similar to those of the leaders of the Social Gospel movement, the utopian writer launched an offensive against the conservative elements of established religion. First, the clergy were accused of being unsympathetic toward the real problems and sufferings of their parishioners. They were characterized as "wily seers...who hold you in fetters,"[163] or actors, "reciting short stanzas of strange, musical gibberish," whose "tales of horrid punishments buzzed constantly in their [the public's] ears—tales cunningly wrought so that no one could disprove them, coming from sources beyond human reach."[164] The horrible effect, claimed Frank Rosewater, was that it dulled people to the "real, active world." He went on to describe the clerics as having lost their humanity, "worshipping apart a cold creed of words."[165]

William Simpson had little patience to spare for the ministers of God. "They are the people," he said, "who have not failed, until recently, to supply you with an occasional change of supernatural pabulum to meet the new wants of a steadily advancing development."[166] They were the ones, added Zebina Forbush, who were "least able to discriminate between the spurious and the real." As a utopian, Forbush knew the clergy would constitute his bitterest opposition and would depict him as opposed to morals, even though his society was founded on the ways of Christ and his law of love.[167]

Utopians who tried to sympathize with the clergy often found them committed to preserving the status quo. Ministers were described as "sincere and honest, but with a limited idea of the spiritualism they essay to teach."[168] Church leaders were seen as "powerful prelates...ambitious of temporal power."[169] Edward Everett Hale, himself a minister, complained as early as 1869 that his role was vague and his work ill defined. He was sure to "give more definiteness to the work of the clergy and the churches" in his utopia, mainly by inaugurating social welfare programs.[170] When a crisis came to the economic order, the utopian often accused the clergy of responding unimaginatively and ineffectually. Frank Rosewater claimed that at such a time, "priests preached economy: prayers ascended in artificial smoke, and burnt incense was given their idol gods to sniff. Moral instincts and moral laws were appealed to."[171] Many a utopian writer acquired a bitter tone when he described the clergy's aloofness and insensitivity to human suffering.

Their strange substitution of theology for piety, of ceremonies for the service of God, of denominational zeal and controversy for religious fervor, and of Church going for loving God and their neighbor would be amusing were it not so tragic.[172]

The ire of these authors also extended to the churches themselves. Like the clergy, they were accused of emphasizing doctrine rather than ethics, religion rather than morality. One writer complained that "in addition to its inability to remedy the labor troubles, our religion had another defect—it did not meet the demand for simple justice."[173] Another cried out, "I want truths which may be apprehended by my reason and experience, which all men may grasp and live by."[174] William H. Bishop, a utopian who made his living writing romances, spoke for many when he wrote: "The Church mourns over sin, and the state punishes it when it develops into crime, but neither the one nor the other actually goes to work in earnest to prevent it."[175]

Stressing, as he did, the hope of creating the kingdom of heaven here on earth, the utopian writer became disenchanted with the otherworldly attitude of the churches. Albert Chavannes complained that "Christianity is losing its hold upon the working classes because they are no longer satisfied with promises redeemable in another world."[176] Man should be devoted to "happiness upon earth," he declared.[177] Richard Hatfield blandly stated that as soon as man "began to dwell upon spiritual things, his efforts were surely vain." He went on to explain that the only good resulting from the existence of the churches was their provision of monasteries to serve as "comforting retreats for the heartbroken and disconsolate."[178] It was far more profitable, complained Fayette Giles, for the orphans in religious asylums to seek their knowledge from "bulletin boards at the doors of newspaper offices" than to listen to the unworldly sentiments of their superiors.[179] On the other hand, when Ephraim Peterson, a newspaper editor in Missouri, accused the church of practicing "frenzied finance," it seemed he was denouncing them for being too worldly. However, his anger arose from their habit of telling people "they are going to get a dividend in the next world on their investments here."[180] Because of the indifference of the church to very real suffering and squalor, which Peterson must have known as a newspaper editor, he refused to be seen attending worship at any church "because no church on earth comes up to my standard of Christianity."[181]

Utopians who condemned the indifference of the church to human suffering were matched by another group of writers who were incensed by the unconcern and even calculated opposition of the church to material and scientific progress. The specter of Galileo's trial and conviction still caused outcry three centuries later, only this time all religions were indiscriminately lumped together as opponents to progress. Mary Lane, an admirer of Francis Bacon, bitterly proclaimed, "Prayer never saved one of my ancestors from premature death.... Prayer will never produce an improved airship."[182] Castello Holford even more bitterly complained about the failure of the Congregational Church to support the smallpox vaccination in colonial times.

The pulpit everywhere thundered against the impiety of vaccination. Smallpox was a wise dispensation of Providence to rid the poor man of the burden of his numerous family; it was a fitting punishment for the sins of the proud and impious. To attempt to escape from or abolish it was a sacrilege.[183]

Such well-known evidence caused other utopian writers to characterize religion as "absurd, irrational and self-contradictory in its dependence upon arbitrary and miraculous power."[184] Winnifred H. Cooley advocated a system of "rational religion" in his utopia to counteract the forces of "dogmatism, superstition, ritualism, emotionalism, and conservatism."[185] Less conciliatory writers happily precluded any vestige of established religion in their utopias.

If, on the one hand, the churches were accused of being too otherworldly and impeding scientific progress, on the other hand, they were condemned for being too much a part of the world the utopian opposed. Henry S. Frisbie, who sympathized with the Haymarket rioters and was a follower of Eugene V. Debs, put the question succinctly: "How shall a leech, being a leech, teach how to remove leeches from the body politic?"[186] More specifically, it was asked how the churches could denounce greed for money when they themselves were guilty of the same crime. "Gold had been their God," proclaimed Bradford Peck, who was a wealthy man himself. "Men went out on Monday, after attending Church services with only prayers on Sunday, with one idea—to make money," he declared.[187] Still another writer described in his bitterness how he had been a spectator at a fashionable wedding:

> ...in one of our Christian Churches, whose pastor and people, paradoxical as it may appear, professed to take the meek and lowly Jesus of Nazareth as an example of their lives. Arranged in gorgeous robes and sparkling with the most brilliant and costly of gems, these "meek and lowly" followers of the Nazarene presented a most striking contrast to that destitution I had just witnessed.[188]

Thus, among these utopian writers an outspoken minority condemned the churches for having failed to exercise their powers for social betterment. To stand idly by to watch their Christian brethren suffer and despair was bad enough, but to ape the very method of that exploitation was too much for some. C. W. Woodridge's representative of the twenty-first century happily pronounced the epitaph of institutional religion in his ideal society. "The Church was the last stronghold of materialism and when materialism passed into the limbo of ancient errors, the Church vanished with it."[189] Bradford Peck's summation of this group's feeling was characteristic. "Notwithstanding all the creeds and all the preaching," he said, "the system of life up to the twentieth century made it utterly impossible for anyone to live a true Christian existence."[190] The churches, these writers felt, had erred by being at once too removed from the real world and too much a part of it.

In summary, institutionalized religion was accused of squabbling over interdenominational differences while ignoring the real suffering of its membership. According to an outspoken minority of utopian writers, both the churches and their clergy had failed to improve the social climate because they either disdained "worldly things" or were too much a part of the greed and materialism of the day. In either case, they compromised their ability to guide the great mass of Christians along the path of justice and love; they abnegated their role as leaders of the flock, a flock that the utopian writer felt was being decimated by the evils of an economic system based on self-interest. The message of Christ failed to reach many people, both high and low.

In his ideal world, the utopian writer sought countermeasures for these failures. He opposed sectarianism with religious tolerance or a universal religion. Both lacked the formality of traditional religion and both were usually based on the ethical teachings of Christ. The utopian critic of traditional Christianity placed great value on man's self-sufficiency and his ability to control his fate by mastering the principles of nature through science. But most of all, the utopian hoped to salvage and preserve what he considered the most valuable contribution of Christianity to the world—the law of love.

Thus, in his discussion of the evils of his day, the utopian attacked a broad range of specific problems, all of which mirrored his larger struggle to retain cherished values in the face of changing times. In the economic realm, the majority of writers counterposed the greed of the businessman, the ruthless and impersonal unconcern of economic enterprise, and the stranglehold of monopoly on the economy against the Christian virtues of altruism and justice. However, the unwillingness of the utopian to condemn the businessman per se, his antipathy toward charity, and his advocacy of such solutions as inheritance taxes and fiat money indicated his acceptance of the basic goals of capitalistic society. His assumption of the spiritual, other-worldly attitude against the gross accumulation of mere wealth had little real conviction behind it. Rather, it was a facade, a handy tool used to condemn those wealthy members of the community who, he feared, would prevent others from attaining comparable wealth and power. Thus the economic values themselves were never really challenged; it was only their application to the few rather than the many that was in question.

With like reasoning, the utopian disavowed all suggestions for a fixed stratification of the social order. Committed to the values of equality and progress as he was, the utopian could not agree to a predetermined place in the social order. Besides, he fully recognized the evils of class consciousness, which he recognized as a necessary prelude to class rebellion. He thought that this upheaval was inevitable once the vast lower classes were deprived of any hope of advancement. The utopian perceived that many signs of this unhappy condition were already in evidence. The scarcity of capital, the special privilege and enormous power of large corporations, the institution of organized charity, and the unrest of the laboring class—all seemed to confirm the utopian's fear of revolution. In short, his fear of social chaos precluded the presence of a large, lower class without any outlet, ideological or real, for their unrest.

Next in importance to the utopian writer was the problem of labor, and it was only logical for him to support its cause while simultaneously denouncing the labor movement. He wanted to see the wages and conditions of the workingman improved, but he did not want to see him permanently identified as a laborer. And because the utopian assumed, rather than defended, the necessity for hard work, he, like the laissez-faire economist, regarded the problems of labor as those of production rather than of human rights. Efficiency was a most important goal for the utopian; therefore, he advocated the efficient allocation of talent and jobs, the stimulation of inventive genius, and laborsaving machinery. In sum, the utopian regarded every worker as a potential businessman and entrepreneur; thus, he supported those measures that would satisfy his enterprising spirit and quest for leisure.

In the political arena, the conflict of values was even more glaring. Because most utopians looked on the simplicity of man in the state of nature as an ideal, if not tenable, goal, they had little patience with the complicated laws and cumbersome legal system of the day. Basically, they wished all power to be in the hands of either the people or their elected representatives. Yet, at least two-thirds of these writers were sufficiently aware of the frailty of human nature to require strict controls for the assurance of the democratic process. They advocated the secret ballot, an educated electorate, voting restrictions, the referendum, initiative, and recall, civil service, free speech, and free press. Ironically, the government became the watchdog of these guarantees. More than half these writers were willing to concede the unworkability of their old laissez-faire beliefs by granting the government extensive controls to curb the increased power of big business. As long as the government was truly representative of the people's wishes, the utopian was content.

Although the problems of health, city living, drinking, and women's rights were given relatively little consideration in these utopias, the immediacy and poignancy of these concerns did as much to stimulate the utopian's anger as anything else. The utopian spoke frankly about the slum-ridden city as well as the dreary farm, and at least four utopias were devoted entirely to the solution of this problem. Once again, it was clear to these authors that natural living and increased technology were not compatible. Inasmuch as crime, drinking, and the exploitation of women were judged environmental problems, they became susceptible to immediate and practical solutions. Thus, in his ideal society, the utopian relied heavily on elaborate schemes for environmental planning and control. The more individualistic utopian counted on the force of public opinion rather than a central planning agency to achieve agreement on proper living conditions; nevertheless, all utopians insisted on well-ordered, mentally and physically healthful surroundings. If these writers had to abandon their values of individualism and self-reliance, at least in part, the majority were willing to do so.

Education and religion, the formative institutions of society, were forthrightly criticized by the utopian for condoning, implicitly or explicitly, the problems of the economic and social order. More than 90 percent of these works provide for universally required or free education. All the utopians considered education a practical instrument for attaining social ends, either as the dispenser of occupational knowledge or as the inculcator of moral virtue. A clear majority of these writers advocated the latter, more traditional point of view.

When it came to religion, however, the organized churches were rebuked both for their concentration on dogma instead of ethics and for their remoteness from the real problems of daily living. Much in the same language as the Social Gospelers, the utopian concluded that a new religion based on the law of love was necessary. Some, however, castigated all religious groups for their anti-scientific and hence anti-progressive attitudes.

Yet, taken as a whole, the presence of a vaguely and loosely organized religion was tolerated, although it was not given an important place in the society of the future. Instead, the ethical system of the utopians was built around the doctrine of love and the golden rule.

Clearly, then, the utopian took exception to almost every phase of his contemporary society. He most of all feared the concentration of wealth in the hands of a relatively few men whose power was well nigh unbounded. Their usurpation of the laws and values considered essential to the American way of life was already evident to the utopian in the form of labor strife, trusts and monopolies, squalor in the cities and land swindles in the country, booms and depressions, political corruption, poor health, and alcoholism. The old values of equality, progress, and hard work were being undermined; the utopian was frightened not only by the presence of these problems, but by the indifference with which they were greeted. Looking ahead, the utopian perceived a dismal and contradictory future, a future he could not abide. Alarmed, his only recourse was to describe painfully the manner in which he thought his contemporaries went astray in the hope that their awakened sense of justice would bring redress and reform.

NOTES

1. William Bishop, *The Garden of Eden, U. S. A.* (Chicago: Charles H. Kerr & Co., 1895), p. 178.
2. Ibid., p. 122.
3. William Simpson, *The Man From Mars* (San Francisco: Bacon & Co., 1891), p. 132.
4. James Cowen, *Daybreak: A Romance of an Old World* (New York: George H. Richmond & Co., 1896), p. 25.
5. Paul Devinne, *The Day of Prosperity: A Vision of the Century to Come* (New York: G. W. Dillingham & Co., 1902), p. 23.
6. Bessie S. Rogers, *As It May Be: A Story of the Future* (Boston: Richard G. Badger, The Gorham Press, 1905), p. 60.
7. William Alexander Taylor, *Intermere* (Columbus, Ohio: Twentieth Century Publishing Co., 1901), p. 43.
8. C. W. Woodridge, *Perfecting the Earth* (Cleveland: Utopia Publishing Co., 1902), p. 216.

9. Bradford Peck, *The World A Department Store* (Boston: Bradford Peck, Publisher, 1900), p. 297.
10. Henry L. Call, *The Coming Revolution* (Boston: Arena Publishing Co., 1895), p. 5.
11. Henry S. Frisbie, *Prophet of the Kingdom* (Washington, D.C.: Neal Publishing Co., 1901), p. 21.
12. Byron Alden Brooks, *Earth Revisited* (Boston: Arena Publishing Co., 1893), p. 99.
13. Frank Rosewater, *'96: A Romance of Utopia* (Omaha: Utopia Publishing Co., 1894), p. 103.
14. John Veiby, *The Utopian Way* (South Bend, Ind.: n.p., 1917), p. 28.
15. [Alonso Van Deusen], *Rational Communism: The Present and Future Republic of North America* (New York: Social Science Publishing Co., 1885), p. 16.
16. Brooks, *Earth Revisited*, p. 35.
17. Jack London, "Goliah," in *Revolution and Other Essays* (New York: Macmillan Co., 1910), p. 98.
18. [William S. Child], *The Legal Revolution of 1902* (Chicago: Charles H. Kerr & Co., 1898), p. 66.
19. R. A. Dague, *Henry Ashton* (Alameda, Calif.: The Author, 1903), p. 200.
20. Rosewater, *'96*, p. 23.
21. Henry L. Everett, *The People's Program: The Twentieth Century Is Theirs* (New York: Workman's Publishing Co., 1892), p. 186.
22. [Child], *The Legal Revolution of 1902*, p. 64.
23. [Edward M. House], *Philip Dru, Administrator: A Story of Tomorrow, 1920–1935* (New York: B. W. Huebsch, 1912), p. 42.
24. Corwin Phelps, *An Ideal Republic; or, A Way Out of the Fog* (Chicago: W. L. Reynolds, 1896), p. 16.
25. Zebina Forbush, *The Co-Opolitan* (Chicago: Charles H. Kerr & Co., 1898), p. 90.
26. Call, *Coming Revolution*, p. 29.
27. Edward Bellamy, *Equality* (New York: D. Appleton & Co., 1897), p. 13.
28. Devinne, *Day of Prosperity*, p. 103.
29. *Man or Dollar, Which?* (Chicago: Charles H. Kerr & Co., 1896), p. 98.
30. [House], *Philip Dru*, p. 8.
31. [Child], *Legal Revolution*, p. 115.
32. Clark Edmund Persinger, *Letters From New America; or, An Attempt At Practical Socialism* (Chicago: Charles H. Kerr & Co, 1900), p. 78.

33. S. Byron Welcome, *From Earth's Center: A Polar Gateway Message* (Chicago: Charles H. Kerr & Co., 1894), p. 214.

34. Albert Adams Merrill, *The Great Awakening* (Boston: George Book Publishing Co., 1899), p. 247.

35. Simpson, *Man From Mars*, p. 116.

36. Costello N. Holford, *Aristopia* (Boston: Arena Publishing Co., 1895), p. 93.

37. Call, *Coming Revolution*, p. 3.

38. Rosewater, *'96*, p. 10.

39. C. A. Steere, *When Things Were Done* (Chicago: Charles H. Kerr & Co., 1908), p. 113.

40. Ibid., p. 115.

41. [Child], *Legal Revolution*, p. 116.

42. Frisbie, *Prophet of the Kingdom*, p. 9.

43. Henry W. Dowding, *The Man From Mars; or, Service For Service's Sake* (New York: Cochrane Publishing Co., 1910), p. 198.

44. Simpson, *Man From Mars*, p. 34.

45. Walter O. Henry, *Equitania; or, The Land of Equity* (Omaha: n.p., 1914), p. 18.

46. J. P. Armour, *Edenindia: A Tale of Adventure* (New York: G. W. Dillingham Co., 1905), p. 125.

47. Taylor, *Intermere*, p. 41.

48. Merrill, *Great Awakening*, p. 51.

49. [House], *Philip Dru*, p. 236.

50. *Man or Dollar, Which?*, p. 119.

51. Bishop, *Garden of Eden*, p. 181.

52. Cowen, *Daybreak*, p. 129.

53. Alfred Hutchinson, *The Limit of Wealth* (New York: Macmillan Co., 1907), p. 60.

54. Brooks, *Earth Revisited*, p. 47.

55. Charles W. Caryl, *New Era* (Denver: New Era Union, 1897), p. 7.

56. Dague, *Henry Ashton*, p. 225.

57. [House], *Philip Dru*, p. 55.

58. London, "Goliath," p. 99.

59. Ibid.

60. [Child], *Legal Revolution*, p. 229.

61. Veiby, *Utopian Way*, p. 76.

62. [Van Deusen], *Rational Communism*, p. 59.

63. Caryl, *New Era*, p. 39.

64. [Mary Lane], *Mizora: A Prophesy*. By Princess Vera Zarevitch (New York: G. W. Dillingham & Co., 1889), p. 128.

65. William Fishbough, *America and the World* (New York: Continental Publishing Co., 1898), pp. 316–17.
66. Cowen, *Daybreak*, p. 94.
67. Caryl, *New Era*, p. 39.
68. [House], *Philip Dru*, p. 222.
69. Henry Olerich, *A Cityless and Countryless World: An Outline of Practical Co-Operative Individualism* (Holstein, Iowa: Gilmore & Olerich, 1893), p. 5.
70. Ibid, p. 35.
71. Simpson, *Man from Mars*, p. 48.
72. Merrill, *Great Awakening*, p. 110.
73. [F. U. Worley], *Three Thousand Dollars a Year: Moving Forward; or, How We Got There* (Washington, D.C.: J. P. Wright, 1890), pp. 22–23.
74. Caryl, *New Era*, p. 153.
75. T. H. Tibbles and Elia M. Beattie, *The American Peasant* (Chicago: F. J. Schulte & Co., 1892), p. 16.
76. Peck, *World A Department Store*, p. 266.
77. [Jacob W. Horner], *Military Socialism* (Indianapolis: The Author, 1911), p. 76.
78. Daniel Bond, *Uncle Sam in Business* (Chicago: Charles H. Kerr & Co., 1899), p. 11.
79. [House], *Philip Dru*, p. 199.
80. Merrill, *Great Awakening*, p. 23.
81. [Samuel Crocker], *That Island* (Kansas City, Mo.: C. E. Streeter & Co., 1892), p. 22.
82. [House], *Philip Dru*, p. 251.
83. Solomon Schindler, *Young West* (Boston: Arena Publishing Co., 1894), p. 210.
84. Cowen, *Daybreak*, p. 251.
85. John Bachelder, *A.D. 2050* (San Francisco: The Bancroft Co., 1890), p. 80.
86. Rev. William S. Harris, *Life in a Thousand Worlds* (Cleona, Pa.: G. Holzapfel, 1905), p. 131.
87. [Horner], *Military Socialism*, p. 76.
88. Forbush, *The Co-Opolitan*, p. 50.
89. Henry, *Equitania*, p. 42.
90. Devinne, *Day of Prosperity*, p. 240.
91. Albert W. Howard, *The Milltillionaire* (n.p., 1906), p. 19.
92. Hutchinson, *Limit of Wealth*, p. 555.
93. [House], *Philip Dru*, p. 41.
94. [George Hamilton Phelps], *The New Columbia; or, The Re–*

United States (Findlay, Ohio: New Columbia Publishing Co., 1909), p. 32.

95. Edward Everett Hale, *Sybaris and Other Homes* (Boston: Fields, Osgood & Co., 1869), p. 176.

96. [Phelps], *New Columbia*, p. 32.

97. Simpson, *Man From Mars*, p. 4.

98. Devinne, *Day of Prosperity*, pp. 54–55.

99. [Ignatius Donnelly], *Caesar's Column: A Story of the Twentieth Century* (Chicago: F. J. Schulte & Co., 1890), p. 28.

100. Milan C. Edson, *Solaris Farm, A Story of the Twentieth Century* (Washington, D.C.: The Author, 1900), p. iv.

101. Herman H. Brinsmade, *Utopia Achieved: A Novel of the Future* (New York: Broadway Publishing Co., 1912), p. 96.

102. Peck, *World A Department Store*, p. 239.

103. Brinsmade, *Utopia Achieved*, p. 23.

104. Edson, *Solaris Farm*, p. iv.

105. [Child], *Legal Revolution*, p. 113.

106. Dowding, *Man From Mars*, p. 236.

107. Hutchinson, *Limit of Wealth*, p. 96.

108. Lena J. Fry, *Other Worlds* (Chicago: The Author, 1905), p. 129.

109. [Lane], *Mizora*, p. 225.

110. [Donnelly], *Caesar's Column*, p. 26.

111. [House], *Philip Dru*, p. 230.

112. Harris, *Life in a Thousand Worlds*, p. 312.

113. Howard, *The Milltillionaire*, p. 5.

114. Brinsmade, *Utopia Achieved*, p. 14.

115. Cowen, *Daybreak*, p. 112.

116. Devinne, *Day of Prosperity*, p. 76.

117. Cosimo Noto, *The Ideal City* (New York: n.p., 1904), p. 63.

118. Schindler, *Young West*, p. 45.

119. Dague, *Henry Ashton*, p. 217.

120. David H. Wheeler, *Our Industrial Utopia and Its Unhappy Citizens* (Chicago: A. C. McClurg & Co., 1895), p. 194.

121. Veiby, *Utopian Way*, p. 59.

122. Ibid, p. 60.

123. Dowding, *Man From Mars*, p. 237.

124. Alcanoan O. Grigsby, *Nequa; or, The Problem of the Ages* (Topeka, Kans.: Equity Publishing Co., 1900), p. 31.

125. Tibbles, *American Peasant*, p. 14.

126. Dowding, *Man From Mars*, p. 240.

127. Richard M. Chapman, *The Vision of the Future* (New York: Cosmopolitan Press, 1916), p. 70.

128. Bishop, *Garden of Eden*, p. 269.
129. Ibid.
130. Devinne, *Day of Prosperity*, p. 115.
131. [Lane], *Mizora*, p. 200.
132. Devinne, *Day of Prosperity*, p. 111.
133. Veiby, *Utopian Way*, p. 58.
134. Harris, *Life in a Thousand Worlds*, p. 197.
135. Welcome, *From Earth's Center*, p. 50.
136. Ibid, p. 226.
137. Henry, *Equitania*, p. 62.
138. Veiby, *Utopian Way*, p. 22.
139. Dague, *Henry Ashton*, pp. 202–3.
140. [Van Deusen], *Rational Communism*, p. 237.
141. D. Lull, *Celestia* (New York: Reliance Trading Co., 1907), p. 103.
142. Merrill, *Great Awakening*, p. 300.
143. Simpson, *Man From Mars*, p. 51.
144. Fayette S. Giles, *Shadows Before; or, A Century Onward* (New York: Humbolt Publishing Co., 1894), p. 22.
145. Ibid., p. 23.
146. Olerich, *Cityless and Countryless World*, p. 315.
147. Phelps, *Ideal Republic*, p. 18.
148. Brooks, *Earth Revisited*, p. 11.
149. Worley, *Three Thousand Dollars*, p. 11.
150. Bishop, *Garden of Eden*, p. 184.
151. Schindler, *Young West*, p. 57.
152. Taylor, *Intermere*, p. 111.
153. Edgar Chambless, *Roadtown* (New York: Roadtown Press, 1910), p. 127.
154. Devinne, *Day of Prosperity*, p. 172.
155. Wheeler, *Industrial Utopia*, p. 12.
156. Noto, *Ideal City*, p. 47.
157. [House], *Philip Dru*, p. 12.
158. Merrill, *Great Awakening*, p. 101.
159. Veiby, *Utopian Way*, p. 25.
160. Harris, *Life in a Thousand Worlds*, p. 97.
161. Dowding, *Man From Mars*, p. 283.
162. Howard, *Milltillionaire*, p. 12.
163. Simpson, *Man From Mars*, pp. 39–40.
164. Rosewater, *'96*, p. 227.
165. Ibid., p. 231.
166. Simpson, *Man From Mars*, p. 41.

167. Forbush, *The Co-Opolitan*, p. 127.
168. Taylor, *Intermere*, p. 114.
169. Ibid.
170. Hale, *Sybaris*, p. 66.
171. Rosewater, *'96*, p. 89.
172. Brooks, *Earth Revisited*, p. 45.
173. Cyrus Cole, *The Auroraphone* (Chicago: Charles H. Kerr & Co., 1890), p. 91.
174. Brooks, *Earth Revisited*, p. 16.
175. Bishop, *Garden of Eden*, p. 254.
176. Albert Chavannes, *The Future Commonwealth; or, What Samuel Balcom Saw in Socioland* (New York: True Nationalist Publishing Co., 1892), p. 19.
177. Ibid, p. 63.
178. Richard Hatfield, *Geyserland: Empiricism in Social Reform* (Washington, D.C.: The Author, 1908), p. 252.
179. Giles, *Shadows Before*, p. 57.
180. Ephraim Peterson, *An Ideal City For An Ideal People* (Independence, Mo.: The Author, 1905), p. 49.
181. Ibid., p. 41.
182. [Lane], *Mizora*, p. 257.
183. Holford, *Aristopia*, p. 165.
184. Woodridge, *Perfecting the Earth*, p. 231.
185. Winnifred H. Cooley, "A Dream of the Twenty-First Century," *The Arena* 28 (November 1902), p. 515.
186. Frisbie, *Prophet of the Kingdom*, p. 20.
187. Peck, *World A Department Store*, p. 5.
188. [Van Deusen], *Rational Communism*, p. 19.
189. Woodridge, *Perfecting the Earth*, p. 232.
190. Peck, *World A Department Store*, p. 5.

4

Types of Utopias

Although utopias have been examined in many ways, in this study no preconceived form was used to categorize these 119 examples; rather, the aim was to type them solely on the basis of their own structures. All similar utopias were collected under one heading, and, it was hoped, the resulting categories would amount to the sum of their common features. Yet, despite the simplicity of the scheme, it became necessary to assign an order of precedence to the features used as a basis of comparison, and therefore each utopia has been classed according to the following criteria: attitude toward government, method of controlling the distribution and production of wealth, historical sources and values, and kind and extent of both environmental and social planning.

The first of these criteria, the utopian's attitude toward the powers of government, was generally the simplest and most decisive way to categorize these works. In the first place, by the end of the nineteenth century political theorists and philosophers were discussing the forms of government far more extensively than any other element in the formation of society; consequently, there was a large range of possibilities. The extremes—anarchy and totalitarianism—represented the boundaries, as it were, within which the utopian could select his form of government. For the most part, he chose to make some compromise and select a middle ground; however, the utopias, taken as a whole group, ranged from near anarchy and distrust for political power in the individualist states, to a form of government very close to the modern totalitarian state.

The second criterion for classifying these works, the method and distribution of wealth, usually coincided with the theory of government. On the one hand, the individualist writers, who supported a laissez-faire policy of government, relied wholly on individual initiative for perfecting their state. On the other hand, the cooperative utopians accepted the principles of modern production; however, they abandoned the wage system. The legal utopians organized their economies on the principles of private enterprise; however, they advocated legislative action and legal sanctions for the many abuses they saw in the capitalist system. Finally, the socialist and totalitarian utopians differed on this point only in degree, attempting to control thoroughly both the production and the distribution of wealth.

Thus far, then, by applying these criteria, the majority of utopias could be classed in the following groups: individualist, cooperative, legal, socialist, and totalitarian. The first and last represented the extremes of the individualist-collective dilemma; those in between characterized some form of compromise. A small number of utopias did not fit any of these categories, primarily because they were less concerned with wealth or government than with creating the proper environment for living a better life. The Greek city-state, as well as some phases of Darwinian evolution, served as models for these writers; therefore, they have been classed in a separate category called the ideal city.

THE INDIVIDUALIST UTOPIA

The glorification and fulfillment of the individual was the *raison d'etre* for society in the individualist utopia. The exaltation of self and the pursuit of self-interest were its greatest values; Francis Bacon, Benjamin Franklin, Charles Darwin, and Ralph Waldo Emerson were its gods. The doctrine of laissez faire and the method of science combined with the euphoria of romanticism to make these writers rhapsodic when speaking of the society of the future. Every idea, value, and program supported their optimistic hopes for the ultimate perfection of the individual: natural selection, the conquest of nature, the millennium, the forces of pure competition, and the eternal laws of supply and demand. The control of one's environment was important, but even more important was the molding of one's character through proper upbringing and education. Society rested ultimately on the virtue of every one of its members; consequently, order, industry, and sometimes love were assiduously cultivated. Conscience, along with the notion that the kingdom of God is within you, was all-important. The unfit and the lazy were ruthlessly persecuted or simply denied access to the perfected land of the future.

The distribution of wealth was not the primary problem of this society. First and foremost, the individualist utopian hoped to create the conditions wherein each person had the greatest freedom to fulfill himself or herself in his or her own way. It was assumed that everyone would be materially satisfied, either through the careful pursuit of his or her interest, the fruits of scientific investigation, or the mutual sharing of all wealth. The method of attaining wealth was important only insofar as it permitted the most diverse expression of individual talent and interest. For this reason, the role of the government or a central planning agency was minimal, if allowed at all. The law, that perennial reminder of human weakness, was hardly necessary; in many societies its use, like that of a vestigial organ, declined to the vanishing point. Politics, too, needed no practitioners in this type utopia. Political management of the economic system was the demon these writers excoriated for having destroyed the conditions of pure competition and the practice of true Christian love. Trusts, monopolies, financial power, political corruption, excessive regulation—all prompted these writers to proclaim the supremacy of personal rights and individual freedom.

Pure Competition

Within the category of individualistic utopias, two authors, John Bachelder and David Wheeler, advocated pure competition as the best means of social organization. When speaking of the economic order, both writers, but especially David

Wheeler, reiterated almost verbatim the words of Adam Smith. According to Wheeler, "the economic man is the competing man."[1] Wealth was gained by selling the product of one's labor, a practice in which "each man gets what he prefers to what he gives."[2] Prices and profits were determined by a rational self-interest. It was assumed that anyone could be successful under this system of mutually advantageous exchanges. "The man who owns anything can sell it and mobilize it; the man who has not anything is free to get the same way as others."[3] Of course, in this utopia "the working man has, indeed, all the motives of the economic man to push him upward by self-help."[4]

This rampant individualism, however, needed checks and balances, even in the utopia that espoused laissez faire. Wheeler demanded a strict application of law to any violent or extra-legal way of acquiring property or wealth. Bachelder relied on the government to control the prices of any corporation that sought to create a monopoly. In Wheeler's utopia, personal property was limited to $100,000. In both utopias, any interference with the "iron law of wages" or the law of supply and demand was immediately punished. "Crushing competition is like damming Niagara," claimed Wheeler.[5] "We have no royal road to eminent attainments or position," declared Bachelder. "Competition tempered with laudable ambition we regard as the true source of inspiration."[6]

The development of character was the chief instrument for order in this society. "The moral law and the moral nature must regulate the conduct of a competitor as it regulates the conduct of a teacher; each has a sphere of self-control."[7] In Bachelder's utopian society, the qualifications for citizenship were "good moral character, intelligence, industrious habits, and good physical and mental condition."[8] This author further believed that it was every person's "sacred duty to labor to make the world better for having lived in it," but the precise method of remaking the world was left to the individual.[9] In short, reform of character was reform of society. "Nothing but industrial intelligence and industrial honesty will save our imperiled millions," claimed Wheeler.[10]

This reliance on an established moral system and the values of the Protestant ethic, a stringent enforcement of law, and the law of supply and demand left little else for these writers to recommend in the way of reform. Bachelder added some rules for social conduct, but concerning social classes he was content to allow a man to be a man for what he was.[11] Since the laborer was always regarded as a potential capitalist, there was little need to discuss social classes. It was understood that as a result of individual differences, some people would be superior and others inferior. This was the natural order of things, and the utopian of this stamp would as soon violate his own conscience as he would this order. Significantly, though, this order did not demand the redistribution of wealth, nor were the superior individuals considered candidates for the greatest share of wealth. "All philosophers are agreed," declared Wheeler, "that abundance seldom or never produces happiness.... Enlightened and moralized human beings have in all times been happy in spite of abundance, and such persons are found in great numbers in our utopia."[12] In sum, competition was seen as a means of personal fulfillment, a stimulus to character development; and the end product, wealth, was only a sign of this greater goal.

Scientism

In another facet of individualistic utopias, the six utopians who advocated the scientific utopia (J. P. Armour, Arthur Bird, Amos K. Fiske, Mary Lane, D. Herbert Heywood, and Bessie Rogers) placed their greatest hopes in man's ability to uncover and utilize the forces of nature. To them, the method of science was a way of life, and only superlatives could describe the extent of its accomplishments. The imagery of the garden, suggesting the Garden of Eden, was typical. "No parts... were given up to the wilderness or desert," said Amos Fiske, "but labor had brought the wilderness into subjection and made the desert like a garden, to minister to the wants of the people."[13] Technological and human advancements abounded in this kind of utopia, including telephones, airships, solar energy, chemical food, perfect health, mental communication, and machinery that matched every human movement. Much of it sounded like science fiction, yet these works were offered in all seriousness by men who made science into a god.

To the writers of this group, science transcended mere matter. In Heywood's utopia, the citizens educated themselves by the mysterious power of mental absorption. When this ability was possessed by the entire population of the world, everyone would be capable of comprehending the mystical force that ruled the universe, thus insuring peace and harmony. In Mary Lane's land of women, everyone possessed "lofty aims, unselfishness in living, perfect love, honor, intellectual grandeur, and universal comfort and luxury."[14] Health was assured in Armour's Edenindia through each person's ability to perceive the laws of nature. Sickness was considered "an ignoble condition, the result of some violation of natural laws."[15] In Bessie Rogers's utopia, thought transference revealed each person's inner thoughts; therefore, secret hatreds, jealousies and suspicions were done away with. To these writers, then, the mysterious forces of nature could only be apprehended by the equally mysterious quality of the human mind. Just as science had begun to conquer the laws of matter, so too, in the society of the future it would extend its province to the laws of the mind.

The Enlightenment ideal of human oneness that these writers espoused produced some uncertainty on the question of individualism. Not all believed in man's ability to govern himself. In Armour's society, the king declared: "You will...realize that the life of an individual is as nothing compared with the continued happiness of my people."[16] On the other hand, Heywood was willing to allow each person "to choose what suits him best, and to work out that idea or thought."[17] The people of Mary Lane's utopia were so perfect that government was unnecessary. Yet, everyone had to contribute his share to the general welfare. "A tree has a million leaves," she wrote, "yet each individual leaf, insignificant as it may appear, has its special share of work to perform in helping the tree to live and perfect its fruit."[18]

Little attention was paid to the form of government or the distribution of wealth. There was no government at all in the utopias of Rogers and Lane, and a benevolent despot in Armour's utopia precluded the need for one. The wealth of the community could be shared equally by the inhabitants, as in the utopias of Heywood and Armour; or, as in the utopias of Rogers and Lane, some could be entitled to more than others. It was assumed in both cases that science would solve the problems of production. The example of Mary Lane's utopia was typical: "Bread came from the laboratory, and not from the soil by the sweat of the brow."[19]

In the realm of social issues, these writers believed most in education and environmental control. Universal education was the great destroyer of castes, except in the utopias of Rogers and Armour. In the former, there was no need for it since "the children are born good; they need no bringing up."[20] In the latter, everyone was required to go to school till the age of twelve, but only 15 percent could go beyond what was required. It was Armour's belief that "it would be interfering with their natural inclination unjustifiably and would result in economic waste by insisting on their having more [education]."[21] Concerning the environment, all manner of improvements were brought about through science. However, the optimism of the scientific outlook prevented these writers from subscribing to the idea of natural selection or the destructive force of nature.

Thus, the value of science, buttressed by Enlightenment thinking as well as the doctrine of evolution, represented the means to a perfect way of life for these five utopians. Their faith was great, not only in the method of science but in human nature as well. Progress was limited only by the human intellect and imagination. Utimately, all would live in comfort, if not in luxury, but more importantly, each person would be free from the cares of survival to develop his higher nature.

Individual Perfection

In the last category of individualistic-minded writers, five utopians (James Cowen, Fayette Giles, Mortimer D. Leggett, D. Lull, and M. Louise Moore) decided to center their reformed societies on the perfected individual. Like the previous types in this group, they were heavily committed to the values of the Enlightenment—science, evolution, and laissez faire. To these could be added Christian love. But even though love was important, it was advocated for the benefit of the giver, not the receiver, who inadvertently gained too. Love was regarded as the molder of better character; by the reform of each person, the society as a whole would benefit. Government, external restraints, even socially propagated, were avoided. Little emphasis was put upon law, for education of the proper sort along with a well-formed environment were enough for the assurance of good conduct by all.

In the utopia of individual perfection, will and conscience were prominent. Leggett, as well as the other members of this group, paid much lip service to the idea of the "regeneration of individuals" through the "blessed gospel of Jesus." "That this gospel contains a panacea for every personal, social, and political evil," he said, "few serious and thinking people entertain an honest doubt."[22] He looked upon society as a composite of human "integers," and he felt that the gospel of Jesus was wonderfully adapted to perfecting these "integers."[23] By the same token, Reverend Lull regarded conscience as "the first, best, and most vital of all human culture." When asked why, he replied: "Because conscientiousness, when by early and right training it becomes general and controlling, solves and simplifies all the problems of human life."[24] In a more secular vein, James Cowen poetically idealized love in the form of the fairest woman in the land. "She seemed as incapable of evil as the birds of the air.... She was guileless by nature, and goodness and truth were as much a part of her as her beauty was."[25]

Thus, for the individualist utopian, innate human goodness precluded a need for government. Fayette Giles insisted that the "rule of the State...should be more advisory than compulsory; that the Government is for and by the people, not the people for the government; and that man is free to do what he will, provided he infringe not the equal freedom of all."[26] In her utopian land, the government had originally managed the railroads and industrial enterprises, but it had not "proved to be advantageous and has now been abandoned."[27] Exactly why, she did not say. Later, she alluded to the superiority of a laissez-faire policy in which "men are free to mine and use silver, or to produce and use agricultural products as they will. Other men are free to refuse or accept them as they will."[28] Self-interest was the guiding principle of the economy.

Mortimer D. Leggett, who looked upon all conduct from a moral point of view, cited the old principle that morals could not be legislated. When they were, he declared, the resulting laws "became dead letters upon the statute-books because of the indisposition or unwillingness of the people to enforce them."[29] The only legitimate activity the government could undertake in these utopias was the education of the children, so that "the moral and social condition... of the masses of people could be raised to as high a standard as possible."[30] Yet even in Cowen's utopia the government could not contribute toward uplifting the public morals because "no one... needs governing."[31] There were no rulers or legislators; the only organization for mutual help was the family, wherein character was so formed that, when the children went forth into the world, no one desired to wrong his or her neighbor.[32]

The distribution of wealth, too, posed no problem for these utopians. Through the advances of science and laborsaving machinery, production was plentiful. The lack of social classes and the oneness of human goodness demanded that some form of equal or common distribution take place. In Cowen's ideal society, all property was owned in common, but individual persons had the right to use it. Leggett allowed those who worked on the land to own it; those who worked in industry shared the profits equally, both worker and capitalist. Unused property was highly taxed. Moore allowed everyone an equitable share of the total production of the community, whereas Giles and Lull retained the institution of private property.

Education and environmental control were important. Leggett, Giles, and Cowen tempered their individualism with a strong faith in evolution and environmental planning. Giles asserted that education "must include a knowledge of the fixed, unchangeable laws of our environment."[33] In her utopia, genealogical records were kept for everyone, and only those individuals possessing the best physiological and psychological traits could marry and reproduce. Leggett admitted that in the process of individual development, "outside influences, environment, surrounding circumstances, had much to do in evolving the desirable and suppressing the undesirable."[34] This was God's law of evolution, he declared. In Cowen's utopia, probably the nearest of any to the ideals of the Enlightenment, scientific training and love for one's neighbor constituted each person's entire education. The utopias of Moore and Lull did not stress the environment as such. They assumed each individual would develop his or her innate goodness to the highest possible degree without any external prodding.

In sum, these five utopians relied almost solely on self-interest and love to bring about an ideal way of life. The only limit to the individualist society was human indifference. Nevertheless, the optimism of these authors was vast. The problems of wealth and survival should disappear, they thought, once the natural, boundless resources of nature were utilized through the mastery of her secrets. Government, law, and political and social organizations were deemed extraneous once individual goodness was allowed to bear its fruit.

THE COOPERATIVE UTOPIA

The values of the cooperative utopia closely corresponded to those of the individualist utopia. Both centered their reform of society on the industry and moral uprightness of the individual; however, the cooperative utopia recognized the greater efficiency and productivity of organizing individual effort into mutually helpful units. The personal virtues of love, order, industriousness, and good conscience were stressed; but the value of equality received priority. Instead of viewing the society and economic order in terms of a one-to-one relationship, as did the individualist utopian, the cooperative utopian thought in terms of groups of individuals that had mutual interests. Ideally, a man could satisfy both his spiritual and his material needs in this utopia; he could retain his own privacy and yet feel free in the company of others.

Intellectually, this utopian was still a child of the Enlightenment, valuing order, efficiency, and the innate goodness of human nature. The value of love was all-important and served as the entire basis for one kind of cooperative utopia, the commune. These utopias used earlier nineteenth-century reform proposals as their models, especially the cooperative and profit-sharing plan of Robert Owen and the Rochdale system; the associational communities advocated by Charles Fourier and his American disciples, Albert Brisbane and Horace Greeley; the syndicalism of the French trade-union movement; and the pure communism of Marx. The cooperative utopian was particularly interested in the common objective of all these systems, namely, to bring about a more direct relationship between a worker and the product of his or her labor. He suspiciously regarded monopolies, trusts, middlemen, and complicated schemes of financing as methods of channeling the product of labor into the hands of the nonproducer. To the cooperative utopian, wealth could only be the direct and sole product of labor.

It was assumed then that if the worker knew he would receive the equivalent of his labor in pay, he would diligently apply himself to his work. Possibly, he could even share his output with a less dextrous or less endowed neighbor who did not produce so much. In fact, this mutual help was thought to be the most satisfying of all the rewards in the system, for it allowed each person to feel responsible for the welfare of his or her neighbor. The cooperative utopian hoped to conquer the problem of efficient production by appealing to each person's sense of duty both to himself and to his or her neighbor. Governments or external coercion were deemed unnecessary. A person agreed either to the equitable sharing of all wealth produced by the community or to a basic salary in proportion to his or her skill. Most often a person did not have a choice. In both cases, however, the middleman was eliminated; the true producer could therefore depend on a just reward.

However, in order to solve the problems of production and distribution without developing the complex organizational apparatus of modern capitalism, this type of utopia was purposely kept small and self-sustaining. It is true that some authors projected beyond the initial, self-contained, exclusive cooperative enterprise to a time when the entire country would participate; but this stage of development was rarely described. Also, because these societies were usually confined to a small area, much emphasis was placed on creating pleasant living conditions. Education was provided, usually without charge. Healthful country living was the usual fare. Simplicity and directness characterized every aspect of living. The fate of one was the fate of all; and with this knowledge in mind, all worked efficiently to maintain and improve the standard of living.

The Commune

The commune was the first cooperative utopia. Advocated by ten authors (Ralph Albertson, Edward Bassett, William Bishop, Thomas Collens, Alcander Longley, Lewis Masquerier, Ephraim Peterson, Titus Smith, J. W. Sullivan, and Mary Tincker), it was an exclusive, self-contained community in which the members agreed to work for the common good according to the preestablished ideals of its founders. Love, altruism, and mutual help were valued most highly; material success was less important. The prototypes for this society were the associational communities advocated by Fourier and the communitarian experiments in America before the Civil War. Their announced purpose was not only the efficient use of common facilities but, more important, the opportunity to work for the common benefit under the guidance of Christian love.

Thus, in Ralph Albertson's Christian Commonwealth Colony, which was typical of the group, love was the central value. "The greatest need of the world," he said, "is its need of love applied to its economic life. We need social reforms, but primarily we need social regeneration. Logically and necessarily redemption will precede reformation and love is the only redemptive force to count on."[35] The true test of Albertson's dedication to Christian love was made when it became clear that the colony's policy of admitting anyone who applied was undermining its stability and order. Nevertheless, he steadfastly refused to bar the door to men and women who sincerely sought salvation through love. He felt that otherwise there would be no excuse for the colony's existence. The fact that Albertson still proclaimed the reformative power of love in his utopia after the colony's failure attested to the strength of his belief.

In connection with the production and distribution of wealth, all members of the community worked together for the common good; in all but one utopia, everyone shared equally in the wealth. It was felt that property ownership developed the acquisitive spirit and its attendant aggressiveness, both of which are alien to the spirit of Christianity. "We do hold," said Albertson, "that property-selfishness is fundamentally and directly responsible for the prevailing conditions in human life in which are cultivated the deepest and darkest passions of all men."[36] Peterson's ideal was to "merge the economic with the spiritual and the moral ethics of Christianity"; therefore, the applicant for citizenship in the Ideal City was required to sell all his property and donate the proceeds to the common treasury.[37] However, the most complete definition of life under the communal system was supplied by Alcander Longley:

Communism means that people should live and work together for their mutual happiness, assistance, and support; hold all their property in common for the use of all; and each work according to his ability and be supplied according to his wants, in accordance with their majority vote.[38]

Yet, these utopians were not oblivious of the possible pitfalls inherent in a system of equal distribution. First, they felt such a system would work only if the members of the community were fully committed to the principles of love and hard work. Thus, even though the rule in Bishop's utopia was that "what is mine is thine," still, the author went on to state: "We don't want our young men to sink into innocuous desuetude simply because the grub is reasonably sure.... We want men and intelligent beings here, not simply well fed and contented animals."[39] Hency, by limiting the membership of their communities and by being highly selective in admission, the policy of equity was more likely to work. Even in the one exception to this policy, in Smith's Altruria, everyone worked from religious conviction, although the spirit of altruism was buttressed by St. Paul's injunction: "He who will not work, neither shall he eat" (2 Thess. 3:10).

In the communal utopia, government and the social classes played negligible parts. Mary Tincker's principle, "We take care of the individual and the state takes care of itself," was representative.[40] Education was important, especially for the inculcation of love. Since the environment was usually a primitive and secluded community, little interest was displayed in this problem. Altogether, the inhabitants of the commune were happy in the knowledge that they lived among persons of similar convictions, that love was uppermost in everyone's mind, that hard work would produce enough for everybody, and that it was a way of life far superior to the one under capitalism in late nineteenth-century America.

The Cooperative Business

Along with the socialist utopia, the cooperative business was the most popular type utopia. It was advocated by sixteen utopians (J.M.D. Bartlett, Charles Caryl, Henry L. Everett, Milan Edson, William Fishbough, Lena Fry, King C. Gillette, Alcanoan Grigsby, Robert Grimshaw, George Morison, Bradford Peck, Corwin Phelps, Isaac Roberts, Morrison I. Swift, William D. Trammell, and F. U. Worley). Unlike the communal utopia, the cooperative business operated on the principles of modern capitalism, but it differed from that system by taking every possible step to assure the highest salary or reward to the most productive workers. Efficiency and the labor theory of value were its ideals. Most often, these utopias resembled a joint-stock company in which the workers received a share in the profits as well as a fixed wage. In other cases, the product of labor was shared equally.

The idea of the cooperative business was derived from the many experiments along these lines in the earlier part of the nineteenth century, including Robert Owen's experiment at New Lanark and the ensuing Rochdale plan, the English cooperative societies, the associational joint-stock companies of Fourier and his followers, and the syndicates of the French trade-union movement. They all commonly possessed a deep hatred for government and any type of regulatory authority that would deprive the producer of a just share in the fruits of his labor. All sought to exclude the middleman, entrepreneur, and financier; likewise, all hoped to return to a life of elemental simplicity.

The basic plan of this utopia was built around some form of joint-stock or profit-sharing enterprise. Like any business, its first concern was to be profitable. Charles Caryl made it quite clear that "this paradise on earth—this goodly place where everybody is to have everything he needs—is planned strictly on a business basis."[41] Usually, a manufacturing, mining, or retail trade enterprise was organized by some wealthy humanitarian or, more often, by selling inexpensive shares to prospective workers. Its methods were such, as Peck stated, "that the unjust division of profit, which now creates so much misery and suffering, through cooperative ownership shall be removed."[42] Efficiency could be attained by "uniting producer and consumer, through mill, farm, supply store, etc. into one combination, eliminating all waste and loss of energy, and for the benefit of all."[43] To King C. Gillette, this plan meant the elimination of insurance, traveling salesmen, brokers, jobbing houses, piecemeal shipping, and innumerable retail outlets. His company would then be in a position "to sell shoes so cheaply that they could compel the public to come to them and pay cash."[44] So ruthless was the demand for efficiency in Bartlett's utopia that "imperfect work was rigidly rejected at the expense of the employee, thereby ensuring the greatest carefulness and exactness."[45]

Under these conditions, it was natural for the utopian of this type to place great faith in the credo of hard work. The hero of Milan Edson's *Solaris Farm* possessed this very necessary principle. "Work I must," he said. "Obstacles seem only to stimulate my ambition to overcome them."[46] The rigors of mental and physical discipline rejuvenated the typical inhabitant of this state. Lena Fry extolled the vigorous life:

These brains of ours need to be kept clear by plenty of rest, good food to keep the body vigorous, lots of pure air, exercise, physically and mentally. If we are attending to these necessities and look upon our bodies as an instrument that must be kept in tune as we would a musical instrument, then harmony will result. Harmony is the secret of concentration. Concentration leads to success.[47]

The moral fervor that characterized this group of utopians made hard work alone insufficient without a higher aim. According to Charles Caryl, the attainment of "the Father's Kingdom on Earth" was the worthy goal he claimed to set for his ideal society.[48] William Fishbough hoped that in his utopia religious bigotry and

> sectarian strife would be supplanted by that better spirit which would grow out of a knowledge of God and His superintending providence as seen in the universal correspondence of His works, and as providing the universal brotherhood of the race under one common and impartial Father.[49]

Both J.M.D. Bartlett and Milan Edson, whose utopias were close to the communal type, spoke glowingly of the value of love. Mrs. Bartlett wrote: "Our only creed is love, and our only purpose is to help each other."[50]

However, unlike the communal utopia, these utopias did not provide for the equal sharing of the wealth produced by the company. In some cases, the workers shared in the profits at the end of the year, but this was the closest they came to the equity plan. All worked for fixed wages and were paid according to skill, productivity, or the difficulty of the task. Often, the onus of a fixed wage was removed by the use of labor checks, which could be traded at a central store for goods produced by the cooperative enterprise. In the utopias of Peck and Worley, a minimum wage of $1,500 and $3,000, respectively, was guaranteed; whereas in Everett's ideal community, no person's estate could exceed $50,000. The basic premise that "labor is capital; money is not capital" underlay the thinking of this group of utopians.[51] They were very sensitive about the question of money; their moral point of view associated it with greed and exploitation. The general feeling coincided with Lena Fry's comment:

> Our members...want something more than money....You can't eat money, but you need a home and clothing....The society wanted men and women to create wealth and those who knew enough to keep it for themselves instead of giving it to the capitalists.[52]

The role of government was by no means ignored. In fact, it was often regarded as a very necessary copartner for ensuring the success of the cooperative enterprise. The natural penchant of the successful cooperative business was to branch out into other industries until virtually every business in the nation was run along the same lines. At that point, the government that represented the collective desires of the people seemed the best form of authority to cope with the vastness of the endeavor. Charles Caryl foresaw the day when the federal government would employ all the men and women who were willing to work to the best of their ability, "if we go about it in a practical way."[53] This idea came very close to the plans of the nationalists and socialists. Ironically, this type of utopian would be the first to disavow any connection with those groups.

Besides efficient production, some utopians ventured to describe higher aims for their ideal societies. Caryl envisioned a material paradise in which each individual would live in a well-ordered community, "securing all the comforts, pleasures, and advantages he can for himself."[54] For Gillette, "the first and most important industry of this new civilization would be to cultivate brains, from which it would hope to reap a continuous harvest of new and scientifically faithful ideas that would promote progress."[55] Few thought this progress would bring monotony. "On the contrary," claims Worley, "with freedom for growth individuality became more marked and diversified than ever."[56]

Thus, from the material prosperity engendered by cooperative enterprise, this group of utopians hoped that the whole fabric of society could be reordered to provide widespread educational and environmental advantages. The cooperative utopian fully believed that by spreading the total wealth of the nation among all those who were industrious, the demands for individual satisfaction and collective security could both be met.

Equality

The distinguishing characteristic of this group of utopians (James Alexander, Alfred Cridge, Henry Dowding, Thomas

Kirwin, Henry Olerich, and D. L. Stump) was their comprehensive and total commitment to the principle of equality. Their ideal lands were neither exclusive communities peopled by a moral elite nor cooperative enterprises dependent on efficiency for their success. Rather, they were whole countries, planets, worlds wherein the citizenry, often representing an advanced stage of evolution, recognized the severe limitations of an individualist outlook. Sometimes, Christian humility was the vehicle of this recognition: "Let him that would be greatest among you be your servant."[57] At other times, the principle of self-interest prevailed: "By doing right things to others, they would in the end be doing the best thing for themselves."[58]

The source of this obsession with equality lay in a curious combination of influences. On the one hand, Henry Olerich attributed his inspiration to the works of Herbert Spencer. On the other hand, Thomas Kirwin claimed to have followed the principles of socialism and Christianity, although he forbade the teaching of theology in the schools and was distrustful of governmental power. Alfred Cridge modeled his utopia on a communitarian experiment in which "the people are rulers themselves."[59] Marx inspired James Alexander, whereas Henry Dowding advocated absolute equality based on Christian humility and love.

The form of utopia advocated by this group of authors usually contained common property, the sharing of wealth on an equity basis, local political autonomy and democracy, communal living, well-planned cities, few laws, and very little financial apparatus. The immediate purpose of such a plan was to realize economic and social prosperity through a "system which recognizes extensive voluntary cooperation as its fundamental principle of production and distribution."[60] Thomas Kirwin asserted that the aim was to remove conflicts of interest through each person's understanding of his allotted or chosen part for the harmony of the entire state.[61] D. L. Stump organized his state to prevent "inherent or guaranteed inequalities in the pursuit of life, liberty, and happiness."[62]

The problem of the distribution of wealth was solved through the common ownership of property. Opposed, as it was, to the long-accepted right to private property, this collective ownership was justified in various ways. "The world was made," declared Stump, "for the use and occupancy of man in the attainment of the highest possible standard of moral and spiritual purity.... The world belongs to its creator."[63] In the same vein, all necessities were free in Dowding's utopia because its citizens were more interested in "the beautiful for its own sake."[64] By contrast, James Alexander settled upon the principle of common ownership simply because he thought no other system could be just.[65]

This group of writers did not turn to the government to bring about the equality they so ardently desired. It was felt that any kind of governmental regulation would bring on some form of coercion; hence, the government's role, as James Alexander explained, was "exclusively advisory." He could find little work for the government in his ideal society because "all productive labor was expended for the creation of common property, to which, when created, every individual had equal title."[66] D. L. Stump felt that all forms of government were "unjust, inhuman and contrary to divine will."[67] The same defiant individualism made Henry Dowding demand that everyone in his ideal society vote and participate in the decisions of government. Only on such condition was the government allowed to have any power in this type of utopia.

As in other individualistic utopias, education and environmental planning were important to this utopian. The teaching of love and service to others was the aim of the educational system; at home, the family was the center of the educative process. Parks, gardens, good roads, and well-planned communities abounded; however, the equality-minded utopian was in the main antipathetic to the city, for he feared that the democratic process would quickly break down with such a vast accumulation of people. Rather, the ideal of the New England town, with its town meeting and close personal relationships, inspired this utopian. Only here could that equality he so earnestly sought be attained.

THE LEGAL UTOPIA

The feature that distinguished this group of utopians most markedly from all others was their attempt to achieve reform through the established political system. These authors felt that, in general, the enactment of proper laws would bring about the desired state of equality and just distribution of wealth. Respect for law, rather than specific individual reforms, was the basis for their ideal domains. Although equality was important, the legal utopia disavowed any interest in sharing the total produce of a community or state. Everyone was expected to work hard, develop his talents and abilities, and achieve success in an honest though profitable way.

It was the dishonest method of attaining wealth that this utopia was created to obviate. Trusts and monopolies were ruled out of existence or taken over by the government, whose obligation to the people was acknowledged and assured by such devices as the referendum, initiative, recall, direct election of all public officials, and a strong civil service. The unjust profit on land was taxed in the manner of Henry George's proposals, and the problems of finance were attacked after the fashion of the Populists. The personal accumulation of wealth was limited by law with such devices as the graduated income tax or inheritance tax. Slums, crime, liquor traffic, political corruption—all were subject to the stringent and omnipresent hand of the law, the law above which no person stood and which no group owned.

The Single Tax

In the first group of writers who believed better laws would bring a better society, Henry George's single tax plan appealed to these seven utopians (Herman Brinsmade, Byron Brooks, Henry Call, Costello Holford, William Simpson, William Taylor, and Byron Welcome) for various reasons. First, George's system was designed to create the least disturbance to the status quo. Like George, Henry Call denounced socialism and asserted that his new republic "does not...demand the entire revolution of existing institutions."[68] Herman Brinsmade boldly declared the same bias: "I am most impressed with the outward signs of the prosperity of the middle classes, the working people of the country."[69] In general, these were conservative writers, fully committed to the middle class ideal and the established political system.

The second reason for the appeal of George's single-tax program was that it preserved the distinction between capital and labor. Unlike the cooperative utopian who took issue with this distinction, these writers agreed that there were two honest ways of accumulating wealth: "One is saving wages, and the other is the profits of capital."[70] In other words, investment as well as labor was considered a legitimate source of wealth. However, the problem that these utopias attacked was the disproportionate accumulation of wealth that accrued to the investor as opposed to the laborer. Thus, great importance was placed on the idea of every man receiving a just return for his labor. Call reasoned that "labor will not pay tribute to capital, because it will not be dependent upon it. Under these circumstances [single-tax], each man's possessions will alone depend upon and be limited by his own exertion and thrift."[71]

The third appeal of the Georgian system was its base in the common ownership of land. This provided a bond among the members of a community while at the same time it served as a check on the atavistic tendencies of one's neighbors. As Byron Brooks claimed: "The origin of property is in nature. The discoverer has no exclusive right to its possession. The ownership of land does not entitle one to its spontaneous product or increase of value."[72]

Furthermore, the common ownership of land appealed to these authors because of their total disdain for the idea of accumulating wealth for its own sake. Time and again they made reference to the Christian duty to share one's wealth. For this reason, Brooks called his system Christian Communism. The hero of Taylor's utopia was "freed of gross materialism," thus allowing his spirit to seek something higher than selfish greed.[73] Costello Holford's hero was similarly freed from avarice, arrogance, love of ostentation and luxury; he desired "power and wealth only that he might do good with them . . . believing that the truest and most acceptable worship of God is doing good to His creatures."[74] In Welcome's society, "the ethics of living equably together made the inhabitants morally superior to all others."[75]

The common ownership of land also served another purpose for these authors; it diminished the power of the government. This group of utopians was unwilling to grant any more power than necessary to the government, even though, under the Georgian system, the government was the collection agency for the single tax. Collecting taxes, however, was not the same as regulating industry. This pleased Byron Welcome. "When the government interferes with private business," he said, "trouble is inevitable."[76] However, far more typical of the group's attitude was that of Henry Call who disavowed socialism but, on the other hand, agreed that the powers of government extended beyond the mere protection of privacy and property. Its true role, he said, was to "serve the whole people acting through their laws, and that the people themselves must first determine their rights before they can be protected."[77]

Science, education, and environmental planning took a prominent place in this type of utopia. It was expected that science would solve the problems of congestion, food production, and health; it had even solved "the rough-knotty problem of labor and production" with technology and laborsaving machinery.[78] Science was mated with the beauties of nature to bring about well-planned cities, parks, gardens, beautiful dwellings, and the widespread use of electric power to reduce smoke and soot. In accordance with the conservative principles of these authors, however, "ostentation of riches is a thing unknown, and there is no ambition to get beyond the general fare in dwellings."[79] All children were educated, usually by the state, because these writers generally believed that "the ignorant may be vicious, and so become a public charge."[80]

Thus, the utopian followers of Henry George were conservative in their attitude toward the social order as well as toward politics and economics. They only advocated that which would bring the least disturbance to the status quo. Their reforms were intended to develop a large middle class and to hinder the formation of an aristocracy by taxing all the sources of permanent power and wealth. True, these utopians also proposed many reforms designed to help the lower classes, such as universal free education and the elimination of slums; but their sympathies largely lay in keeping the small businessman, wage earner, and property owner prosperous. The single tax met all these requirements.

Government Regulation

Eleven utopians (Frederick Adams, Albert Chavannes, Ernest Fitzpatrick, Alverado Fuller, William S. Harris, Edward House, Alfred Hutchinson, John Macnie, Albert Merrill, Wayland Spaulding, and Chauncey Thomas), whose sympathies paralleled those of the single-taxers but who thought that system too limited, advocated a broad legislative program. They also were primarily interested in the development of the middle class. Their ideal was stated as follows: "Here at last was a rich, prosperous, and happy nation; no squalor, no ragged clothes, no careworn faces."[81] "Neither was there tremendous difference in wealth."[82]

Ideologically, this group was strongly committed to the values of hard work and the equality of opportunity. The Reverend W. S. Harris dealt severely with "any person becoming rebellious and refusing to work."[83] Strength of will, otherwise known as resolution, transformed the meaning of work in Edward House's utopian land. In reference to his own day, House declared: "Life would have for us a different meaning if we would resolve and keep the resolution, to do the best we could under all conditions, and never fear the result."[84] In Harris's utopia, the result was that "the average wealth of the laborers increased."[85] Thus, when the law removed the artificial inequities imposed on the ordinary citizen, it was the belief of these utopians that all, by dint of hard work, could readily attain a comfortable existence.

The organization of this type of utopia usually centered around some legal mechanism that prevented the accumulation or control of large amounts of wealth by any one person or group. Taxes of all kinds, guaranteed work, social security, minimum wages, and a limit on personal property were all advocated for this purpose. Edward House had the most comprehensive plan for equalizing the wealth. Borrowing heavily from George's program of taxing land values, he proposed a general tax on realty along with a 20 percent tax on improvements on city property. A graduated income tax completed his tax program; however, the corporations bore the brunt of his reforms. A federal incorporation law with franchise taxes was imposed. All corporations were required to have their books examined by representatives of both the government and the people who sat on the board of governors. Natural monopolies were run by the government; holding companies were banned. The problems of labor were resolved by compulsory arbitration, the eight-hour day, pension and insurance plans, and employment bureaus. A federal commission regulated all corporations. To these restrictions, Wayland Spaulding added a child-labor law, a stock commission, and a 2 percent limit on annual profits.

Besides economic restrictions, two members of this group, Frederick Adams and Albert Chavannes, advocated political reforms. In Adams's state, the President and his cabinet were to be elected by popular vote. The citizenry was to be adequately represented by congressmen from districts that were reapportioned every four years. The people as a whole decided on the laws; they also had the power to remove judges from the Supreme Court. With these safeguards, Adams felt he could allow the government to run any industry in competition with private enterprise, print fiat money, and own and operate the railroads. In short, political democracy was regarded as the people's check on the very necessarily augmented governmental power.

For Chavannes, the most important problem was the reconcilement of personal liberty with an adequate distribution of wealth. More clearly than most utopians, he perceived the difficulty of regulating an economic order that basically relied on individual initiative. Yet in the early days of his utopian commonwealth, experience showed that "as soon as a man gets a little power, he is sure to use it to his own advantage and usually it works badly for the community."[86] Therefore, no one could gain admittance to this land without a certificate of good character. However, when individuals still persisted in hoarding money, it became necessary for the government to fix wages and profits and, in short, take over the running of private enterprise. In the end, the hero proclaimed himself both an individualist and a communist. Nevertheless, he went on to complain of being prevented from doing "more as I would like to."[87]

Thus, for Chavannes as well as the other members of this group, utopia was a compromise. Few ideal lands were filled with such contradictions as these. Only here could Albert Merrill declare on the same page that the greatest production of wealth could take place only when industry was absolutely free from government interference, but that the production became inefficient with the increase of monopoly.[88] Thus, to prevent the inefficiency of monopoly, it was necessary to employ coercion, regulation, and the inevitable government control. In few other places was the utopian dilemma so clear. On the one hand, the utopian tried to cling to the older value of laissez faire, while, on the other hand, he saw that injustice was inevitable unless there was some regulation.

Environmental control was not a prime concern in these utopias. However, a number of writers felt that when economic enslavement ceased, progress in the social realm would occur. Hutchinson best expressed their views when he declared: "When the mind is free to act, unhampered by the stress of poverty, the intellectual faculties of a person are developed to that highest degree of perfection."[89] Many applied the increase in government revenue from taxes to public works projects whose purpose was to beautify the countryside. However, aesthetic considerations were usually placed in the background.

Thus, by chipping away at the abuses and inequalities of the economic system, these utopian writers hoped to build up a body of law that would make the unjust accumulation of wealth virtually impossible. For them, justice meant equality. As Merrill indicated in one of his four maxims for social content, "Equal distribution of wealth is necessary for the greatest production of wealth."[90] With this goal in mind, the possibility for progress was limited only by the capacity of the guardians of that principle to legislate its existence.

Populism

Within the group of those who decided to work within the status quo, the populist utopians (Daniel Bond, William S. Child,

Winnifred Cooley, Samuel Crocker, Ignatius Donnelly, Henry Morris, John McCoy, T. H. Tibbles, and the anonymous author of *Man or Dollar, Which?*) differed from the other legal utopians in that their reforms exactly matched those of the Populist party during the 1890s. In fact, two members of this group, Ignatius Donnelly and Thomas Tibbles, were well-known Populist leaders. All of the writers in this group served as propagandists for the Populist cause.

As was characteristic of the Populist movement in general, these authors wrote with sanguinity and a sense of immediacy. Their common belief was: "We are in the dying hours of the Competitive system. The old house is falling to ruin and the new is not yet built."[91] Not only was the economic system failing; some writers even concluded that insurrection was imminent. Only by the immediate application of drastic reform measures did the populist utopian think it possible once again to "bend every force toward the serious business of making life worth living."[92] He sensed that he stood at the crossroads of history. "This is a great age," said William S. Child, "but we should never forget that the foundation was being laid by suffering humanity since the days of Adam."[93] The great age Child referred to was the utopian era of the near future that would have the prescience to adopt the Populist reforms. Only then, claimed Tibbles, will we have learned "to find some sweetness in everything," and once again "believe in the brotherhood of man."[94]

With this sense of urgency, the populist utopian set to work listing all the laws that would abolish "giving any man an advantage over any other man or tending to concentrate wealth in the hands of a few."[95] Henry Morris summed up their goals:

To establish, maintain and operate throughout the United States, post offices, railroads, canal lines, roads, highways, bridges, bicycle roads, public parks, gardens, baths, savings banks, banks of deposit and exchange, universities, colleges, schools, institutions for the reformation and confinement of criminals, homes for the helpless and indigent, asylums and sanitariums for the treatment and maintenance of the insane, idiotic, feebleminded, blind, deaf, and dumb and other unfortunates, and hospitals and dispensaries for the sick.

To provide speedy means for the condemnation and restoration to the people of the United States of all lands, water, coal, minerals of all kinds, mineral oils, natural gasses, mineral and medicinal water, now the subject of monopoly.[96]

The instrumentality for accomplishing this program was the government, or, as Ignatius Donnelly called it, "their own government, which so cares for humanity and strives to lift it up."[97]

This governmental power, however, did not assume the proportions it could under the socialist state. It was pointed out that for years the socialists had looked to the postal service as an excellent illustration of collective ownership; and though Daniel Bond agreed, he felt it necessary to add that "the compulsion to work must come within a man, not without."[98] He emphasized that it was the role of the government not to say you shall work, but that you may work.[99] Furthermore, equal pay was not the reward for work provided by the government, as some socialists proposed. "We shall not seek to produce uniformity of recompense for all kinds of work," declared Ignatius Donnelly.[100] In general, it was felt that too much governmental control over the daily activity of the citizens would stifle initiative and bring about a monotonous uniformity.

Though the government had much to do with creating the conditions for the more equitable distribution of wealth, the real basis of reform in the populist utopia came from the spirit of human oneness and cooperation it engendered. The expressed ideal for the inhabitants of this state was to "live as one family."[101] Many felt that "to conspire against another is like conspiring against oneself."[102] Some sought to return to the "neighborliness and spirit of cooperation" that characterized American life before the Civil War.[103] This quest for identity with his neighbors permeated the whole tone of the populist utopian's society.

Thus, the populist utopian hoped to achieve his goals through the power of a truly representative government. Although he recognized the value of hard work and individual initiative, he realized that individuals were helpless in the face of the power and wealth of large coroporations. Yet, needing and wanting the goods these corporations provided, the populist utopian was not willing to legislate them out of existence. Rather, he placed them under control of an even larger organization—the government—in the hope that political democracy would be ensured without establishing, at the same time, an "aristocratic plutocracy."[104]

THE SOCIALIST UTOPIA

The socialist utopian hoped to reorganize the economic order so as to create a more equitable distribution of wealth. His goal was virtually the same as that of the cooperative and legal utopian; however, he possessed fewer qualms about using a centralized authority to achieve it, primarily because he was certain that organization was the hallmark of the times, and he preferred an organization that was answerable to all the people. After all, reasoned this particular utopian, the magnates of industry and the financial world were answerable only to themselves, and it was clear that their sense of obligation to the community was extraordinarily shortsighted.

But beneath these authors' dislike of the so-called robber baron was an admiration for his methods and accomplishments. Many a socialist utopian admitted that, by placing his faith in centralized government, he was in effect creating one large monopoly to replace the many smaller ones. Ingeniously, he argued that if monopolies were defended on the principles of economy, mass production, and efficiency, so, too, the socialist state could be upheld as the logical culmination of the same principles. In a socialist state, however, the profits would be distributed to the people at large instead of finding their way into the pockets of a few individuals.

The appeal of this reasoning was enormous; and, in the face of it, even the most advanced thinkers of the day found it difficult to support their innate suspicion of governmental power. Nevertheless, socialism remained a threat to the established political system. And yet, both the followers of Edward Bellamy and the pure socialists decided that the advantages of such a system far outweighed its disadvantages, especially in light of the crisis they all felt was impending. No group more outspokenly criticized the establishment than the socialist utopian. These writers harbored a typical mistrust of politics and politicians, and they did not have to look far to find evidence for their view. Thus, the political apparatus in their ideal societies was kept to a minimum. Instead, a board of governors, much like that of a corporation, coordinated the problems of production and distribution according to the principles of efficiency and equality. It was assumed that if the people were given their daily bread, their complaints would cease. The problems, therefore, were chiefly technical and could be solved by observation and objectivity. The variability of human nature was not part of the equation for happiness in the socialist state.

Thus, a curiously conservative air hung about this most radical of utopias. Organized much like a corporation, it rewarded the industrial virtues of hard work and thrift. Although each person would receive a share of the ever-increasing wealth of the community, each person was also expected to match his or her private needs with those of the community. The same standards were applied to both education and environmental planning; there was little room for personal idiosyncrasy, even though the need for personal satisfaction was acknowledged by most of these writers.

The Nationalist Utopia

Because Edward Bellamy's utopia provided the impetus for the subsequent proliferation of utopias during this era, it could be expected that he would have imitators, although they vigorously denied the "socialist" label. His detractors were many, a fact that probably stimulated further support. Altogether, eight writers (John Brant, Paul Devinne, Ludwig Geissler, C. S. Griffin, George Phelps, Frank Rosewater, Solomon Schindler, and Mrs. C. H. Stone) came to his aid.

In essence, Bellamy tried to achieve a greater and more just distribution of wealth by organizing the forces of labor into an industrial army whose officers would run the state as well as the economy. Everyone, through the device of credit cards (much like the labor checks of the communal utopias), received an equal share of the yearly production. Thus, labor was the sole determinant of price, and efficiency was assured through the national organization of all industries. Incentives to work hard were provided by promotions to positions of greater responsibility that were accompanied by great social prestige.

In the nationalist utopia, efficiency was the highest value. The superiority of the system impressed its devotees in various ways. John Brant claimed: "We have done away with such work as looking for advertising, seeing that competitors do not get too much business and all that sort of thing."[105] According to Solomon Schindler, the nationalist system allowed the people of America to do what they could not do before—"to subdue all those natural resources by the aid of which we create sufficient wealth and secure a comfortable existence for all."[106] With a trained and organized industrial army, asserted Frank Rosewater, "there was no longer a limit to opportunity for production"; therefore, "wealth began to accumulate at a wonderful rate."[107] Thus, the highly organized nationalist system seemed far superior to these authors than the haphazard economic policies of their own day. With the Spencerian theory of evolution as reference, Brant considered nationalism an example of evolutionary progress to a complex, and therefore higher, form of life.[108]

Despite the lavish praise for this new economic order, these writers were still concerned with the possibility of corruption at its very heart. On the one hand, Bellamy allowed suffrage only to the retired members of the industrial army, that is, those over the age of forty-five. On the other hand, Brant separated the political and industrial functions of the state, giving the former the higher power, but making it ultimately responsible to the universal electorate. Another solution to the problem, proposed by Paul Devinne, limited the entire function of the government to the inspection and regulation of production and consumption. He felt that if any corruption entered this domain, the people, in their role as consumers, would be immediately aware of it.[109] George Phelps excluded the idea of making a profit in any governmental operation for, he said, "the only excuse for government...is to secure the well-being of both [sic] its sovereign, its subjects, and its servants—the whole people."[110]

Even though the nationalist utopian believed that "a nation is measured by the justice with which its wealth is distributed," his state was designed to deal with far more than wealth.[111] Education, social habits, and environmental planning were at least as important. The charity and philanthropy of their own day was replaced by an organized effort to benefit the minds and bodies of the citizenry. All surplus wealth and unused labor was to be utilized for "some ornamental public improvement."[112] Ignorance was considered the archenemy of progress; therefore, the state attempted to educate its youth so that they "may not find themselves strangers in a strange world."[113] Strength of character, a most necessary quality in this utopia, was not allowed to be developed by chance.[114] Even the rearing of children, long thought a natural instinct, bowed before the organizational talents of these utopians.[115]

Gadgetry and innovation naturally fascinated these efficiency-minded writers. Despite their socialistic inclinations, they were not above admiring a John D. Rockefeller or a Thomas Edison.[116] Bellamy's penchant for convenience led to the invention of covers for streets and sidewalks during rain or snow storms. Cleanliness was an obsession in Devinne's state, and all the writers in this group relied on laborsaving machinery to make up for the man-hours lost through early retirement at the age of forty-five. Rosewater banished fences, backyards, and ugly signs.

Thus, every aspect of the nationalist society bowed before the genius for arranging. The haphazard character of their present society horrified these utopians. Their rage for order demanded satisfaction in the form of an all-powerful central authority that would ruthlessly eliminate inefficiency in the economic order and, at the same time, benevolently attend to the wishes of the people.

Socialism

Taken together with the nationalist utopians, more authors chose to form their ideal societies around the socialist state than any other type. Altogether, sixteen writers (Henry Allen, Cyrus Cole, Robert A. Dague, Zebina Forbush, Henry Frisbie, James M. Galloway, Lawrence Gronlund, Edward Everett Hale, William Dean Howells, Jack London, Thomas McGrady, Cosimo Noto, Clark Persinger, Henry Salisbury, C. A. Steere, and Alonzo Van Deusen) chose socialism for their ideal state. Primarily, their choice was born out of extreme dissatisfaction with the economic order under capitalism. In every discussion of capitalistic society, said Cosimo Noto, our last comment must always be: "It made beasts of men."[117] Jack London bemoaned the strife, the opposition of classes, and the stifling of the very spirit of man.[118] He maintained that "man has risen from the vitalized slime of the primeval sea to the mastery of matter, but he has not yet mastered society."[119] Alonzo Van Deusen simply looked on the existing order as selfish, incoherent, haphazard, and unharmonious—mainly because it was based on individual effort.[120] He maintained that liberty came from order, and that only under the socialist system could the order for personal liberty be provided.

Aware of the stigma attached to their cause, these writers, in an effort to reach the widest possible audience, went out of their way to cite the benefits that would accrue to the individual under socialism. Zebina Forbush asserted: "The cooperative commonwealth is organized to produce a better and stronger man mentally, physically, morally, and spiritually."[121] She reasoned that under socialism the rich were not permitted to rob the poor, the strong prey on the weak, or the keen exercise their faculties at the expense of the dull because all shared the wealth equally. For the same reason, Clark Persinger promised liberty and true freedom.[122] Robert A. Dague explained how the socialistic system "levels down the millionaire and levels up the masses." With the accumulation of property, he said, "comes hope and education, and intelligence and aspiration."[123]

Yet, despite attempts to placate the individualists, the socialist utopians demanded that all means of production be owned and operated by the government. Although Forbush assured that no citizen would be disturbed in the enjoyment of his or her personal property, her republic was dedicated to the proposition that "the machinery of production belongs to the people in common."[124] Clark Persinger described what qualities this government should have.[125] First, he said, it must be efficient, even to the smallest detail. Second, it must be immediately responsible to the will of the people, even to the extent of changing the whole form of government if the people should so desire. Third, it must be free from corruption. The only method for ensuring the accomplishment of these goals in Persinger's state was a system of public censure whereby any civil servant suspected of corruption was immediately subject to an investigation and the possible loss of his job. The system depended on the interest and vigilance of the public at large, an assumption readily granted by all these writers, except Zebina Forbush who suspected that the great mass of people were indifferent to everything but their own immediate welfare.[126]

When it came to work and possessions, however, there was no argument about the people knowing their basic interests. The efficiency of centralized planning provided such an abundance of wealth that even with an equal share of this output, few would have reason to quibble. The success of the socialist state rested upon the principle of preventing waste and maintaining a proper system of distribution of the products of labor.[127] Under this system, Jack London maintained, "food and shelter... are well nigh automatic."[128]

Yet the worker had to contribute his share, too. The values of the Protestant ethic were as strong in the socialist utopia as in the most individualistic ones. No compromise was made here. "The *sine qua non* of citizenship was the badge of the worker. Idlers, drones, parasites, and dilettanti might commit suicide or starve; but no adequate provision was made for them to live."[129] Promotion was earned only through the efficiency of the worker, and though it brought no increase in salary, the resulting prestige and honor reflected the individual's worth to the total welfare.[130]

Environmentally, the socialist utopian promised much. In this cooperative state, everyone had a stake in the appearance and quality of his or her living conditions. Edward Everett Hale made each citizen responsible for any dirt, rubbish, or disarray in the street on which he or she lived.[131] Slums were replaced with beautifully landscaped streets and homes. "The massive blocks of the lower town had given way to immense palaces, surrounded by wide lawns, fountains, trees and gardens."[132] The workers could look forward, upon their retirement, to enjoying all this beautiful scenery as well as to the serene contemplation of higher, intellectual pursuits.[133] Somehow, it was felt that the beautification of one's environment increased one's propensity for cooperation and noble action.[134] Jack London characterized the effect of his well-planned socialistic state as "a reign of universal laughter."[135]

Thus, a selfish, competitive, and haphazard world would be replaced by an orderly, efficient one. Few of these writers anticipated any shortcomings in their system, although two of them, Forbush and Dague, felt it would be a long time before the citizenry could relinquish their habit of competition for that of cooperation. And the cornerstone of the socialist utopia—a benevolent government—depended upon the cooperative spirit of the people for its solidity. These writers unanimously assumed that this spirit would be forthcoming once each worker knew that he or she would receive a just portion of the total wealth of the state. Altogether, the goodness of human nature, which the competitive system suppressed, would blossom forth, and a new way of life would being.

THE TOTALITARIAN UTOPIA

Although totalitarianism had not been formulated as a political philosphy at this time, a few utopians loved order so much that when they came to outline their ideal societies, the result closely resembled the modern totalitarian state. Individual persons, society, and its institutions could not be trusted to bring about the refinements in the organization of life that these authors wished. Instead, the state, anonymous and all-powerful, possessed total authority to conform the lives of its citizens to its ideal. The state's economic and political power was at least as extensive as that of the socialist utopias, but it was in the social realm that this state exercised its greatest authority. The proper and equitable distribution of wealth was an assumed fact. Political arrangements were minimal or entirely ignored, and often a dictator or benevolent despot obviated the need for a political organization.

Philosophically, these writers often spoke of selective breeding and the improvement of the race. Charles Darwin and Herbert Spencer received due recognition as the progenitors of this ideal land; however, a number of these writers also had a nostalgic longing for the olden times of philosopher kings. They had a special reverence for Plato's *Republic*, and one writer, Jacob Horner, spoke glowingly of Peter the Great.

However, the rigid and stern regulation of life in the totalitarian state received its justification from more immediate goals: the perfection of the race, the eradication of ignorance and disease, the control of the environment, and the personal security arising from a well-defined place and role in society. Added to these factors was the very simple conviction that order could only be imposed on people from without. Rarely did the utopian show less faith in the ability of individuals to pursue their own best interests. The totalitarian utopian often asserted that the interests of individuals should always be those of society, and that in the case of a conflict, those of society should prevail. Characteristically, however, this type of utopia rarely offered a rationale for its form; rather, in the manner of its leaders, it asserted what was best, then insured the elimination of all practical dissent.

Totalitarianism

Seven authors (Richard Chapman, Albert Howard, Frank Hatfield, Richard Hatfield, Walter Henry, Jacob Horner, and Henry P. Mendes) subscribed to the totalitarian form of society. Science and its implied order was their highest value. In Frank Hatfield's utopia, scientists constituted the highest class and were granted the greatest social honors. In Richard Hatfield's society, philosophers were those who utilized the laws of science; they were given a higher place than scientists, who were considered more collectors of fact. Richard Hatfield placed Darwin among the scientists and awarded philosopher's rank to Herbert Spencer, John Fiske, and Prince Peter Kropotkin.[136] Richard Chapman's ideal land was organized to provide for the "expert observation and authoritative restraint" of every person from the moment of conception to his or her death.[137] Chapman believed that through the application of the scientific method, human faculties could be developed to the highest degree. This love of science even extended to the prosaic duties of the housewife, who in Jacob Horner's society "knows how to manage scientifically."[138]

On the matter of government, there was little dispute. In Albert Howard's utopia, a fabulously rich millionaire solved all problems with his wealth; yet, the benevolent despot was peculiar only to Howard's utopia. In Henry Mendes's utopia, a Board of Pastors, similar to the idea of "elders" in the Jewish community, controlled virtually every aspect of society, including marriage. The rest created anonymous organizations called the "state," from which decrees and guidance emanated in a paternalistic way. Walter Henry's summation of the tasks of the totalitarian government was representative:

> In Equitania, the government gives all of its subjects an equal chance, helping all who may need it in getting suitable employment, improving or making tolerable their environment in living and in work, in seeing to it that the strong do not unfairly impose upon the weak, nor the learned and shrewd take undue advantage of the ignorant, and that everyone shall have a fair chance to earn a living and get food, shelter, and clothing... and that he have opportunity for real recreation.[139]

In addition to these goals, the state in this type of utopia served as a collection agency for all personal information about its citizens. The government gathered statistics on every aspect of living "with a wealth of detail transcending the wildest dreams of the present day statistician."[140] In Chapman's ideal state, every person was awarded a number, twenty digits long, tatooed on his or her arm so that no one could get lost or conceal his or her identity. Love also fell under the province of government regulation. Only those considered genetically suitable for propagation were allowed to marry in the states of Richard Chapman, Albert Howard, and Richard Hatfield. Represented by an official whipping master, the state in Walter Henry's utopia saw to it that all parents performed their duties toward their children. Furthermore, all criminals, insane persons, and social deviates were sterilized.

Despite some token pronouncements about the value of equality, these societies were usually organized with a clearly defined class structure. In Jacob Horner's Militaire, there were generals and privates, although everyone worked the same hours. Chapman allowed his educational system to differentiate between the superior and inferior minds of its students. Frank Hatfield classed people according to their productivity, with laborers on the lowest level, then supervisors, and finally scientists and spiritual leaders. Even in Walter Henry's Equitania, there were, ironically enough, six classes of citizens: plain citizens (all male voters), counselors (mothers), associates (wives), matrons, defectives and degenerates, and finally, criminals and offenders.

These social strata were created in the totalitarian utopia in order to justify the inequitable distribution of wealth. If an individual was a member of one of the lower social classes, it was reasoned that he would be more willing to recognize the justice of a proportionately lower salary. The motto "Equal pay for equal work" prevailed, except in Horner's utopia.[141] There, despite social differentiation between generals and privates, everyone received the same pay.

Thus, the state determined what wealth would be produced to whom it would be given, what significance it had, and even whether it could be inherited by a person's heirs—that is, if a person was permitted to have heirs. Marriage, education, work—all were undertaken under the paternal eye of government regulation. The ideal of totalitarian society was best expressed by Richard Hatfield: "Love your race—it will give new charm and value to your life."[142]

THE IDEAL CITY

A small number of utopians limited their horizons to the immediate problems of city life. Each of the writers in this group presumed that a healthful and orderly physical environment was a necessary condition for a healthy and orderly mental and spiritual existence. The idea was an old one, and two of the authors had the Greek city-state clearly in mind. Yet history did not have to provide any precedents for this type solution. It was obvious to any viewer of the contemporary scene that problems concerning a healthy environment were multiplying as fast as the extraordinary migration to the cities. Yet, none of these utopias proposed to set up exclusive communities in the virgin countryside, where overcrowding would be minimized and factories less obtrusive. Rather, they concentrated on perfecting life in the city itself. In short, they accepted the growth of the city as a natural and proper development.

Because these authors were grouped through the physical form of their utopias rather than according to any ideological commitment, it would be natural to expect a diversity of values and goals. Some believed in the capitalistic system, others denounced it in favor of an uncontrolled individualism, still others advocated equality. All were aware of the great possibilities of science and devoted much space to portraying all kinds of technological wonders. However, little social planning took place, even though two writers advocated selective breeding. Thus, intellectual discussions were inappreciable in this type of utopia, where the practical necessities of rearranging the environment took precedence.

The Model City

Six authors (Edgar Chambless, William Harben, Warren Rehm, H. George Schuette, John Veiby, and C. W. Woodridge) organized their utopias around the concept of the ideal city. Their general attitude was best summed up by C. W. Woodridge's rhetorical question: "Who wouldn't prefer a world that he could fix up to suit him rather than one that he must take ready made."[143] They steadily fixed their vision on some form of the garden of paradise. Most often they neglected to describe how this ideal was to be achieved; rather, they made up for their lack of detail with a rhapsodic enthusiasm. As Edgar Chambless declared: "See to it that the plenty which fills them [sic] storehouses is distributed with the freedom of the rain and the sunshine which falls alike on the just and the unjust, to whosoever hath need."[144] Chambless never indicated how the storehouses were filled in the first place.

In like manner, this type of utopian tried to satisfy everyone in the realms of social status, law, and government. According to H. George Schuette: "All should possess and be perfectly equal; for man to man is brother."[145] Just the opposite conditions applied to John Veiby's land. "If the republic of our own making shall endure," he said, "we must give individuals of the most various types an opportunity to have it their own way, and facilitate change in customs or morals to meet the demand of the individuals."[146] Veiby went so far as to declare that even if all the people in his utopian state were happy and content, perfection would not have been achieved; for the happiness would be that of animals, and the people would lose "the self-consciousness born of pain and opposition."[147] Schuette, on the other hand, desired that none be extremely rich or poor; "the golden mean is best for individuals and the public welfare."[148]

How, then, did these writers picture their ideal cities? Edgar Chambless, who worked as a clerk in the New York patent office, devised an ingenious scheme to prevent overcrowding in the city. He created one continuous city from New York to San Francisco consisting of an endless two-story building that provided habitation for the entire population. Thus, a small group of immediate neighbors would prevent the loneliness that afflicted farm and country people, while at the same time the shape of the building prevented a large group of people from massing in any one place.

William Harben's ideal society, set in the year 10,000, had sufficiently evolved from the "animalistic" time during the late nineteenth century, so that thought transference, mind-reading, and mental telepathy had allowed the doctrine of brotherly love to prevail. "If a man had an evil thought, it was read in his heart and he was not allowed to keep it."[149] In addition, vegetarianism, crystal buildings, airships, and heat from the center of the earth made this world akin to paradise.

Warren Rehm's practical city was a combination of Puritan practicality and Greek aesthetics. Each lot, block, and building was regulated by size, shape, and appearance according to the principles of practicality and beauty. Only five thousand people were allowed in each ideal city; tramps were banned as well as those who refused to comply with the city charter. The Greek ideals of democracy and physical fitness were fostered. But the basis of it all was hard work. "Nothing is impossible to industry"; "Genius is the born love of hard work"; "Talent is the acquirement of the love of hard work"—these were the mottos taught in the schools of Rehm's practical city.[150]

Like Rehm, H. George Schuette held the Greek city-state as his ideal. In fact, his was the only utopia set in the past—specifically, America before discovery. According to the story, four hundred Greeks found their way to the uninhabited shores of America, in order to establish a democracy based on the principle of equality. So absolute was this equality that it was decreed: "No citizen should attempt to change his building, home, or surrounding grounds so that it looks like an improvement over his neighbors."[151] However, this uniformity caused dissention. The policy was modified so that in the future the citizens of this Greek city-state spent their energy on physical culture and personal beauty. Soon a race of "perfect, strong, beautiful, noble, courageous, wise men and women" emerged.[152] All activity was then focused on the preservation of this condition.

John Veiby's ideal city was based on the practical motto: "Try everything and cleave to that which is good."[153] In his state, the government regulated education, transportation, and some industries only because Veiby felt that the ordinary citizen should be preoccupied solely with that which was creative; all other activities were left to either the government or chance, mostly the latter. The only important stricture was the ancient motto: "To thine own self be true." Otherwise, each person decided for himself or herself how best to live.

Finally, the utopia of C. W. Woodridge resembled a giant public works project. Set in the year 1913, it started with a plan to employ the idle United States Army without glutting the labor market. A city, Fort Goodwill, was built for their residence as they planted trees, irrigated and plowed the vast Western deserts. So successful was this plan, that soon its progenitors were preaching its message to the entire world. "There are other deserts to water, other barrens to plant, other waste places to clothe with verdue," they claimed. "Go ye out into the world and open the gates of paradise to all its people."[154] Soon the unemployed joined in this project; then people left their regular work to harness the power and beauty of the world.

Ultimately, Woodridge maintained that mankind would work in order to live, not live in order to work, but only when the garden of paradise had been created.

Thus Woodridge, like the other utopians in this group, felt that some moral purpose ultimately gave meaning to their actions. The environment was only an external symbol of an internal peace and order; yet it was believed that if one could create these external conditions, the very turmoil within people would subside. This goal was probably the most grandiose of all the utopian groups and, at the same time, the least specific. Nevertheless, these writers made up in enthusiasm what they lacked in concreteness.

In summary, the following number of authors advocated each type of utopia: individualist (13), cooperative (32), legal (27), socialist (25), totalitarian (7), and the ideal city (6). The last category, the ideal city, must be excluded from any evaluation of this proportion, since the problems and solutions they represented were unique to that group only.

Of the remaining 104 authors, a majority advocated an increase in governmental power. The socialists and totalitarians were the most outspoken of this majority; however, those most interested in preserving the form of the present society, the legal utopians, clearly proposed an increase in governmental control over the many abuses they decried, even though they tried their best to minimize that increase. Only the individualist and cooperative utopians, constituting about 40 percent of the whole group, were loath to augment the government's jurisdiction over daily life. Even so, these groups thought mainly in terms of small, exclusive communities; and within those communities, the central authority often had as much power as the most centralized utopias. Only two authors actually advocated a return to pure laissez faire, whereas a number of scientific utopias simply ignored the problem altogether. Thus, for those utopians who dealt with the problem, a large majority were on the side of increased governmental authority.

The question of the distribution of wealth produced almost a total unanimity. The question here was whether to divide it equally or in accordance with merit. In terms of values, the difference of opinion centered around the distinction between equality of wealth and equality of opportunity. Those advocating equality of opportunity—that is, the individualists—prevailed, but only by a slight majority. The policy of dividing the total output of a community equally among its members violated some of the very basic values of these utopians—the right of private property and the idea of hard work. The legal, cooperative business, and individualist utopians were all heavily committed to these principles. Furthermore, their morally supported belief in a system of rewards and punishments for all human activity proved a great obstacle to the principle of equity in the matter of physical goods. Despite these hindrances, a surprisingly large number of utopians (43 percent) incorporated the equal sharing of wealth into their ideal societies.

The values of these writers were drawn mainly from a small group of very influential reformers in the eighteenth and nineteenth centuries: Adam Smith, Robert Owen, Charles Fourier, Charles Darwin, Herbert Spencer, Henry George, Laurence Gronlund, and Edward Bellamy. None of the utopias was truly original in form; each of the utopian societies copied the suggestions and ideas of one or more of these figures. The younger utopian writers, who were mainly influenced by the post–Civil War figures, more readily chose the collectivist form of utopia, whereas the older authors cast their individualist societies in the image of the earlier figures, Adam Smith and Robert Owen.

NOTES

1. David H. Wheeler, *Our Industrial Utopia and Its Unhappy Citizens* (Chicago: A. C. McClurg & Co., 1895), p. 63.
2. Ibid., p. 61.
3. Ibid., p. 127.
4. Ibid., p. 231.
5. Ibid., p. 243.
6. John Bachelder, *A.D. 2050* (San Francisco: Bancroft Co., 1890), p. 76.
7. Wheeler, *Our Industrial Utopia*, p. 60.
8. Bachelder, *A.D. 2050*, p. 20.
9. Ibid., p. 37.
10. Wheeler, *Our Industrial Utopia*, p. 298.

11. Bachelder, *A.D. 2050*, p. 51.
12. Wheeler, *Our Industrial Utopia*, p. 11.
13. Amos K. Fiske, *Beyond the Bourne* (New York: Fords, Howard, & Hulbert, 1891), p. 88.
14. [Mary Lane], *Mizora: A Prophesy* (New York: G. W. Dillingham & Co., 1889), p. 103.
15. J. P. Armour, *Edenindia: A Tale of Adventure* (New York: G. W. Dillingham & Co., 1905), p. 111.
16. Ibid., p. 35.
17. D. Herbert Heywood, *The Twentieth Century: A Prophesy of the Coming Age* (Boston: F. B. Heywood, Publisher, 1890), p. 22.
18. [Lane], *Mizora*, pp. 92–93.
19. Ibid., p. 39.
20. Bessie S. Rogers, *As It May Be: A Story of the Future* (Boston: Richard G. Badger, Gorham Press, 1905), p. 57.
21. Armour, *Edenindia*, p. 51.
22. Mortimer D. Leggett, *A Dream of a Modest Prophet* (Philadelphia: J.B. Lippincott & Co., 1890), p. 86.
23. Ibid.
24. D. Lull, *Celestia* (New York: Reliance Trading Co., 1907), p. 141.
25. James Cowen, *Daybreak: A Romance of an Old World* (New York: George H. Richmond & Co., 1896), p. 225.
26. Fayette S. Giles, *Shadows Before; or, A Century Onward* (New York: Humbolt Publishing Co., 1894), pp. 135–135.
27. Ibid., p. 84.
28. Ibid., p. 94.
29. Leggett, *The Dream*, pp. 126–27.
30. Giles, *Shadows Before*, p. 147.
31. Cowen, *Daybreak*, p. 56.
32. Ibid.
33. Giles, *Shadows Before*, p. 21.
34. Leggett, *The Dream*, pp. 126–27.
35. Ralph Albertson, *The Social Incarnation* (Commonwealth, Ga.: Christian Commonwealth Publishers, 1899), p. 4.
36. Ibid., pp. 40–41.
37. Ephraim Peterson, *An Ideal City For An Ideal People* (Independence, Mo.: The Author, 1905), p. 8.
38. Alcander Longley, *What Is Communism?* (St. Louis: n.p., 1890), p. 1.
39. William Bishop, *The Garden of Eden, U.S.A.* (Chicago: Charles H. Kerr & Co., 1895), p. 122.

40. Mary Agnes Tincker, *San Salvador* (Boston: Houghton, Mifflin & Co., 1892), p. 99.

41. Charles W. Caryl, *New Era* (Denver: New Era Union, 1897), p. 15.

42. Bradford Peck, *The World A Department Store* (Boston: Bradford Peck, Publisher, 1900), p. 316.

43. Ibid., p. viii.

44. King C. Gillette, *The Human Drift* (Boston: New Era Publishing Co., 1894), p. 14.

45. J.M.D. Bartlett, *A New Aristocracy* (n.p.: Bartlett Publishing Co., 1891), p. 307.

46. Milan C. Edson, *Solaris Farm: A Story of the Twentieth Century* (Washington, D.C.: The Author, 1900), p. 5.

47. Lena J. Fry, *Other Worlds* (Chicago: The Author, 1905), p. 138.

48. Caryl, *New Era*, p. 33.

49. William Fishbough, *America and the World* (New York: Continental Publishing Co., 1898), p. 314.

50. Bartlett, *A New Aristocracy*, p. 274.

51. Corwin Phelps, *An Ideal Republic; or, A Way Out of the Fog* (Chicago: W. L. Reynolds, 1896), p. 178.

52. Fry, *Other Worlds*, p. 44.

53. Caryl, *New Era*, p. 22.

54. Ibid., p. 71.

55. Gillette, *The Human Drift*, p. 121.

56. [F. U. Worley], *Three Thousand Dollars A Year: Moving Forward; or, How We Got There* (Washington, D.C.: J. P. Wright, 1890), pp. 52–53.

57. Henry Dowding, *The Man From Mars; or, Service For Service's Sake* (New York: Cochrane Publishing Co., 1910), p. 176.

58. Henry Olerich, *Modern Paradise* (Omaha: Equality Publishing Co., 1915), pp. 71–72.

59. Alfred Cridge, *Utopia; or, The History of an Extinct Planet* (Oakland, Calif.: Winchester & Pew, 1884), p. 15.

60. Henry Olerich, *A Cityless and Countryless World: An Outline of Practical Co-Operative Individualism* (Holstein, Iowa: Gilmore & Olerich, 1893), p. 6.

61. [Thomas Kirwin], *Reciprocity in the Thirtieth Century: The Coming Cooperative Age* (New York: Cochrane Publishing Co., 1909), p. 110.

62. D. L. Stump, *From World to World* (Asbury, Mo.: World to World Publishing Co., 1896), p. 7.

63. Ibid., p. 21.

64. Dowding, *Man From Mars*, p. 199.
65. James B. Alexander, *The Lunarian Professor* (Minneapolis: n.p., 1909), p. 70.
66. Ibid., p. 114.
67. Stump, *From World to World*, p. 22.
68. Henry L. Call, *The Coming Revolution* (Boston: Arena Publishing Co., 1895), p. 216.
69. Herman H. Brinsmade, *Utopia Achieved: A Novel of the Future* (New York: Broadway Publishing Co., 1912), p. 44.
70. William Simpson, *The Man From Mars* (San Francisco: Bacon & Co., 1891), p. 69.
71. Call, *The Coming Revolution*, p. 208.
72. Byron A. Brooks, *Earth Revisited* (Boston: Arena Publishing Co., 1893), p. 104.
73. William A. Taylor, *Intermere* (Columbus, Ohio: Twentieth Century Publishing Co., 1901), pp. 126–27.
74. Costello Holford, *Aristopia* (Boston: Arena Publishing Co., 1895), p. 183.
75. S. Byron Welcome, *From Earth's Center: A Polar Gateway Message* (Chicago: Charles H. Kerr & Co., 1894), p. 73.
76. Ibid., pp. 87–88.
77. Call, *The Coming Revolution*, p. 216.
78. Taylor, *Intermere*, p. 88.
79. Simpson, *Man From Mars*, p. 161.
80. Brooks, *Earth Revisited*, p. 66.
81. Albert A. Merrill, *The Great Awakening* (Boston: George Book Publishing Co., 1899), p. 39.
82. Ibid., p. 105.
83. W. S. Harris, *Life in a Thousand Worlds* (Cleona, Pa.: G. Holzaphel, 1905), p. 140.
84. [Edward M. House], *Philip Dru, Administrator: A Story of Tomorrow, 1920–1935* (New York: B. W. Hueback, 1912), p. 33.
85. Harris, *Life in a Thousand Worlds*, p. 246.
86. Albert Chavannes, *The Future Commonwealth; or, What Samuel Balcom Saw in Socioland* (New York: True Nationalist Publishing Co., 1892), p. 145.
87. Ibid., p. 131.
88. Merrill, *The Great Awakening*, pp. 206–7.
89. Alfred Hutchinson, *The Limit of Wealth* (New York: Macmillan Co., 1907), p. 225.
90. Merrill, *The Great Awakening*, pp. 206–7.
91. Daniel Bond, *Uncle Sam in Business* (Chicago: Charles H. Kerr & Co., 1899), p. 32.

92. Winnifred H. Cooley, "A Dream of the Twenty-First Century," *Arena* 28 (November 1902), p. 515.
93. [William S. Child], *The Legal Revolution of 1902* (Chicago: Charles H. Kerr & Co., 1898), p. 66.
94. T. H. Tibbles and Elia M. Beattie, *The American Peasant* (Chicago: F. J. Schulte & Co., 1892), p. 25.
95. [Ignatius Donnelly], *Caesar's Column: A Story of the Twentieth Century* (Chicago: F. J. Schulte & Co., 1890), p. 31.
96. Henry O. Morris, *Waiting for the Signal* (Chicago: Schulte Publishing Co., 1897), p. 343.
97. [Donnelly], *Caesar's Column*, p. 47.
98. Bond, *Uncle Sam in Business*, p. 13.
99. Ibid., p. 30.
100. [Donnelly], *Caesar's Column*, p. 121.
101. [John McCoy], *A Prophetic Romance, Mars to Earth* (Boston: Arena Publishing Co., 1896), p. 38.
102. Tibbles, *The American Peasant*, p. 20.
103. *Man or Dollar, Which?* (Chicago: Charles H. Kerr & Co., 1896), p. 173.
104. [Samuel Crocker], *That Island* (Kansas City, Mo.: C. E. Streeter & Co.,, 1892), p. 88.
105. John Brant, *The New Regime: A. D. 2202* (New York: Cochrane Publishing Co., 1909), p. 58.
106. Solomon Schindler, *Young West* (Boston: Arena Publishing Co., 1894), p. 172.
107. Frank Rosewater, *'96: A Romance of Utopia* (Omaha: Utopia Publishing Co., 1894), pp. 128–29.
108. Brant, *The New Regime*, p. 45.
109. Paul Devinne, *The Day of Prosperity: A Vision of the Century to Come* (New York: G. W. Dillingham & Co., 1902), p. 234.
110. [George H. Phelps], *The New Columbia; or, The Re–United States* (Findlay, Ohio: New Columbia Publishing Co., 1909), p. 64.
111. Brant, *The New Regime*, p. 99.
112. [Phelps], *The New Columbia*, p. 49.
113. Devinne, *Day of Prosperity*, p. 172.
114. Ibid., p. 173.
115. Schindler, *Young West*, p. 200.
116. [Phelps], *New Columbia*, p. 38.
117. Cosimo Noto, *The Ideal City* (New York: n.p., 1904), p. 359.
118. Jack London, "Goliah," in *Revolution and Other Essays* (New York: Macmillan Co., 1910), p. 75.
119. Ibid., p. 74.

Types of Utopias   139

120. [Alonzo Van Deusen], *Rational Communism: The Present and Future Republic of North America* (New York: Social Science Publishing Co., 1885), p. 50.
121. Zebina Forbush, *The Co-Opolitan* (Chicago: Charles H. Kerr & Co, 1898), p. 51.
122. Clark E. Persinger, *Letters From New America; or, An Attempt At Practical Socialism* (Chicago: Charles H. Kerr & Co., 1900), p. 77.
123. Robert A. Dague, *Henry Ashton* (Alameda, Calif.: The Author, 1903), p. 217.
124. Forbush, *The Co-Opolitan*, p. 14.
125. Persinger, *Letters From New America*, p. 60.
126. Forbush, *The Co-Opolitan*, p. 35.
127. Dague, *Henry Ashton*, p. 226.
128. London, "Goliath," p. 105.
129. C. A Steere, *When Things Were Done* (Chicago: Charles H. Kerr & Co., 1908), pp. 115–16.
130. Forbush, *The Co-Opolitan*, p. 72.
131. Edward Everett Hale, *Sybaris and Other Homes* (Boston: Fields, Osgood & Co., 1869), p. 80.
132. Henry B. Salisbury, *The Birth of Freedom: A Socialist Novel* (New York: Humbolt Publishing Co., 1890), p. 138.
133. Cyrus Cole, *The Auroraphone* (Chicago: Charles H. Kerr & Co., 1890), p. 195.
134. [Henry F. Allen], *The Key of Industrial Co-Operative Government* (St. Louis: The Author, 1886), p. 29.
135. London, "Goliah," p. 81.
136. Richard Hatfield, *Geyserland: Empiricisms in Social Reform* (Washington, D.C.: The Author, 1908), p. 143.
137. Richard M. Chapman, *The Vision of the Future* (New York: Cosmopolitan Press, 1916), p. 9.
138. [Jacob W. Horner], *Military Socialism* (Indianapolis: The Author, 1911), p. 46.
139. Walter O. Henry, *Equitania; or, The Land of Equity* (Omaha: n.p., 1914), p. 33.
140. Chapman, *Vision of the Future*, p. 29.
141. Ibid., p. 68.
142. Hatfield, *Geyserland*, pp. 210–11.
143. C. W. Woodridge, *Perfecting the Earth* (Cleveland: Utopia Publishing Co., 1902), p. 93.
144. Edgar Chambless, *Roadtown* (New York: Roadtown Press, 1910), p. 180.
145. H. George Schuette, *Athonia; or, The Original Four Hundred* (Manitowoc, Wis.: Lakeside Co., 1911), p. 385.

146. John Veiby, *The Utopian Way* (South Bend, Ind.: n.p., 1917), p. 92.
147. Ibid., p. 13.
148. Schuette, *Athonia*, p. 446.
149. William Harben, "In the Year Ten Thousand," *Arena* 36 (November 1892), p. 747.
150. Warren S. Rehm, *The Practical City* (Lancaster, Pa.: The Lancaster County Magazine, 1898), pp. 19–20.
151. Schuette, *Athonia*, p. 426.
152. Ibid., p. 414.
153. Veiby, *The Utopian Way*, p. 38.
154. Woodridge, *Perfecting the Earth*, p. 217.

5
Utopian Values

Like the intellectual systems the utopian adopted, his values were very much a part of his time. The most popular value, equality, had its roots in the natural-rights philosophy and the quest for political democracy prevalent in the late eighteenth century. The value of hard work had an even older heritage, arising out of the turmoil of the Protestant Reformation and becoming a part of the value system that came to be called the "Protestant ethic." Its praises were sung in America by the Puritan divines as well as Benjamin Franklin; by the end of the nineteenth century it received its greatest impetus from those economic theorists who advocated the labor theory of value. Christianity, of course, had a long heritage, but the utopian, as did his counterpart in the Social Gospel movement, placed special emphasis—almost to the exclusion of everything else—on the doctrine of Christian love. Apparently, it was the only universally applicable part of that body of doctrine that could cut across the many beliefs, isms, and creeds that flooded the scene at the end of the nineteenth century.

So, too, the idea of progress, born during the time of the European Renaissance, was rekindled by the theory of evolution, and both became part of the utopian creed. The spirit of individualism, with its wellsprings in the romanticism of the earlier part of the century, had already begun to wither, but not before it had left its grandiose vision of human dignity firmly imprinted on the utopian mind. In short, at the very moment of his birth, the utopian inherited a whole system of values, some complementary to and others estranged from his milieu; yet, all were destined to play a large part in the life of each utopian.

The most significant part of the utopian's discussion of these values, however, lay in the varying degrees of emphasis and meaning he placed on them. Not every writer accepted the full implications of these values; indeed, regarding individualism and equality, the writer often had to make a choice. There were also differences between the equality of opportunity and that of possession, between the idea of work supported by either the values of the Protestant ethic or the labor theory of value, between a moral code applied through either the individual conscience or social pressure, and between an individualism based on either self-interest or a concern for others. The opposition implied by these choices revealed a more fundamental conflict: that between the individual and society. The degree to which the utopian emphasized one over the other determined which type of utopia he was more likely to advocate and which solutions he favored. Many writers heroically tried to incorporate the good of both extremes, but those with any respect for consistency abandoned the attempt and cast their lot with one side or the other.

EQUALITY

Equality was the most important value for the utopian in his judgment of any state or society. The phrase quoted most frequently in these works was from the Declaration of Independence: "All men are created equal." The most popular utopian, Edward Bellamy, chose the word "equality" for the title of his sequel to *Looking Backward*.[1] And when, in the fall of 1886, he began writing his most famous work, the idea of equality was uppermost in his mind; his stated purpose was "to reason out a method of economic organization by which the republic might guarantee the livelihood and material welfare of its citizens on a basis of equality corresponding to and supplementing their political equality."[2] The utopian often spoke eloquently about "the keystone of our national arch—human equality, the climax of human civilization and happiness,"[3] or about "human brotherhood and the equal rights of man."[4] With the same thought in mind, he frequently blamed the disorder of social conditions on "a contemptuous disregard" for this principle.[5] His disillusionment with his own era stemmed from his conviction that the people "were neither free nor equal in any ordinary sense of the word."[6]

The utopian justified his belief in the principle of equality in many ways. Because of his commitment to Enlightenment thought, he argued that all men were free and equal by virtue of every individual's possession of the "right to life, liberty, and the pursuit of happiness."[7] As suggested by another part of the Declaration of Independence, men were also equal because they were created by God. To the religious utopian, this meant that "all men were equal before God," that is, they all possessed a soul and were all subject to God's judgment.[8] For others, it simply meant that "God created this beautiful world for all people."[9] Being members of the same species, a fact given much prominence by the idea of evolution, also served the utopian's argument. While trying to mock the eternal quest for social status, James B. Alexander offered the following suggestion:

Every man's ancestral tree is just the same height as all the rest, his lineage is just as long and his pedigree must contain practically the same number of terms whether we reckon back to Adam or to the original protoplasm.[10]

To Byron Books, it should have been obvious to all that "we are all members of the same family."[11] He did not feel there could be much argument over this biological fact. However, Cyrus Cole thought it necessary to call upon a scientific hypothesis—namely, that "matter in its ultimate state was homogeneous, that is, consisted of atoms all alike," to support his stand for equality.[12]

Yet the word "equality" had many different meanings for these authors. The adjectives "political," "social," "individual," or "economic" often qualified this word for a clarification of its meaning. Many controversies of the time centered on the difference between the equality of opportunity and the equality of possession, and this, too, was important to the utopian. When

Henry Call complained that his contemporaries "missed the substance of freedom and found only its shadow," he was referring to the lack of political independence available to the average citizen.[13] On this point, over 90 percent of the utopians agreed. Political equality was the very basis of the democratic state, and all but a few of the most powerful utopian state governments allowed the voice of the people to be heard.

Though there was less unanimity on the question of social equality, still, a majority of writers specifically advocated a classless society. Byron Brooks represented this group when he declared:

There is no downtrodden class—in fact, there is but one class...a human being, a man or woman is of far more consequence than any possible position or title whatsoever. They have no titles, no uniforms, no manner or kind of social mark of distinction. Personal worth is the only thing that is respected.[14]

Many authors allowed different social levels in their ideal societies, but moderated their effect by emphasizing humility and the golden rule. The Reverend W. S. Harris created a state in which, though there were social levels, "no one feels himself beneath or above another, and no one feels embarrassed in the presence of a superior intelligence."[15] Finally, a few agreed with Jacob Horner's contention that "men were not equal mentally, morally, or physically, and that in every well-regulated society, some must command and others obey."[16] However, even in Horner's utopia, all children went to the same kind of school to receive the same education, and "the sons of generals have no privileges the sons of privates do not have."[17] Thus, on the social level, the utopian generally made provision in his ideal state for the mutual respect for all persons, even though a large minority set up social classes as a sign of inevitable differences among people.

However, in America, as most utopians recognized, social equality was directly related to the value of one's possessions. In fact, C. A Steere achieved social equality by first putting everyone on the same economic level. Yet, he still made allowance for individual differences:

This new conception of equality does not necessarily mean that a board of competent anthropologists, sociologists, chemists, and phrenologists have met in conclave and solemnly and learnedly announced that every citizen of the commonwealth was endowed with the same mental and physical characteristics and capacities. Far from it. It signifies, rather, that classes have been abolished by the expropriation of the national resources, thus putting all upon the same economic level. Social, political, and legal inequalities could not exist.[18]

Many utopians, however refused to erase individual differences by putting everyone on the same economic level. They concurred with the prevailing notion that success in the economic realm was a sign of and a reward for unusual ability, perseverance, and skill. In this regard, Alfred Hutchinson felt it necessary to affirm that "there never had been and there never will be an equality among men."[19] In this statement, he denied the existence of an absolute individual equality; like other utopians of this stamp, he preferred to speak of the equality of opportunity, an equality that allowed each person to start his or her way in life on an equal footing and yet be rewarded in proportion to his or her efforts. Under these conditions, the utopian could proudly boast that his ideal country was "a land of absolute individuality as well as absolute equality."[20] What he meant was that everyone had equal opportunity "for physical and mental development and in securing the pleasures and comforts of life"; however, because of individual differences, not everyone would acquire the same quantity of comfort, pleasure, or mental and physical well-being.[21] Each was free to pursue his or her own interests in his or her own way, and it was presumed that not everyone's interests would coincide.

On the other hand, a very large group of utopians felt that everyone had certain basic needs that had to be satisfied. Individual differences could be tolerated, but only after these needs were provided. If certain people, by virtue of their excessive wealth, prevented others from obtaining the means to survive, then some central authority would forcibly have to create an equality of possession and wealth whereby everyone was at least guaranteed food, clothing, and shelter. This more desperate view of the economic crises gloomily assumed that the problem was too large to be solved by the equality of opportunity or other individualistic measures. Nevertheless, many who advocated the equal distribution of wealth recognized that it could readily undermine the idea of a personal reward for personal effort; therefore, they tried to compensate for the potential loss of this worthwhile value by making some form of altruism a socially desirable habit. Furthermore, conscious of the stultifying sameness that could result from the equal distribution of wealth, this type of utopian went to great lengths to avoid that result. Edward Bellamy declared: "While we insist on equality, we detest uniformity and seek to provide the greatest possible variety of tastes in our expenditure."[22]

Nothing pleased these utopians more than the vision of the members of a great middle class enjoying the fruits of their labor, with very few people, or none at all, on the extremes of the social scale. A minority of utopians preferred to restore equal opportunity and a laissez-faire system to attain this end, but most agreed that an all-powerful central authority could only summon enough power to grant social and economic equality. Some of this latter group advocated the equal distribution of wealth and a classless society; others preferred to allow individual differences to be represented by various social classes while yet retaining an equal distribution of wealth. Except for the handful who built their states around benevolent despots, all not only agreed to the necessity for political equality, but also supported the idea that "the foundation principle of true civilization was an impartial enforcement of equity."[23]

WORK

Although the reformer of this era dreamed constantly of the millennium, he suffered no illusions about the necessity for hard, difficult work to obtain it. Not one of these books presented the presumably ideal conditions where all the comforts of life were available with the pressing of a button or the flick of a finger. In fact, quite a number of utopians considered their states perfect when "there will be something for everybody to do and everybody will be doing it."[24] The utopian was clearly committed to the values of the Protestant ethic. He hated waste, inefficiency, and idleness because they were morally objectionable as well as inconvenient. Even the man who refused to condemn the souls of the unemployed knew that their presence was a hindrance to progress. If the world were to improve with the passing of each day, all must work; the harder everyone worked, the sooner everyone would arrive at a state of perfect bliss and happiness. Whether people were building God's kingdom of heaven on earth or were looking toward the triumph of human reason, it mattered little. The basic ingredient was the same—hard work.

To some utopians, work was somehow connected with a moral purpose. First, there were those utopians, mindful of the doctrine of the talents, who regarded work as the price one paid for one's salvation. To them it was necessary to "consider your existence as sacred, and have a purpose worthy of it."[25] This statement presupposed God as the final judge and arbiter of the worth of one's life. It made sense, therefore, to answer the question, "What should be the highest and noblest ambition of every human being?" with the reply, "It is to fill the place in life for which he was intended."[26] In the language of the Protestant ethic, work was called duty, and its instrument of fulfillment was called conscience. Since every man possessed a conscience, "every man is his own monitor, and he needs no other. He knows his duty and he has that within him which keeps him up to it more effectively than any outside influence could."[27] The sense of obligation that this line of reasoning demanded of one was total and complete. The ultimate judgment of God rested on the fulfillment of one's duty, and the question was often asked, "What does it profit a man if he gain the whole world, and by it lose all that God intended should be his?"[28] To the believer, this question had only one answer.

This idea of duty required that its adherents not only work, but perform their work well. "Distinction and excellence for its own sake" was extolled;[29] for if God was worthy of the best, a man could ill afford to use his talents "making inferior goods to meet the consumer's ideas as to price."[30] The ideal manner of going about one's work was described by Thomas Kirwin:

The workers are so deeply interested and earnest in their occupations that they give no time or thought to anything else; and besides, their natural dignity would keep them from trifling talk and actions at such a time.[31]

Strict adherence to the demands of the task at hand was an absolute necessity. If this condition were fulfilled, success was assured; however, if success were not forthcoming from a worthy effort, then a person could rightly say he was not fitted for a certain kind of work. The doctrine of the talents allowed some people more ability than others, and a humble realization of that fact was necessary at the approach of each task. Bradford Peck complained that much waste and inefficiency resulted from those blinded by their own egotism into thinking they could occupy any position. As he saw it, "There were many people trying to fill a position in life for which they were not fitted."[32]

Twelve years later, Bradford Peck blamed everyone who failed to seek work best suited to his talents, Edward House blamed society for not allowing each individual to perform a task wherein he or she could exercise his or her best talents. In fact, the ultimate goal of House's utopia was to provide the conditions in which "every child born of woman may have an opportunity to accomplish that for which he is best fitted."[33] Although work was still the criterion of worthiness for Edward House, this shift in emphasis from individual to social responsibility can be attributed to a disenchantment with the individualistic ethics of religion as well as to the inroads made by Social Darwinism. The utopian came to realize that the problems associated with a man's occupation were matters of economic and social planning. A mere reliance on blame and conscience to correct misfortunes attributable to uncontrollable fluctuations in the business cycle seemed futile. The doctrine of the talents could only work when equal opportunity existed.

A number of utopians became further disillusioned with the doctrinal justification of work because it was often used as a rationale by businessmen to support their morally questionable intentions. A few utopians, in all sincerity, gave credence to this commercial attitude. T. H. Tibbles was representative; he advised businessmen to "elevate the morals of your workmen and you promote the interests of your company."[34] His application of the moral code to the workman's interests was even more dubious when he advised the entrepreneur against hiring men to work on Sunday, since he will cause his men "to be reckless in handling a machine that cost fifteen to twenty thousand dollars."[35]

This merging of the doctrine of the talents into the doctrine of wealth as a sign of election was recognized and deplored by the majority of utopians. Alfred Hutchinson spelled out the relationship. "Work with all thy might, thy genius, and thy power," he said, "to accumulate all the wealth possible." However, he was quick to add that this wealth must be acquired by "fair and honorable means."[36] Yet, most utopians compared this latter admonition to a straw thrown to the wind. "It is not by honest acts of labor that such fortunes can be acquired," claimed Henry L. Call;[37] and Costello Holford, himself a doctor, outrightly accused the rich of being "dissolute gentlemen."[38]

The majority of utopians thus came to value work for its own sake or for certain practical ends and not as a means to riches or a necessary path to eternal salvation. To Solomon Schindler, a follower of Bellamy, work was simply that which "brings happiness and gives satisfaction."[39] A character representing Paul Devinne's utopia stated his feeling thus: "Work ennobles us, you know."[40] William Bishop, whose community was run as a business, claimed: "There is poetry in well-directed labor and a feeling of independence in the knowledge that one is earning one's way in the world without the help of one's ancestors."[41] Both James B. Alexander and Edward Bellamy thought of work as a practical way of returning one's obligation to society. Young West in Bellamy's *Looking Backward*, after being introduced to the new world of 2000 A.D., felt "an overmastering desire to roll up one's sleeves and do something toward rendering an equivalent for one's living."[42] Finally, there were those, such as James Cowen, who extolled the "love of the work itself."[43]

Yet even these reasons seemed insufficient to replace the value of work as a means to money or a path to salvation. A more basic and compelling idea could be found in these novels. Somehow, probably through the influence of John Locke as well as David Ricardo's labor theory of value, the utopian concluded that human labor was the sole source of wealth. Furthermore, there was a very elementary and direct connection between labor and its product, whereby it was believed that all time and energy expended must have its immediate and fruitful result. In his attempt to retain this simple relationship, the utopian resented what he called "artificial" methods of acquiring wealth. Most of all, he complained of the manipulation of capital, land speculation, and special-privilege legislation, which he felt did not result in any real, usable product. William S. Child insisted that "all wealth is the product of labor. True values may be increased by law or speculation, or as in the case of land, by settling the country, but nevertheless, all actual wealth is the product of labor."[44] In the same vein, Edward House apologized for the capitalist's ignorance of this creed. "Good man that he means to be," House claimed, "he does not know, perhaps he can never know, that it is labor, labor of the mind and of the body, that creates, not capital."[45] In short, the majority of utopians agreed "that in the last analysis it is by labor that all are supported."[46]

Within these thoughts were the seeds of revolution; yet, only a few utopians related the idea of the exploited laborer to his own era. Albert Merrill complained that "the laborer, the real producer of all wealth, got only a bare living,"[47] whereas Henry Olerich, an admirer of Herbert Spencer, demanded that all wealth produced by labor should belong to the producer.[48] Nevertheless, the utopian's fear of permanently fixed social classes, especially the lower classes, prevented him from forming a rationale for revolution. Far more representative was the attitude of Mary E. Lane, who regarded labor as the necessity of life and who claimed that this "law of social equality" accounted for the superiority of the citizens in her utopia.[49]

The consideration of labor by many utopians as the sole source of communal wealth gave it a central place in their utopias. Since progress was most often measured in terms of the total goods and services produced in a society, the amount of physical and mental effort expended was deemed directly proportional to that goal. According to Cyrus Cole, "Labor is thought to be the most important factor of progress" for this very reason.[50] The motto of William Simpson's utopia—"toilers with a will"—

represented the general feeling. Perhaps the clearest statement in support of this idea was made by David H. Wheeler:

Abundance has meant what it meant in old Rome, a big feast and a "good time generally." In Utopia it must mean just plain work, and more of it rather than less. For we desire to keep abundance; and that means labor and thrift. The industrial ideal not only requires every man to produce as much at least as he consumes; it also requires him to convert his consumption into products or into character and that means building by effort the virtues of the industrial life.[51]

Thus, if the utopian society sought "the satisfaction of every want,"[52] it required the total participation of every member of the community. Then, claimed William Bishop, the whole citizenship of the country would be kept in luxury, but only if "there were no waste or foolish extravagance."[53] He had little patience with the unproductive member of the community. Whether the utopian's commitment to the idea of work stemmed from the values of the Protestant ethic or from his love of efficiency and progress mattered little. The inefficient and the idle were universally censured. The morally inclined utopian chose to preach industry while direly warning those who faltered that "if a man will not work, neither let him eat."[54] These utopians, more often than not, excluded the lazy from their utopian society. Ephraim Peterson, a newspaper editor in Missouri, thought them unworthy to become citizens "by reason of their bad character and habits, of which they will not repent."[55] However, he allowed them to be fed outside the walls of his ideal city, but only if there was a surplus.

By the same token, the efficient-minded utopian chose to cut off the nonproducer from his livelihood and his usual rights as a citizen. Most agreed with Clark Persinger that "the idle man is an alien, without income or vote."[56] The typical method of securing for the worker his just due in these utopias was to substitute labor checks for money. In this way, a man could purchase goods only in proportion to the worth of his contribution to the total wealth of the community, thus ensuring that "no man is plundered and no man starved, who is willing to work."[57] The more sympathetic utopians allowed the drones of society to perform their quota of labor by participating in public works projects instituted by the government for that purpose.[58] Some utopians simply left it up to public opinion, "which is most potent in this age and which strongly condemns a useless and idle life."[59] Finally, a whole array of incentives, including retirement plans, guaranteed work, machinery for the duller, repetitive jobs, diversified tasks in each job, and most of all, ready promotion for good work induced the members of utopia to contribute their greatest efforts of mind and body for the creation of an ideal place in which to live.

In short, the utopian was unanimously committed to the value of hard work as a necessary condition of progress. Some judged progress in terms of eternal salvation, but they were in the minority. Moral condemnation of the idle and unproductive, though evinced by some utopians, did not appeal to the majority who preferred to think constructively in terms of efficiency and social planning. They were willing to recognize larger social forces as causes of unemployment and unproductive labor and, consequently, felt that society, ideally, should make it possible for all to work. This, it was judged, would more than adequately provide the necessary goods and services to satisfy every want and mark the society as a progressive one.

MORALITY

Although uninterested in Christian doctrine, the utopian showed marked concern for the correct behavior of the inhabitants in his ideal society. Yet, any criterion of correctness implied a standard of value, and more often than not, the standard was expressed in moral terms. The words "conscience," "duty," "selfishness," "pride," "justice," and other evidences of moral judgment occurred on almost every page of these works. The utopian found it impossible not to think in terms of human will and responsibility, the only frame of reference for ethical judgment he knew. When he condemned the wealthy, he cited the long-established moral bias against materialism. In praising the value of work, he alluded to what he called "the industrial virtues"—honesty, truth, fidelity, diligence, and thrift. His optimistic faith in the future was partly tinged with a belief in the millennium and the ultimate triumph of God's goodness and justice. The value of equality was largely based on his conviction that all men were alike in their possession of a soul; by the same token, the utopian alluded to this belief when he argued for the infinite worth of each individual person. Likewise, the utopian's insistent condemnation of organized religion only proved more conclusively his desire to see his world organized and imbued with the principles of justice and order. In short, it was virtually impossible for the utopian to dissociate himself from the Christian moral tradition, despite his professed allegiance to science and the values of the Enlightenment.

In spite of the varieties of social organization created by these authors, there was unanimous consent concerning the need for a clear and universally applicable code of conduct for the citizens of utopia. In the economic realm, there was common agreement on the principle of establishing a sense of obligation to the community in preference to the unregulated accumulation of private wealth. The politician was conceived of as a representative of either his constituents or certain principles, but never of himself. Socially, the utopian agreed to the importance of the family and to the need for establishing rules governing the upbringing of children. There was also a consensus on what would be the most important rule governing ethical behavior in all these realms, that is, the golden rule, or the Christian law of love. Practically everyone supported Byron Brooks's contention that "morality is the basis of all true civilization and of the safety of the state,"[60] and William Leggett's statement that "any plan or system of reformation that failed to elevate or restore a sense of justice...between man and man, must prove a failure."[61]

However, the utopians could be about evenly divided on the question of what or who would be the monitor for this ethical code. One group spoke in terms of conscience and individuals, another spoke of education or the state; inevitably, some spoke of both. But when Cyrus Cole commented that "religion ranks above everything in the social and moral growth of nations," he virtually stood alone in advocating organized religion as the guardian of public morality.[62] Far more typical was the comment of Byron Welcome, a member of the Populist party, who tolerated the presence of religious groups but interpreted the biblical injuction, "Go ye preach the gospel to all people," to mean "preach until social conditions are right, then preaching is no longer necessary."[63] Like Welcome, the utopian considered religion an embarrassing reminder of human frailty and weakness, something that his optimism rebelled against, but that his practical sense did not fail to take into account.

It was natural, then, that the more conservative utopians—those who advocated the individualistic, cooperative, and legal utopias—would regard morality as a matter of conscience. They viewed society as Ralph Waldo Emerson did, as the sum total of individuals, and they assumed that if every individual were true to the moral dictates of his conscience, the entire society would be perfect. They believed that "each individual in a great measure became [in utopia] a law unto himself, and that was the law of perfect righteousness unfolding itself in the hearts and minds of the people."[64]

Because this type of utopian believed in conscience as the ultimate arbiter of right and wrong, he did not place much faith in law or conventional guides to conduct. Rather, he believed, along with James Cowen, that "the incentive is in the love of our work and the consciousness that we are doing something to make someone a little happier and the world a little better."[65] A large percentage of this group insisted on the final disappearance of all legal apparatus before utopia could be attained. Society would be perfected, they held, by man, who "only has the immortal arbiter within, saying do right, abhor the evil."[66] For this group, society existed to enhance the perfection of each individual; for as Byron Brooks went on to say, "Man only has the faculty of distinguishing truth, of delighting in its possession, of developing it in his life."[67] The old moral terms "human will," "responsibility," "punishment and reward"—all construed in terms of the individual—were at the center of their ethical system. And because the psychology of laissez faire, making one's own way, and the Horatio Alger mentality suited this individual-centered ethic, there were a substantial number of members of this group who would agree with David H. Wheeler's contention that "there can be no reasonable doubt that modern industry is the best moral gymnasium ever offered to mankind in our practical life."⁶⁸ There could be no doubt, either, that many in this group were suspicious of politics and government and anything else that would encroach on their highly personal view of man's place in the world.

The counterpart of this group, mainly those utopians who advocated a socialistic or highly centralized state, were not willing to do away entirely with the stimulus of individual reward and punishment. They emphasized the ideas of equality and social justice and were harsher in their judgment of economic failure and the great disparity between rich and poor. The term "selfishness" appeared frequently in their works, and they were willing to insist that "righteousness under commercialism is an absolute impossibility."⁶⁹ Representative of this group's attitude was C. W. Woodridge's righteous comment: "It is easier for a camel to pass through the eye of a needle than for a rich man to enter into citizenship in utopia."⁷⁰ Many members of this group angrily denounced the institution of private property. Common or state ownership of property seemed an appropriate solution, for it meant "social redemption of the race."⁷¹ As Ralph Albertson viewed the contemporary scene, he commented, "The root of social wrong is selfishness and the chief bulwark of selfishness is the institution of private property."⁷² Many agreed to this interpretation of social justice based on individual moral virtue. Ephraim Peterson went so far as to judge that "the present condition of things cannot be improved upon" because of the system of "every man for himself, privately owned property, interest, rent, profit."⁷³ To be sure, the utopian of this group criticized almost every aspect of the status quo, but he rarely advocated revolution or spoke of class warfare. Instead, he proposed a moral transformation in which justice would be applied equally and in which unlimited self-aggrandizement would be punished, even if it meant the entire re-creation of the foundations of society.

The utopian appealed to his reader in the language of the moral crusader. Perhaps he shrewdly guessed it was the most persuasive appeal he could make, but more than likely, he chose to write in terms of his Christian heritage because he was convinced of its rightness. He denounced the cause of the

Christian churches insofar as they removed themselves from the problems of the day, but this did not prevent the utopian from making appeals to conscience or a sense of social justice.

PROGRESS

If there was any one idea that could motivate the utopian observer to commit himself to a future state—even prompt his writing a utopia—it was the idea of progress. Though conditions of the time disenchanted him, it was mainly one theoretical condition—the lack of progress—that appalled him the most. Progress for what? Equality of opportunity, material prosperity, the advantages of leisure and learning—it really did not matter, so long as there was evidence of improvement. The notion of progress was contained in every popular ideology of the day: evolution, Christianity, enlightenment values, scientism, even Marxism.[74] "It is the general belief," commented John Ira Brant, "that now almost anything you can imagine is possible."[75] G. H. Phelps, a follower of Bellamy, gave voice to the view that "in actual practice, we discover that the universal trend of all things is toward improvement, and that essential perfection is the ultimate destiny of things."[76]

Certainly, the idea of progress became synonymous with the thought of the utopian writer. Clark Persinger dedicated his book to those who "are seriously seeking the betterment of present social conditions, and not those who regard the present order as a satisfactory one."[77] In fact, for the utopians, it was no less than necessary to subscribe to the doctrine of progress. In James Cowen's utopia, an advanced thinker of the future state admonished his American visitor: "A firm faith that victory will come and that the golden age is before you will be a great help in your struggle with evil. Lay hold of the faith. It is yours."[78] Milan Edson translated this advice into the dogmatic conclusion that "the object and purpose of this planet is the evolution of human beings, their continued growth and development, until the state of perfection is reached.... All energies flow toward this end."[79] Later he alluded to the advent of the millennium,[80] which both Byron Brooks and John Bachelder believed was imminent.[81] In short, any ideology that embraced an element of hope about the future was seized by the utopian and pressed to his purpose.

However, although these writers clung desperately to the idea of progress, not all were convinced that the mere passage of time automatically brought improvement. According to Mrs. J.M.D. Bartlett, it was concentration on the present that brought success. "If that is rightfully spent," she said, "the future will take care of itself."[82] Nor did all agree that a state of perfection was imminent. Clark Persinger warned that the first generation would realize that "their lot in life, while improved—and vastly improved—would not be made perfect."[83] Alcanoan Grigsby, though an ardent advocate of future progress, had doubts: "In every age, and in every condition of life, man has been building in the direction of his ideals, but never reaching them."[84] At the opposite extreme, Henry Dowding's exuberant judgment of man's progress in mastering his world led him to the unhappy questions, "Is it conceivable that mankind will pause?" "May we not find other worlds to conquer?"[85]

To all these objections, the confirmed believer in progress had ingenious, logical answers. Henry Dowding found an answer to his own dilemma. When his highly evolved and advanced state was characterized as a "sluggish race of people... with no wars, no class distinction, nothing to worry about," the advocate of that state replied: "It is the attraction of lofty ideals of future glory which disturbs the race and animates the people to struggle."[86] The fallacy of the more serious objection of never attaining perfection and therefore having a hopeless goal was similarly exposed. The error, claimed the more sophisticated utopian, was in confusing progress and perfection. The idea of progress was a process, not an absolute. It was never meant to be attained wholly. "Life consists in the eternal aspiration for some beloved purpose. Could this purpose be absolutely discovered or removed, there would be nothing left to life."[87] In terms of happiness and suffering, Cyrus Cole reached the same conclusion:

Science has demonstrated that happiness and suffering were relative.... A condition of uninterrupted happiness, no matter how various and dissimilar the causes which produce it, if long continued, must finally result in unconsciousness. "No suffering, no pleasure" is a true statement. Evil and suffering are thus as essential to life worth living as are virtue and pleasure.[88]

This denunciation of the absolute, fixed world of perfection allowed the utopian to look forward to an ever-improving world, an idea close to the doctrine of evolution, even closer to the ever-present notion in the utopian mind that the world was unfinished and America's job was to finish it. Whether the task could be accomplished, and even less so, when it could be accomplished, was never a question. To revel in the process constituted the greatest happiness possible. Forbush's borrowed words of Shakespeare described the utopian's mood well: " 'Time's noblest offspring is her last,' and we may hope that such offspring is this day born, and that it will thrive and continue to grow until time is no more."[89]

Having committed himself to constant improvement, the utopian could almost alleviate his despair over the present, which he regarded merely as a stepping stone to a better, improved world. "What more glorious privilege than to live in the Twentieth Century,"[90] Herbert Heywood declared. Paul Devinne, a severe critic of the status quo, was still able to state unabashedly, "Yes, we can readily see that mankind has made progress and has grown better and more rational."[91]

A natural and expected consequence of this exuberance was the association of the spirit of progress with its chief instrumentality, the state. No doubt a good deal of the feeling became translated into imperialism and the idea of manifest destiny. One would expect statements such as Fayette Giles's description of American cultural dominance of the Western hemisphere one hundred years hence.

Old America, with its annexation of Cuba, Canada and British America, is indeed an enchanted land—of vast cities, forests, and fields, prairies and snow-capped mountains; a land in which the fragrance of the rose is somewhere ever present, within whose borders are found the fruits of every zone, the flowers of all climes, and grain and herds with which to fill the stores of earth and feed a whole hungry world.... A rich land—better than the Eden of old.[92]

But the most important significance of this lyric statement of American superiority was its singularity among all the utopian writers. Few concluded that nation and progress were synonymous, or, perhaps, it was so tacitly understood, it needed no utterance. However, the utopian writer was less interested in nations, boundaries, states, or particular loyalties than he was in the all-pervading struggle of man against nature and man against himself. The whole world was his province. He truly felt that "our age is rushing in great forces, the ripening of thought. The conflicts of mind are over. The earth yields her secrets at our desire. The stars write their victory on the open sky."[93]

Thus, to the utopian, progress was not an elaborate doctrine, as it was to the eighteenth-century thinker, or a historical inevitability, as it was to the Marxian dialectician. True, Darwin and Spencer contributed greatly to the utopian's hopes for the future; nevertheless, his commitment to progress was primarily a simple feeling that tomorrow would be better. So essential was this feeling that quite a number of utopians could not conceive of the day when man ceased to hope for something better. The idea of progress negated the notion of an absolute, fixed world and also removed any despair that might have resulted from matching an absolute ideal with an imperfect present. Rather, the utopian advocated constant change, which presented continual challenges to his ability to improve and perfect.

INDIVIDUALISM

Although only a minority of these writers could be considered individualists of the Emersonian stamp, a great number were deeply committed to the ideal of personal satisfaction. Many realized that man was no longer a master of all he surveyed, as Thoreau contended; nevertheless, they dedicated their utopias to the task of conquering the mysteries of nature through science. The utopian's reliance on free will, reward, and punishment; his commitment to the values of hard work and equality; and his hope for steady improvement of the race—all centered on his belief in the innate worth of each individual person. The fact that he cared at all to write a utopia indicated a concern for the fate of his fellow citizens. Although self-interest was denounced, and altruism was cultivated in these ideal societies, few utopians came to regard the state as a living, organic thing; rather, some considered its role negative, while most were willing to increase its powers only when the people it represented had the ultimate say. In short, the utopian thought mainly in terms of a personally oriented world.

The individualist utopian revealed himself in many ways. He fully believed that "the inner life of the individual will assert its supremacy without the assistance of artful pretense."[94] He spoke frequently of character building, inner courage, and the fierce but strengthening daily sustenance of competition. He firmly believed that man was a "free moral agent" and that "he ought to be the builder and artificer of his own character... for real worth, will power and moral strength can come in no other way." He thought to depend on circumstances, surroundings, or favorable conditions produced "boneless, nerveless, and insipid youths."[95] Heredity, one's companions, or "some other equally foreign thing" received the blame for what the individualist felt should squarely rest on the shoulders of the person himself.[96]

Similarly, competition was hailed as the "source of mental, physical and spiritual progress."[97] In fact, the lack of free, open, total competition proved disconcerting to this type of utopian. The principle that "nothing but skill determines the contest, and the public can never lose by it"[98] could not be applied to an artificially regulated system "whereby a favored few are permitted to rob the many."[99] In such a society, hope for character development seemed small. Forbush was willing to admit that her own society still developed character, but "the most remarkable character and the most admired in it are the modern Shylocks."[100] Others, more pessimistic, viewed the passing of the "old lessons of self-restraint, prudence, and self-denial." A few old teachers of those lessons were still around, claimed David Wheeler, but their "voices are faint."[101]

For the individualist, the idea of a utopia at first seemed anomalous. If he thought, as Hutchinson did, that "while the government should say what the individual might do and what he might not do, as a free agent, it was not for the government to be the active agent in doing those particular things,"[102] then government became a body without power, a mere recommending agency. However, the individualistic utopian usually had more in mind. The government's role was to suppress or "clear away the foulness of imperfect character,"[103] whereby certain individuals trespassed on the rights of others. They considered it necessary for the government to regulate and even legislate a state of pure competition and to prevent combinations or groups of individuals from monopolizing and dominating one commercial enterprise. The state fostered "every industrially trained man, who has in him some stuff of the pioneer, to live close to a frontier to be crossed by effort to press the unknown into the service of humanity."[104]

Yet the word "individualism" was equated by some with selfishness, so universally condemned by the utopian writer. Because he witnessed such deprivation, the utopian came to believe that people were selfish, unmindful of others. Under these conditions, "individualism" was really another term for "ruthless exploitation." Edward Bellamy claimed: "It was in the name of individual liberty, industrial freedom, and individual initiative that the economic government of the country was surrendered to the capitalists."[105] James Cowen accused "excessive individualism...with its selfish disregard for others," as the cause for the downfall of many an enlightened nation of the past.[106] For Albert Chavannes, individualism meant "that form of action followed by undeveloped organisms to secure self-preservation."[107]

Bitterness and cynicism characterized other statements on individualism. In a story by Jack London, the new leader of the people had to destroy some old individualistic stalwarts of the status quo. To justify his action, he offered the following rationale:

What are a few paltry lives? In your insane wars you destroy millions of lives and think nothing of it. In your fratricidal commercial struggle you kill countless babes, women, and men, and you triumphantly call the shambles "individualism."[108]

Later, when the socialist leader triumphed in the revolution, the few individualists left were described as "men who yearned for the flesh pots and cannibal feasts of old, creatures long of teeth and savage of claw who wanted to prey upon their fellowmen."[109] In Forbush's utopia, individualists were kept out of the state legislature by simply ruling that "the honor was unaccompanied by compensation."[110] Woodridge asked "to count that man as an enemy... whoever seeks for himself or for any individual privileges not open to all."[111] Even Edward Everett Hale, a staunch pleader for moral virtue, became angry when he viewed the slum conditions in Boston. One of his characters stated:

I know that you hate to be constantly making laws and controlling people... and I know your father says that government is best which governs least, but I think something might be done to give these people a better chance.[112]

Conscious of the immoral connotations of his ideology, the individualist utopian sought to transcend the label of selfishness. Without relying on unearned gifts from the state, he would strive through his own moral courage and God-given talents for the betterment of mankind. All selfish motives were subsumed in a benevolent altruism. He might agree that "self-gratification is the end of one's acts; but, sometimes," he was quick to add, "we can be more gratified by devious routes, that is, helping others."[113] Thus, it was morally acceptable to utilize one's abilities for the service of others. According to James B. Alexander:

With us the greatest liberty is accorded to the individual, but so well grounded is our predisposition to work for the benefit of the community that no one has any fear or suspicion that another is not doing what he ought, or is able to do for the common good.[114]

To some utopians, this was individualism in the highest degree; it could neither be called selfish, nor was it morally suspect. In fact, some claimed that it was "pleasing in the sight of God to see men strive for the public good."[115] The moral code dictated that one was duty-bound in conscience to work for the common good. Mrs. J.M.D. Bartlett recognized this when she called for the need of "basing all reform, all happiness, all prosperity upon the code of ethics which while it demands the highest development of the individual, yet takes its inspiration from the thought of the common welfare."[116] To her, the highest moral development demanded an "unselfish desire for the prosperity of others."[117]

Thus, the freedom implied by individualism was not the freedom of the savage, "with no arts or sciences to aid him, and all the world his enemy."[118] Rather, it was the freedom to share one's knowledge and ability. In other words, the utopian observer recognized the absurdity of complete reliance upon the self when confronted with the complexity and interdependence of society. Freedom was not absolute freedom. "We are free to choose to run the race," claimed David Wheeler, but once this "noble athletic game has started, slugging is no part of it, tripping up a competitor is no part of the race, and striking below the belt is not a principle of industrial knightly contests."[119] Training and endurance counted, but not with an eye for oneself alone. There were rules and there was a code; everyone was bound by some law. This in itself added to a person's freedom; for if the rules were known, "such knowledge makes men more self-reliant, and knowing their own rights, are all the more ready to accord others the same rights and not infringe upon them."[120] In Thomas Kirwin's utopia, this ideal became a reality when "every man is practically a law unto himself, and needs no coercion to make him act justly toward his fellow men."[121]

In this statement, the very need for society was questioned. Some utopians foresaw this predicament. Forbush recognized that

this proposition carried to its logical conclusion would abolish all co-operative effort, and as society, even in its lowest forms, rests upon co-operation, all society is, if judged by that standard, but weakening in its effects.[122]

To be an individualist in this sense meant to be antisocial, a designation few utopians wished applied to their philosophy.

They would rather admit, "Man is a gregarious social being and is not born for himself alone, but for mankind."[123] An effort to resolve the paradox of how much a person could be an individual and also part of society was made by Richard Hatfield when one of his characters announced:

One who belongs to society must sacrifice a part of his individuality. One who sacrifices a part of his individuality is degraded in self respect, unless he is philosophical enough to recognize that it is noble to pay tribute to others which is the price of a happy social life.[124]

Thus, according to the majority of individualistic utopians, "true individuality is best exemplified in a condition of society where every man and woman will willingly and gladly bear their share of the general burden of life."[125] This not only produced "a robust manhood with respectful independence" but was also intended to provide a better world "improved by his efforts and accomplishments."[126]

These values to which the utopia adhered, therefore, contributed much toward his picture of a steadily improving, universally beneficial existence of abundance and happiness. Order was the first requirement in the utopian land. It was fostered in the utopian system of values by demands for an ethically viable moral code that would be clear and acceptable to all. The golden rule and the law of love met these requirements in the utopian mind, because love was the one moral value that satisfied the giver and receiver simultaneously, and it turned the destructive and potentially chaotic value of self-interest into something positive and helpful. So, too, equality was advocated partly to allay any possible strife arising from a conflict between the haves and the have-nots. If equality of opportunity were established, then at least everyone could apply his strength and skill to his work, receiving the fruits of his labor if successful and having no one to blame if he failed. Likewise, if the total wealth were distributed equally, no one could be envious of his or her neighbor, and each person could rest in the knowledge that he or she was working for the common good. In both types of equality, the ability to work, a very important value to the utopian, was guaranteed. On the conceptual level, the idea of progress also supported the utopian penchant for order by its implication of constant improvement in the natural order of the world.

The second requirement of the utopian's ideal society—material abundance—also coincided with these values. Hard work, supported by the moral values of the Protestant ethic as well as the individualist's creed, provided a most necessary ingredient. It received a further impetus, of course, when the worker realized he would receive the true value of his labor through the application of the equity principle. So, too, progress necessitated a mastery of the natural forces of the universe, and its much lauded instrument, science, would overcome many an obstacle to the goal of human abundance. Furthermore, the self-reliance engendered by the spirit of individualism spurred the inventive skill and genius necessary to master those forces.

The final and ultimate requirement for the utopian society—personal happiness and fulfillment—was furthered in large measure by attaining these other goals; however, something else was required. The alternate degradation and insufferable pride so long associated with social classes would be impossible in a world built on the principle of a classless society. Work for everyone afforded a personal leisure that could go a long way toward individual fulfillment. Similarly, the satisfactions associated with the spirit of altruism could be overwhelming in themselves, and, significantly, even the staunchest individualist took this value into account.

NOTES

1. It is interesting to note that one of the earliest utopias written in America, which appeared anonymously in Philadelphia in 1802, was entitled *Equality*.
2. Edward Bellamy, *Looking Backward: 2000–1887* (Boston: Ticknor, 1888), p. v.
3. William Alexander Taylor, *Intermere* (Columbus, Ohio: Twentieth Century Publishing Co., 1901), pp. 41–42.
4. Ernest Hugh Fitzpatrick, *The Marshall Duke of Denver; or, The Labor Revolution of 1920* (Chicago: Donohue and Henneberry Co., 1896), p. 201.

5. Ibid.

6. Edward Bellamy, *Equality* (New York: D. Appleton & Co., 1897), p. 5.

7. Henry L. Call, *The Coming Revolution* (Boston: Arena Publishing Co., 1895), pp. 7–8.

8. Henry W. Dowding, *The Man From Mars; or, Service For Service's Sake* (New York: Cochrane Publishing Co., 1910), p. 201.

9. Paul Devinne, *The Day of Prosperity: A Vision of the Century to Come* (New York: G. W. Dillingham & Co., 1902), p. 59.

10. James B. Alexander, *The Lunarian Professor* (Minneapolis: n.p., 1909), p. 99.

11. Byron Alden Brooks, *Earth Revisited* (Boston: Arena Publishing Co., 1893), p. 55.

12. Cyrus Cole, *The Auroraphone* (Chicago: Charles H. Kerr & Co., 1890), p. 59.

13. Call, *The Coming Revolution*, p. 7.

14. S. Byron Welcome, *From Earth's Center: A Polar Gateway Message* (Chicago: Charles H. Kerr & Co., 1894), p. 72.

15. Reverend W. S. Harris, *Life in a Thousand Worlds* (Cleona, Pa.: G. Holzapfel, 1905), p. 196.

16. [Jacob W. Horner], *Military Socialism* (Indianapolis: The Author, 1911), p. 77.

17. Ibid., p. 38.

18. C. A. Steere, *When Things Were Done* (Chicago: Charles H. Kerr & Co., 1908), p. 116.

19. Alfred Hutchinson, *The Limit of Wealth* (New York: Macmillan Co., 1907), p. 6.

20. Taylor, *Intermere*, p. 48.

21. John Bachelder, *A.D. 2050* (San Francisco: Bancroft Co., 1890), p. 16.

22. Bellamy, *Equality*, p. 31.

23. [Henry Francis Allen], *The Key of Industrial Co-Operative Government* (St. Louis: The Author, 1886), p. 23.

24. Richard M. Chapman, *The Vision of the Future* (New York: Cosmopolitan Press, 1916), p. 73.

25. Richard Hatfield, *Geyserland: Empiricisms in Social Reform* (Washington, D.C.: The Author, 1908), p. 31.

26. Walter O. Henry, *Equitania; or, the Land of Equity* (Omaha: n.p., 1914), p. 57.

27. James Cowen, *Daybreak: A Romance of an Old World* (New York: George H. Richmond & Co., 1896), p. 237.

28. Bradford Peck, *The World A Department Store* (Boston: Bradford Peck, Publisher, 1900), p. 38.

29. *Man or Dollar, Which?* By a Newspaperman (Chicago: Charles H. Kerr & Co., 1896), p. 106.
30. John Ira Brant, *The New Regime: A.D. 2202* (New York: Cochrane Publishing Co., 1909), p. 17.
31. [Thomas Kirwin], *Reciprocity in the Thirtieth Century: The Coming Cooperative Age.* By William Wonder (New York: Cochrane Publishing Co., 1909), p. 203.
32. Peck, *World A Department Store*, p. 302.
33. [Edward M. House], *Philip Dru, Administrator: A Story of Tomorrow, 1920–1935* (New York: B. W. Huebsch, 1912), p. 58.
34. T. H. Tibbles and Elia M. Beattie, *The American Peasant* (Chicago: F. J. Schulte & Co., 1892), p. 374.
35. Ibid., p. 375.
36. Hutchinson, *Limit of Wealth*, p. 28.
37. Call, *The Coming Revolution*, p. 35.
38. Costello, N. Holford, *Aristopia* (Boston: Arena Publishing Co., 1895), p. 71.
39. Solomon Schindler, *Young West* (Boston: Arena Publishing Co., 1894), p. 24.
40. Devinne, *Day of Prosperity*, p. 124.
41. William Bishop, *The Garden of Eden U.S.A.* (Chicago: Charles H. Kerr & Co., 1895), p. 168.
42. Bellamy, *Looking Backward*, p. 29.
43. Cowen, *Daybreak*, p. 237.
44. [William S. Child], *The Legal Revolution of 1902.* By A Law Abiding Revolutionist (Chicago: Charles H. Kerr & Co., 1898), p. 143.
45. [House], *Philip Dru*, p. 10.
46. C. W. Woodridge, *Perfecting the Earth* (Cleveland: Utopia Publishing Co., 1902), p. 15.
47. Albert Adams Merrill, *The Great Awakening* (Boston: George Book Publishing Co., 1899), p. 96.
48. Henry Olerich, *A Cityless and Countryless World: An Outline of Practical Co-Operative Individualism* (Holstein, Iowa: Gilmore & Olerich, 1893), p. 90.
49. [Mary Lane], *Mizora: A Prophesy.* By Princess Vera Zarovitch (New York: G. W. Dillingham & Co., 1889), p. 75.
50. Cole, *The Auroraphone*, p. 134.
51. David H. Wheeler, *Our Industrial Utopia and Its Unhappy Citizens* (Chicago: A. C. McClurg & Co., 1895), pp. 292–93.
52. Call, *The Coming Revolution*, p. 35.
53. Bishop, *The Garden of Eden*, p. 177.
54. [Child], *The Legal Revolution*, p. 255.

55. Ephraim Peterson, *An Ideal City For An Ideal People* (Independence, Mo.: The Author, 1905), p. 25.
56. Clark Edmund Persinger, *Letters From New America; or, An Attempt at Practical Socialism* (Chicago: Charles H. Kerr & Co., 1900), p. 73.
57. [Ignatius Donnelly], *Caesar's Column: A Story of the Twentieth Century*. By Dr. Boisgilbert (Chicago: F. J. Schulte & Co., 1890), p. 32.
58. D. L. Stump, *From World to World* (Asbury, Mo.: World to World Publishing Co., 1896), p. 30.
59. [Kirwin], *Reciprocity in the Thirtieth Century*, p. 63.
60. Brooks, *Earth Revisited*, p. 91.
61. Mortimer D. Leggett, *A Dream of a Modest Prophet* (Philadelphia: J. B. Lippincott & Co., 1890), p. 41.
62. Cole, *The Auroraphone*, p. 181.
63. Welcome, *From Earth's Center*, p. 179.
64. [F. U. Worley], *Three Thousand Dollars A Year: Moving Forward; or, How We Got There* (Washington, D.C: J. P. Wright, 1890), pp. 81–82.
65. Cowen, *Daybreak*, p. 236.
66. Brooks, *Earth Revisited*, p. 96.
67. Ibid.
68. Wheeler, *Our Industrial Utopia*, p. 296.
69. Peterson, *An Ideal City*, p. 17.
70. Woodridge, *Perfecting the Earth*, p. 145.
71. Ralph Albertson, *The Social Incarnation* (Commonwealth, Ga.: Christian Commonwealth Publishers, 1899), p. 22.
72. Ibid., p. 16.
73. Peterson, *An Ideal City*, p. 17.
74. Marxism's great appeal—the historical inevitability of equality—never seemed to capture the public imagination in America probably because the ideas of progress and equality were so much a part of the more popular and traditional sources of American values.
75. Brant, *The New Regime*, p. 65.
76. [George Hamilton Phelps], *The New Columbia; or, The Re-United States*. By Patrick Quinn Tangent (Findlay, Ohio: New Columbia Publishing Co., 1909), p. 1.
77. Persinger, *Letters From New America*, preface.
78. Cowen, *Daybreak*, p. 81.
79. Milan C. Edson, *Solaris Farm: A Story of the Twentieth Century* (Washington, D.C.: The Author, 1900), p. 72.
80. Ibid., p. 132.

81. Brooks, *Earth Revisited*, p. 16; Bachelder, *A.D. 2050*, p. 41.
82. J.M.D. Bartlett, *A New Aristocracy* (n.p.: Bartlett Publishing Co., 1891), p. 275.
83. Persinger, *Letters From New America*, p. 50.
84. [Alcanoan Grigsby], *Nequa; or, The Problem of the Ages* (Topeka, Kans.: Equity Publishing Co., 1900), p. 293.
85. Dowding, *Man From Mars*, p. 334.
86. Ibid., pp. 233–34.
87. Albert W. Howard, *The Milltillionaire* (n.p., 1906), p. 4.
88. Cole, *The Auroraphone*, p. 127.
89. Zebina Forbush, *The Co-Opolitan* (Chicago: Charles H. Kerr & Co., 1898), p. 48.
90. D. Herbert Heywood, *The Twentieth Century: A Prophesy Age* (Boston: F. B. Heywood, Publisher, 1890), p. 21.
91. Paul Devinne, *The Day of Prosperity: A Vision of the Century to Come* (New York: G. W. Dillingham & Co., 1902), p. 157.
92. Fayette S. Giles, *Shadows Before; or, A Century Onward* (New York: Humbolt Publishing Co., 1894), pp. 9–10.
93. Heywood, *The Twentieth Century*, p. 21.
94. [Henry Francis Allen], *A Strange Voyage* (St. Louis: Monitor Publishing Co., 1891), p. 64.
95. Henry, *Equitania*, p. 35.
96. Ibid.
97. Forbush, *The Co-Opolitan*, p. 29.
98. Welcome, *From Earth's Center*, p. 139.
99. Forbush, *The Co-Opolitan*, p. 84.
100. Ibid., p. 72.
101. Wheeler, *Our Industrial Utopia*, p. 282.
102. Hutchinson, *The Limit of Wealth*, p. 208.
103. Wheeler, *Our Industrial Utopia*, p. 282.
104. Ibid., p. 303.
105. Bellamy, *Equality*, p. 9.
106. Cowen, *Daybreak*, p. 100.
107. Albert Chavannes, *In Brighter Climes; or, Life in Socioland* (Knoxville, Tenn.: n.p., 1895), p. 166.
108. Jack London, "Goliah," in *Revolution and Other Essays* (New York: Macmillan Co., 1910), p. 87.
109. Ibid., p. 101.
110. Forbush, *The Co-Opolitan*, p. 54.
111. Woodridge, *Perfecting the Earth*, p. 169.
112. Edward Everett Hale, *Sybaris and Other Homes* (Boston: Fields, Osgood & Co., 1869), p. 173.

113. Chavannes, *In Brighter Climes*, p. 181.
114. Alexander, *The Lunarian Professor*, p. 68.
115. H. George Schuette, *Anthonia; or, The Original Four Hundred* (Manitowoc, Wis.: Lakeside Co., 1911), p. 424.
116. Bartlett, *A New Aristocracy*, p. 286.
117. Ibid., p. 306.
118. C. S. Griffin, *Nationalism* (Boston: The Author, 1889), p. 70.
119. Wheeler, *Our Industrial Utopia*, p. 293.
120. [Kirwin], *Reciprocity*, p. 40.
121. Ibid.
122. Forbush, *The Co-Opolitan*, p. 34.
123. Schuette, *Anthonia*, p. 424.
124. R. Hatfield, *Geyserland*, p. 87.
125. [Kirwin], *Reciprocity*, p. 111.
126. Bachelder, *A.D. 2050*, p. 77.

6
Conclusion

The utopian movement in post–Civil War America began with the publication of Edward Everett Hale's *Sybaris and Other Homes* in 1869; however, the production of utopias for the next twenty years was sparse, indeed. By 1889, only ten more had appeared. Then, in the next ten years, the amazing total of fifty-six utopias was published. Clearly, the success of Edward Bellamy's *Looking Backward*, published in 1888, popularized a form of writing most suited to reflect general and widespread discontent. Utopias were written and published in all sections of the country, from San Francisco to New York, from New Orleans to Chicago. Teachers, journalists, lawyers, doctors, politicians, clerics—just about every professional walk of life had its contributors to this form of writing, confirming the view that these writers were mainly from the upper middle class.[1] By 1917, one hundred nineteen utopias advocated just about every reform advanced during that era, and some others besides.[2]

Intellectually, the utopian courted only those parts of his heritage that supported his optimistic belief in progress; for his most often-expressed purpose was to attain a "heaven on earth" in which pastoral simplicity reigned alongside a bounteous plenty. It hardly occurred to most utopians that one was inimical to the other; and significantly, whenever the tenets of his intellectual heritage suggested such a dichotomy, he put them in the background or ignored them entirely.

The well-ordered world of the enlightenment thinker who

believed in progress, the perfectibility of man, and the conquest of nature served as the wellspring for the utopian's optimism. However, when the doctrine of man's innate goodness and the pursuit of self-interest logically extended to the political and economic policies of laissez faire, the utopian tempered his belief with another eighteenth-century doctrine of egalitarianism and the even older idea of Christian love. Likewise, when the method of science required the rejection of evidence from tradition and authority—in a word, the past—most showed themselves far more partial to the tradition of John Locke, the Declaration of Independence, and Christian love than to the more contemporaneous doctrines of socialism and "conservative" Darwinism.

Ironically, this commitment by the greater majority of utopians to the optimistic beliefs of the Enlightenment worked against them when they exposed the evils of the entrepreneurs and plutocrats, for they justified their ways in terms of the selfsame concepts used by the utopians: natural law, individualism, self-interest based on the perfectibility of man, and the conquest of man's problems through science and technology. In fact, it was the depersonalization of life caused by industrialization and urbanization that roused the most outspoken commentary from the utopian; and yet these failures were supported by the same commitment to progress and science on the part of the wealthy entrepreneur and businessman.

The utopian was not oblivious of this contradiction, however, and his espousal of the doctrine of Christian love was intended to counterbalance it. His indifference, and sometimes antagonism, toward the rest of the body of Christian doctrine, especially that which emphasized man's propensity toward evil and God's power of retribution, demonstrated his secularization of love into a social force that would bring about his most cherished value of equality. Religion was important to the utopian only because it supported an ethic wherein conscience and concern for others aided society in its role of preserving order. The established churches, with their creeds, dogmas, rituals, and concern for sectarian uniqueness instead of the welfare of their membership, alienated the utopian's interest in religion as such, and, much like the Social Gospelers, he sought to create a new religion based entirely on a respect for the visible welfare of one's fellow man.

In form, this new religion, a kind of secularized utopianism, owed much to the idea of evolution, especially the concepts advanced by Herbert Spencer, for it changed what were once mere hopes into the respectability of a historically inevitable paradise. This change was probably one of the most radical shifts in thinking from the pre–Civil War period in America to the post–Civil War era. The utopian writer was simply reiterating what came to be a firm belief in his time—that the quality of society did not depend upon the sum total of individual human wills, as Emerson had believed, but that society itself was more than the sum of its parts; it had a life and will of its own that followed the forces of nature. It was the dream of Auguste Comte coming true, for all that had to be done was to find the laws that govern human conduct, just as Isaac Newton had discovered them concerning gravity and force, and paradise would be within reach.

Although the revolutionary character of this idea escaped most utopians, the notion did much to make the idea of socialism more palatable. At least 20 percent of these writers openly espoused socialism as a form of government in their ideal societies, and another 20 percent had governments that were socialistic in form. The utopians, as well as many of their contemporaries, saw the government as the only force powerful enough to curb the excesses of the competitive spirit and laissez-faire capitalism—the common problem most cited in these works. True, the utopian had little practical experience with socialism, as Erich Fromm points out in his introduction to Bellamy's *Looking Backward*: "He [referring to Bellamy] did not see the dangers of a managerial society.... He did not recognize that the bureaucrat is a man who administers things and people, and who *relates himself to people as things*. The system tends to produce machines that act like men and men who act like machines."[3] The real appeal of socialism, however, lay in its guarantee of economic equality. This is the value that stood at the center of all the utopian's hopes and wishes for the society of the future.

In fact, the entire intellectual commitment of the utopian

writer can best be interpreted in the light of his values. Unlike his European counterpart, the American utopian was not committed to an idea for its own sake. His pragmatic quest rested in an ingrained belief in the value of equality. His intellectual commitments—the perfectibility of man, the conquest of nature, the methods of science, Christian love, and cooperative evolution—supported his desire for a fair chance to share in the fruits of his labor, which, in turn, would entitle him to the higher things in life: companionship, peace, security, respect, leisure, and the enjoyments of nature. The heart of his ideal society concentrated on wiping out the extremes of the social scale. The rich and the poor would disappear in future generations. Depending upon how optimistic or pessimistic these writers were concerning human nature, they chose either to merely require an equality of opportunity or to guarantee equality in the distribution of wealth. By far, the large majority worked out a system to provide a fairly equal distribution of wealth. Some, like Bellamy and his many followers, tried to give more money for the less desirable jobs and awarded prestige for the professional and creative work in his society; all persons in this society retired after twenty years of work. Still the authors, such as Edward Everett Hale, depended upon Christian love and charity to create a balance of wealth. None doubted, however, that a greater equalization of wealth and the quality of life was necessary.

Even so, the socialist ideal of equality did not lessen the utopian's belief in the value of hard work, a value he or she espoused only slightly less than equality. The Puritan work ethic had deep roots in the consciousness of these writers. Work was the expression of self, and the satisfactions that accrued from it were considered the same as those of the creative artist. When the utopian did believe in equality of opportunity, he or she was really fostering a personal fulfillment through the creativity of work or through the wealth accumulated from hard work. Even in the most benevolent society, those who refused to work, excepting women and children, were either punished or banished as a blight upon society.

Underneath this persistent dedication to the values of equality and hard work was a deep and abiding moral sense, a commitment to the traditional Christian virtues: honesty, thrift, prudence, fortitude, temperance, and justice (very little was said about chastity). These virtues, in turn, provided the inner drive for the desire to work, create, improve oneself, and finally, enjoy one's success. However, there were rewards and punishments. In rejecting organized religion, the utopian was careful not to reject its system of ethical reinforcement. One of the chief arguments against any system that advocated material equality was that it stifled the inner drive for accomplishment. In the utopian's mind, however, was the backup system of Christian virtue and love. Accomplishment became an end in itself, a moral virtue. Even in the socialistic utopias that deemphasized individual conscience, great attention was paid to a socially sanctioned system of praise and punishment; everone may have received the same salary, but some had the privilege of command while others followed. In these cases, social prestige replaced accomplishment for its own sake, and the transition from organized religion to individual conscience to a system of socialized rewards and punishments was complete.

In this grandiose vision of creative employment, the utopian hoped to resolve the traditional dilemma between personal freedom and the demands of the common good. In delineating the problems of his time, the utopian provided a comprehensive list of all those things that stifled his hopes for the reconcilement of these opposites. By far the largest protest was against those practices that denied the possibility of everyone's reaching and maintaining a state of middle-class affluence. Significantly, the greed and selfishness of the wealthy evoked the steadiest indignation from these writers; other practices and policies that reinforced the wealth of these few—organized charity, class division, monopolies, and the scarcity of capital—were denounced for the same reason. This solidification of social classes and the power structure was what the utopian feared the most. As a representative of that middle class who fully thought hard work must have a just and equitable reward, he grew more indignant with the increasing evidence of political corruption, economic insecurity and inefficiency, corrupt journalism, education for the few, and a clergy subservient to their benefactors—in short, the growing power of the plutocrats.

Against these considerations, the utopian painted the kind of society that would more closely resemble his belief in egalitarianism and progress. The resulting composite utopia could be described thus: a country in which everyone was assured of a job to satisfy his talents and abilities; sufficient pay to provide the necessities of life; only nominal class division; state control over the money supply and the larger industries; an eight-hour day or less; an assured political democracy; an independent press and an outlet for the voice of the people; control of the environment by the government to ensure clean, pleasant living conditions and the elimination of slums; a state health program; lighter burdens for the housewife; free education for all; and the right to worship as one pleased.

Not all the desires of the utopians can be enumerated in such a composite picture. The progress that utopians envisioned cannot be measured wholly in terms of salary, leisure, job security, or even a beautiful home in a countrified city. To be sure, the utopian advocated all these things, but he also wanted personal satisfaction in life. His type of solution indicated what kinds of satisfaction he desired most.

The range of utopian solutions went from the extremes of individualism to authoritarianism, each representing opposite values. The authoritarian, socialistic, and nationalistic utopians sought the security of personal comfort above all, even at the sacrifice of individual freedom. For them, the definition of freedom was negative, that is, freedom from starvation and physical want. For the individualist utopian, freedom was the ability to be creative in one's work, to superimpose one's mind and ideas over nature and society, and, paradoxically, to give oneself to the group in return for the pleasure of their company. When the individualist spoke of equality, he meant equality of opportunity; all men started as equals, but talent, energy, and genius would decide who would excel and reap the greater reward.

Proportionally, the individualistic utopians were outnumbered, by a slight margin, by those who advocated collectivist solutions. Their sources stemmed mainly from eighteenth-century enlightenment thought, the tradition of Christian moralism, and early nineteenth-century reformers such as Robert

Owen, Claude-Henry St. Simon, Charles Fourier, and the communitarians, whose ideals of communal integrity and security appealed to this type of utopian. They conceived of society as a composite of individuals, and their values were viewed in terms of personal ethics. On the other hand, though the collectivists were not above reinforcing their highly organized society with a system of personal ethics, their highest values were to the group or to society as a whole. The collectivists were influenced more by contemporary writers and movements, such as Herbert Spencer, Henry George, populism, and socialism. They recognized that some form of complex organization was required to deal with the forces unleashed by the Industrial Revolution and that the selfish desires of the few had to be controlled by a larger power than an aristocracy of wealth, a power that could represent the wishes of the people as a whole.

The logical solution for the collectivist utopian was some form of socialism, and significantly many more utopias conformed to the socialist model than the utopians themselves were willing to recognize. Bellamy's use of the term "nationalism" to describe his socialist state adequately avoided the stigmatizing label. In typical American fashion, the utopian was less committed to the ideology of socialism than he was to a practical solution for a dilemma represented by historical fact. But it was the individualist utopian whose proposal was more revolutionary, for he denied the flow of history that clearly demanded more power for the state, not less. He refused to recognize that the power of one organization, the trusts, could only be controlled by the power of another equally big, the government. Instead, the individualist utopian preferred to do away with a need for both, and he looked forward to a time when law and all it represented could be swept aside and the very nature of man could be transformed.

However, the individualists and collectivists together represented a one-sidedness that many utopians considered as dangerous as allowing the status quo to prevail. A large number sought a middle ground that avoided the evils of the extremes. Even though their solutions were mainly derivative—for the most part from Henry George, the Populists, and other political reforms—this type of utopian was sharply aware of the dangers of sacrificing personal freedom for the sake of collective security. He was willing to increase governmental power only to the extent of curbing the plutocrats who prevented an equitable distribution of wealth. In other words, the extent of governmental power was determined by the degree to which the utopian thought the industrial powers of his day departed from the egalitarian and democratic tradition. In this respect, the utopian who sought the middle ground prefigured the course that the progressive leaders, as well as later reformers, would take. Although not necessarily a tribute to either their prophetic powers or their influence on subsequent history, their decision did nevertheless represent a triumph of mental balance, especially in the light of their trying to preserve the dual tradition of individualism and equality.

In a larger vein, the utopian movement can be considered a part of the general protest at the end of the nineteenth century against the forces of disintegration and decay. It can be classed with other voices of protest: the Social Gospelers, the economists of the American Economic Association, the social scientists, the poets and literary protesters; as well as all the political reform groups: Populists, progressives, nationalists, and the many small-town politicians who took issue with the corrupters and grafters.[4] The utopian novelist can be counted among those thinkers whom Eric Goldman described as having "developed ideological acids capable of dissolving every link in conservatism's steel chain of ideas."[5] In fact, the utopian was especially helpful in breaking the chain of ideas that forced so many to justify the status quo; for, even if his portrait of the ideal society was unacceptable in its details, he forced the general reader to look at his traditional way of life in a new light, and this process of questioning was the very basis on which subsequent reforms were built. Hence, the utopian acted as a "devil's advocate" of the American system. Although the utopian's efforts have been labeled both as a "bypath far removed from the mainstream of American literature"[6] and as having "no great circulation or influence,"[7] ironically, the basic premise they all possessed—namely, that the status quo needed a change if America were to survive—has been historically vindicated.

NOTES

1. Allyn B. Forbes, "Literary Quest for Utopia, 1880–1900," *Social Forces* 6 (December 1927), p. 188.

2. "Although the lack of literary merit of many of these [utopian] novels explains their neglect, the mere number of them testifies to their significance in the social and intellectual life of the period" (Elizabeth Sadler, "One Book's Influence: Edward Bellamy's *Looking Backward*," *New England Quarterly* 17, [December 1944], p. 541).

3. Erich Fromm, introduction to *Looking Backward*, by Edward Bellamy (1888; reprint ed., New York: Signet Classic, 1960), pp. xi–xii.

4. By "the poets" I mean those included in Robert Walker's study, *The Poet and the Gilded Age* (Philadelphia: University of Pennsylvania Press, 1963), in which he concluded: "If there is one single preoccupation which gives to this verse a common tone, it is the sense of persistent objection to things as they appeared to the poet" (p. 276.)

5. Eric Goldman, *Rendezvous with Destiny*, rev. ed. (New York: Vintage Books, 1959), p. 81.

6. Robert L. Shurter, "The Utopian Novel in America, 1880–1900," *South Atlantic Quarterly* 34 (April 1935), p. 144.

7. Charles E. Merriam, *American Political Ideas* (New York: Macmillan Co., 1920), p. 437.

Bibliography

PRIMARY SOURCES

Adams, Frederic U. *President John Smith: The Story of a Revolution.* Chicago: Charles H. Kerr & Co., 1897. Based on the overriding principles of equal rights and rule by the majority, this book projects the reorganization of the country along these lines after a popular revolt occasioned by the reelection of the Republicans in 1900. Supposedly written in 1893, it incorporated many reforms of the Populists.

Albertson, Ralph. *The Social Incarnation.* Commonwealth, Ga.: Christian Commonwealth Publishers, 1899. Written by one of the leaders of the internationally famous Christian Commonwealth community in Georgia. This book attempted to perpetuate the ideal of the colony by describing how to apply Christian love to every aspect of daily life.

Alexander, James B. *The Lunarian Professor.* Minneapolis: No publisher, 1909. Set in the twenty-fourth century on the moon, this society, described as the highest stage of evolution, depicts an ideal life based on the common ownership of goods.

[Allen, Henry Francis]. *The Key of Industrial Co-Operative Government.* By Pruning Knife. St. Louis: The Author, 1886. A book, claimed by the author to have been written in 1875, that projects an ideal state on Venus. All people live according to the golden rule and expand their energies in the conquest of nature.

———. *A Strange Voyage.* St. Louis: Monitor Publishing Co., 1891. Although it is a revision of the above book, its political and social structure is the same. Dedicated to the Farmer's Alliance and Industrial Union, it revealed less patience with the lazy and unfit while adding intuitive thought transmission as a cure for the problems of misunderstanding.

Armour, J. P. *Edenindia: A Tale of Adventure.* New York: G. W. Dillingham Co., 1905. Set on an isolated island inhabited by the descendants of Henry Hudson, this utopia is ruled by a benevolent despot who utilizes the modern inventions of the outside world. The laws of nature are the predominant criteria of all good and bad. Natural instinct is exalted; health is largely a matter of the mind.

Bachelder, John. *A.D. 2050.* San Francisco: Bancroft Co., 1890. Written in reaction to the "communistic" state of Bellamy's utopia, this ideal society embodies the virtues of free enterprise from which the inefficiencies of monopolistic capitalism have been eliminated. This highly organized society rewards the fit and punishes the indolent and the poor. Supply and demand govern everything. Technology rules.

Bartlett, J.M.D. *A New Aristocracy.* New York: Bartlett Publishing Co., 1891. Love for one's neighbor, industrial thrift, and social well-being—all activated by good conscience—are the cornerstones of this plan for society. In the form of a romance, this is the story of a woman whose love for the wayward and the poor dominates her life to the extent that she conquers her aristocratic fiance's snobbishness. A cooperative shoe factory becomes an ideal community. The example of Christ dominates throughout.

Bassett, Edward Barnard. *The Model Town; or, The Right and Progressive Organization of Industry for the Production of Material and Moral Wealth.* By Beta. Cambridge, Mass.: Printed for the Author by H. O. Houghton & Co., 1869. A model town based on the cooperative efforts of this Christian community forms the basis of this ideal place, which is self-sufficient. Property is private, but hard work and sharing are the chief values of this agrarian community.

Bellamy, Edward. *Looking Backward: 2000–1887.* Boston: Ticknor, 1888. Bellamy, in the most popular of the utopian novels, described an ideal society in which each person has a chance to employ his talents through an elaborately organized and highly centralized system of production and distribution. Its goal was to provide an individual sense of personal fulfillment while avoiding the fluctuations of the laissez-faire economic system of the time.

———. *Equality.* New York: D. Appleton & Co., 1897. The dialogue between Julian West and Doctor Leete continues in polemical fashion in this sequel to the above book. Bellamy emphasizes equality as the basic value of his system; however, in an attempt to answer nine years of objections, little room is left for the romance that added to the popularity of the earlier work.

Bird, Arthur. *Looking Forward: A Dream of the United States of America in 1999*. Utica, N.Y.: L. C. Childs & Son, 1899. Written by a former diplomat to Haiti, this book projects America's rule of the entire Western Hemisphere by 1999. Many mechanical improvements usher in an era of Christian brotherly love; however, the peace is kept by America's overwhelming air power.

Bishop, William. *The Garden of Eden, U.S.A.* Chicago: Charles H. Kerr & Co., 1895. This isolated community, set in the hills of West Virginia, is supported by a wealthy philanthropist who wishes to return to a life of true Christianity. Communal living, health, science, and women are all eulogized. Seclusion from the world is considered necessary for the success of this venture.

Bond, Daniel. *Uncle Sam in Business*. Chicago: Charles H. Kerr & Co., 1899. The economy and public welfare of this society are run by a government whose administrators and laws are solely determined by a vote of the people. Written in the form of letters to someone in England, this book, which borrowed much from Populism, explains how the socialist revolution took place in America at the turn of the century.

Brant, John Ira. *The New Regime: A.D. 2202*. New York: Cochrane Publishing Co., 1909. Set in the year 2202, this book is a thinly disguised story of a man who is brought back from amnesia to view an advanced stage of his own society, a highly centralized state with some local autonomy. The society is organized for the sake of efficiency and brother love.

Brinsmade, Herman H. *Utopia Achieved: A Novel of the Future*. New York: Broadway Publishing Co., 1912. A story, set in the year 1962, of a society in which industrial efficiency, vegetarianism, and healthful living do much to make it ideal. The single-tax system is employed. John D. Rockefeller, J. P. Morgan, and Thomas A. Edison are favorably mentioned.

Brooks, Byron Alden. *Earth Revisited*. Boston: Arena Publishing Co., 1893. By the year 1992, a system called Christian Communism is established to ensure that all men are in fact treated equally. Wealth and selfish ambition are deplored; science and evolution receive the highest praise.

Call, Henry L. *The Coming Revolution*. Boston: Arena Publishing Co., 1895. Economic equality is the cornerstone of this utopia. Written in essay form, it predicts a gradual and peaceful revolt against the unequal distribution of wealth. Many ideas are borrowed from Herbert Spencer and the Populist movement.

Caryl, Charles W. *New Era.* Denver: New Era Union, 1897. A profit-sharing plan in which the investors and workers are organized into the New Era Union and live in the New Era Model City, which is planned to the last detail. Organized according to military lines and set near Denver, it uses the profits from its mining operations to invent new methods of production and efficiency. The author, an admirer of Edward Bellamy, proposed New Era Model Clubs to foster the movement on a national basis.

Chambless, Edgar. *Roadtown.* New York: Roadtown Press, 1910. In this book dedicated to J. P. Morgan, the author, a patent examiner, proposes a plan to solve the increased urbanization and problems of large cities. Environmentalism and equality are important values.

Chapman, Richard M. *The Vision of the Future.* New York: Cosmopolitan Press, 1916. A highly detailed set of rules for social and personal behavior precludes what the author thinks are the two major problems of his time: ignorance and disease. Having no one financially dependent upon another is the economic goal of this highly autocratic state that organizes production and distribution of all goods. Much value is placed on environmental influences.

Chavannes, Albert. *The Future Commonwealth; or, What Samuel Balcom Saw in Socioland.* New York: True Nationalist Publishing Co., 1892. Socioland, whose capital is called Spencer, subscribes to the principle that whatever promotes the general welfare also promotes personal happiness. Written in the form of letters from this land in Africa in the year 1950, this utopian romance records much frank discussion of the individualist-collectivist dilemma. The ultimate aim is to make law unnecessary and altruism prevail. The principle of hard work is central.

―――. *In Brighter Climes; or, Life in Socioland.* Knoxville, Tenn.: No publisher, 1895. A continuation of the above in which the equal distribution of wealth is achieved. The motto of the state is: "In Each Other We Trust." The rules for entering this exclusive community are more stringent than in the earlier work; otherwise, there are few changes of importance.

[Child, William Stanley]. *The Legal Revolution of 1902.* Chicago: Charles H. Kerr & Co., 1898. A group of reformers legally effect a revolution by achieving populist reforms at a constitutional convention. William Jennings Bryan is elected first president of the new state. Work for everyone is its motto. All private wealth is limited.

Cole, Cyrus. *The Auroraphone*. Chicago: Charles H. Kerr & Co., 1890. A theory of equality, based on the physical principle that ultimately all atoms of the world are the same, is advocated in this society. The government is the sole employer. The golden rule and inventive genius are the two guiding principles.

Collens, Thomas Wharton. *The Eden of Labor; or, The Christian Utopia*. Philadelphia, Pa.: Henry Carey Baird & Co., 1876. Both an anti-utopia and a utopia in which both states are shown to differ according to the selfishness of their inhabitants. In the ideal state, the principle of Christian charity prevails, and all workers equally share the fruits of their labor. Based on the labor theory of value. In the selfish state, the rich get richer by exploiting the poor, who get poorer.

Cooley, Winnifred H. "A Dream of the Twenty-First Century," *The Arena* 28 (November 1902), pp. 511–16. Succinctly written, this utopia takes the form of an old woman's dream. Politically, many of the populist reforms are initiated. All industry is nationalized, and the emphasis is on hard work. "Social control" ensures the correct attitude of citizens before adulthood. Set in the twenty-first century, where rational science is the most admired intellectual activity.

Cowen, James. *Daybreak: A Romance of an Old World*. New York: George H. Richmond & Co., 1896. Love of neighbor imbues this society with universal peace and commercial success. Energy is concentrated upon the mastery of nature. A classless society. The political structure is replaced by a mutual aid society. All property is held in common.

Cridge, Alfred Denton. *Utopia; or, The History of an Extinct Plant*, Oakland, Calif.: Winchester & Pew, 1884. A pre-Bellamy utopia written in the form of a pamphlet. All land and wealth are held in common in this pure democracy. Communal living and honorable work have a central role along with mechanical invention and science.

[Crocker, Samuel]. *That Island*. Kansas City, Mo.: C. E. Streeter & Co., 1892. This political allegory seethingly satirizes both Republicans and Democrats in the whole of the nineteenth-century America. It ends in the twentieth century with the triumph of a third political party that is strikingly similar to the Populists. Written by a Midwesterner, much attention is given to farm problems.

Dague, Robert A. *Henry Ashton.* Alameda, Calif.: The Author, 1903. A wealthy reformer transforms an island he owns into an ideal state by giving the people full control of the government, which, in turn, regulates all production and consumption. Elimination of waste is an essential goal.

Devinne, Paul. *The Day of Prosperity: A Vision of the Century to Come.* New York: G. W. Dillingham & Co., 1902. Organized along the same lines as Edward Bellamy's utopia, this country is ruled by a board of industrial and professional representatives. All aspects of life are centrally planned; there are no social classes. The highest value, order, is demonstrated in the setting of an elaborately and beautifully recreated New York City.

[Donnelly, Ignatius]. *Caesar's Column: A Story of the Twentieth Century.* By Dr. Boisgilbert. Chicago: F. J. Schulte & Co., 1890. A propaganda piece for the Populist party, for whom the author was vice presidential candidate in 1900. Much of the book, written in the Armageddon genre, concerns the demagogic portrayal of the people's cause against the plutocracy. Set in Africa, the Populist party platform rules this utopia to which the hero and heroine flee in the end.

———. *The Golden Bottle: or, the Story of Ephraim Benezet of Kansas.* New York: D. D. Merrill Co., 1892. Many erudite allusions and a fascination for practical invention and power fill this sequel to the above book. However, reforms take place on a worldwide basis when the internationally organized proletariat finally triumphs. A satire on the gold standard is partly intended. The book ends with a highly romantic eulogy of womanhood.

Dowding, Henry W. *The Man From Mars; or, Service For Service's Sake.* New York: Cochrane Publishing Co., 1910. Service is the highest value of this story about an elaborately organized utopia, which is recounted by a visitor from Mars. Utilities are run by the government; otherwise, an altruistic, private enterprise produces most of the goods and services. No monopolies are allowed. The final object of all effort is to enjoy the arts, fine literature, and good company.

Edson, Milan C. *Solaris Farm: A Story of the Twentieth Century.* Washington, D.C.: The Author, 1900. Written to eulogize the effects of living close to the soil, this utopia also places high value upon social equality and technological progress. Communal self-sufficiency eliminates more complicated contemporary problems. The author, who calls himself a humanitarian, expresses interest in spiritualism and communication with dead.

Everett, Henry L. *The People's Program: The Twentieth Century Is*

Theirs. New York: Workman's Publishing Co., 1892. A social plan designed to alleviate the plight of the workingman. Cooperative factories produce more than enough to provide luxury and leisure for the workers; nevertheless, everyone works, and there is work for all. An authoritarian government controls monopolistic industries and regulates the economy.

Fishbough, William. *America and the World*. New York: Continental Publishing Co., 1898. Profit-sharing, joint stock companies enroll the entire population according to skills and interests. Nonworkers and the wealthy are banished. A board of philosopher wise men rule the legislature composed of company representatives. Science and efficiency are given much adulation. This book was purportedly written in 1881, just before the author died. It was published by a friend.

Fiske, Amos K. *Beyond the Bourne*. New York: Fords, Howard and Hulbert, 1891. This culmination of evolutionary development ends in world unity. Free trade, one language, and worldwide communication, both mental and physical, have resulted from a complete mastery of nature. Purportedly written in 1873 by the author, who was a staff member of the *New York Times*.

Fitzpatrick, Ernest Hugh. *The Marshal Duke of Denver; or, The Labor Revolution of 1920*. Chicago: Donohue and Henneberry Co., 1896. This anti-plutocratic novel ends with the triumphal forces of organized labor earning the passage of a graduated income tax and the printing of fiat money. Political corruption is punishable by death, and all labor problems are settled by mandatory arbitration. An elaborately planned, park-studded city of Denver replaces Washington as the capital of the nation.

Forbush, Zebina. *The Co-Opolitan*. Chicago: Charles H. Kerr & Co., 1898. Equal opportunity is accomplished in this society with the elimination of private property. Competition stimulates progress; everyone must work. Railroads and efficient machinery create ample profits that are shared by all citizens equally. This exclusive community is set in Idaho.

Frisbie, Henry S. *Prophet of the Kingdom*. Washington, D.C.: Neal Publishing Co., 1901. Social and economic equality are achieved through socialism. The law of love is the mechanism of success in this society, which culminates in the establishment of the kingdom of heaven on earth. It is written in biblical form and language.

Fry, Lena J. *Other Worlds*. Chicago: The Author, 1905. A profit-sharing, communal business succeeds through the middlemen. Bartering replaces the need for money and its attendant evils. Hard work, just rewards, and a central distribution system preclude what the author thought was society's greatest evil—trusts.

Fuller, Alverado M. *A.D. 2000*. Chicago: Laird & Lee, 1890. Apparently written in 1887 by the author, an Army Lieutenant, this utopia abounds with engineering and mechanical marvels. A clear, rigid legal system is administered by a large civil service that also runs all utilities and some businesses. A tax on excess profits and limited land possession prevent economic abuses. A large Army undertakes public works projects when not at war.

Galloway, James M. *John Harvey: A Tale of the Twentieth Century*. Chicago: Charles H. Kerr & Co., 1897. The state, which is the sole employer, rents all land for private use. This all-powerful state is run by a democratically elected legislature. Set in 1935, the story is told in the form of a conversation between a visiting Englishman and John Harvey, founder of this fictitious communal society located near Pike's Peak.

Geissler, Ludwig A. *Looking Beyond*. New Orleans: L. Graham & Son, 1891. This attempt to defend Edward Bellamy from a detractor, Richard Michaelis, counterposes all Bellamy's proposals to those in the latter's book, *Looking Forward*. It does not differ from Bellamy in any way.

Giles, Fayette S. *Shadows Before; or, A Century Onward*. New York: Humbolt Publishing Co., 1894. In this Eden of 1993, the world is organized along republican principles, each country related to the world government as each state is related to the federal government. Paternalism and monopoly are things of the past. Physical fitness is stressed along with severe restrictions on alcohol and marriage. Electricity is the panacea of the technological world.

Gillette, King G. *The Human Drift*. Boston: New Era Publishing Co., 1894. The author envisions a joint-stock shoe company branching out into other sectors of the economy until it controls all the material resources of the nation. It then establishes a society devoted to the principle of material equality. Everyone is required to work up to the age of forty. Much stress is put on the industrial virtues and science.

———. "World Corporation." Boston: The New England News Co., 1910. A World Corporation is formed to bring all nations and peoples together into one corporate body in order to share in the production and distribution of wealth. Labor units determine share of wealth. Politics is banned; education and intelligence are exalted.

Griffin, C. S. *Nationalism*. Boston: The Author, 1889. Equal distribution of goods and compulsory work create social equality in this utopia, modeled after Edward Bellamy's work. Laborsaving machinery and advanced technology have a central place in this highly planned country in which the government owns and operates all means of production. The author was also much influenced by Laurence Gronlund.

Grigsby, Alcanoan O. *Nequa; or, The Problem of the Ages*. By Jack Adams. Topeka, Kans.: Equity Publishing Co., 1900. In a land called Altruria, everyone works to abolish poverty and reshape the environment to accord with human needs. The economy is organized around a consumer's cooperative. It is also a religious organization that stresses selflessness. Landlords, middlemen, loafers, and money are all banned from this community.

Grimshaw, Robert. *Fifty Years Hence; or, What May Be in 1943*. New York: Practical Publishing Co., 1892. Trade unions, full employment guaranteed by the government, and profit sharing remove the economic problems of this society. A single, universal religion is organized around the principle of charity. Science is the highest value, and evolutionary progress demands selective breeding and environmental conditioning.

Gronlund, Laurence. *The Cooperative Commonwealth*. London: No publisher, 1886. An ideal socialist society designed to give workers the fruits of their labors. Indebted to German socialist thinkers and John Stuart Mill, his cooperative society becomes subordinate to the Supreme Will of the universe.

Hale, Edward Everett. *Sybaris and Other Homes*. Boston: Fields, Osgood & Co., 1869. Set in the ancient state of Sybaris, this society, unlike Carthage which believes in commerce, aims to develop each individual to his or her highest capacity while protecting the rights of all. Private gain at the expense of others is condemned. The government regulates all industry and operates the railroads. The churches are responsible for eliminating crime and poverty in this minister's utopia. Punctuality and democracy are important values.

Harben, William. "In the Year Ten Thousand," *Arena* 36 (November 1892), pp. 743–49. Mind reading, mental telepathy, pacifism, and brotherly love characterize this advanced state in which an old man describes how barbaric life was in the late nineteenth century.

Harris, Reverend William S. *Life in a Thousand Worlds*. Cleona, Pa.: G. Holzapfel, 1905. A traveler visits many worlds in the solar system, some satirizing earth, others proposing solutions for earth's problems. A composite, ideal society contains compulsory work, private but government-regulated enterprise, a locally autonomous political system, an advanced technology, and a central place for the church. An elaborate code of social mores is instituted by law. Strict adherence is required.

Hatfield, Frank [pseud.]. *The Realm of Light*. Boston: Reid Publishing Co., 1908. The government, run by a president elected for life, paternally owns and rules this simple African community. All equally share wealth; however, there are three classes of citizens—laborers, supervisors, and scientists and spiritual leaders. The highest value is the promotion of the general welfare. Everyone has a number.

Hatfield, Richard. *Geyserland: Empiricisms in Social Reform*. Washington, D.C.: The Author, 1908. Common ownership of property and government distribution of goods obviates the need for money in this utopia. The state controls production, work, marriage—everything. The good of the race is the criterion for all decisions of state. Selective breeding has provided perfect health and physiology in the inhabitants who are also expected to be altruists.

Henry, Walter O. *Equitania; or, The Land of Equity*. Omaha: No publisher, 1914. There are six classes of citizens in Equitania, a state set up in accordance with the American political system but with a strong emphasis on the separation of church and state. The government controls natural resources and regulates private enterprise; however, it mostly punishes criminals and the indolent. Efficiency in every sphere of living is the highest goal.

Heywood, D. Herbert. *The Twentieth Century, A Prophesy of the Coming Age*. Boston: F. B. Heywood, Publisher, 1890. Mechanical wonders abound in this country where the citizens have a mental perception of the mysteries of nature and the universe. Intensity of activity and concentration satisfy all necessary needs and provide much leisure. All wealth is equally distributed, and all organizations are eschewed in this psychologist's utopia.

Holford, Costello N. *Aristopia*. Boston: Arena Publishing Co., 1895. The story begins with the discovery of America and the settlement of Jamestown; then, it recounts American history as it could have been were it run by enlightened men. All land belongs to the state, which also controls manufacturing. Handsome rewards for invention stimulate technological progress. Few laws are necessary, and free education is provided for all.

[Horner, Jacob W.]. *Military Socialism*. Indianapolis: The Author, 1911. In this militarily organized, socialist state all products of labor belong to the government, which pays everyone in accordance with their rank. Promotion is attained by popular election. The government is run by a council of generals who make laws for every aspect of living. Hard work and chastity are the most important virtues. The author admired Peter the Great.

[House, Edward M.]. *Philip Dru, Administrator: A Story of Tomorrow, 1920–1935.* New York: B. W. Huebsch, 1912. Philip Dru, fabulously talented leader of the American republic, scourges the excessively wealthy capitalists with taxes and prosecution in order to bring about a more equitable distribution of wealth. Economic reforms abound. Equality of opportunity is the goal of the economic order, and the government takes sufficient power to achieve this end. The author owes much to Henry George and Herbert Croly.

Howard, Albert W. *The Milltillionaire.* By M. Auburre Hovorre. No place: No publisher, 1906. A millennium with state hotels, hospitals, elaborately planned cities, aerial ships, electric subways, and free education is provided by a fabulously rich man who owns all the land on earth. Universal charity precludes a need for religion. Love of truth is the highest value. Material welfare is more than adequately provided by seven months of compulsory work from everyone. No deviation is allowed.

Howells, William Dean. *A Traveler from Altruria.* New York: Harper Bros., 1891. Altruria embodies the values of equality and concern for others as it mirrors the contradiction between this ideal and the reality of American society in Howells's time. The ironically minded Altrurian explains how all wealth is equally divided and how each man chooses the kind of work he thinks he can do best. There are no cities in Altruria; the home and the local community are the centers for living. Simplicity, beauty, and Christian charity are extolled.

———. *Through the Eye of the Needle.* New York: Harper Bros., 1907. A sequel to the above book, this novel reemphasizes the impossibility of attaining a well-ordered livable world without disengaging from a ruthless pursuit of wealth and the value of self-interest. Altruism is only possible, maintains the author, when everyone begins to seek the simple beauties of life.

Hutchinson, Alfred. *The Limit of Wealth.* New York: Macmillan Co., 1907. A limit of $10,000 on private wealth is intended to correct two evils: the selfish accumulation of money and the lack of equal opportunity. All surplus wealth is collected by the government to be spent on public employment projects that do not compete with private enterprise. A remarkably foresighted book set in the mid-twentieth century.

[Kirwin, Thomas]. *Reciprocity in the Thirtieth Century: The Coming Cooperative Age.* By William Wonder. New York: Cochrane Publishing Co., 1909. In the year 3079, the people in their collective capacity own everything except personal property, which may not exceed $50,000. Only positive thinking is allowed; no tragedies, evil, scandal, or badness can be the subjects of communication. Electricity is the panacea for progress. Law and politics are minimal.

Lane, Mary E. *Mizora, A Prophesy.* By Princess Vera Zarovitch. New York: G. W. Dillingham & Co., 1889. This federal republic in the center of the earth is dominated by women who have mastered the secrets of nature. Laws are almost unnecessary for these enlightened, reasonable people. Wealth is abundant; there is more than enough for everyone, although selfishness is not permitted. The author admires Francis Bacon.

Leggett, Mortimer D. *A Dream of a Modest Prophet.* Philadelphia: J. B. Lippincott & Co., 1890. Individual reform through character building and religious education obviates the need for law, government, and money in this society. Everyone works together and shares in the return from their labors. Technological accomplishment is a natural byproduct of the power of the human will, which is developed to a high degree. The golden rule reigns in this world of Mars, a thousand years hence.

London, Jack. "Goliah." In *Revolution and Other Essays.* New York: Macmillan Co., 1910. A scientist who has mastered the secret of energy threatens the world into living in peace under socialism. The absence of private property reduces crime and other evils attributed to the capitalist economic system.

Longley, Alcander. *What Is Communism?* St. Louis: No publisher, 1890. Communal living is the ideal of this society in which all work for the common support, and all share alike. All major decisions affecting the general welfare require unanimous consent. The author, who lived in communities for forty years, poses this work as a handbook for the ideal community.

Lull, D. *Celestia.* New York: Reliance Trading Co., 1907. Unlimited agreeableness is the dominant characteristic of this society wherein conscience prevents crime, poverty, and disorder. The government also helps by providing annuities for the poor and free education to everyone. All are indoctrinated in the correct habits of good thinking.

[McCoy, John]. *A Prophetic Romance: Mars to Earth.* By Lord Commissioner. Boston: Arena Publishing Co., 1896. The world government of Mars controls a few large industries and regulates others, but it tries not to take too large a role in the private part of the economy. Education inculcates a love of home and country. The land is fully developed and well ordered with the help of much energy that is spent on science. All live as one family.

McGrady, Thomas. *Beyond the Black Ocean.* Terre Haute, Ind.: Standard Publishing Co., 1901. Written by a Catholic priest from Bellevue, Kentucky, in order to advance the cause of socialism, this book depicts a cooperative commonwealth in which the product of labor is the sole source of wealth. The government tax on land or its rent recalls Henry George's Single Tax. Laziness is the greatest sin.

[Macnie, John]. *The Diothas; or, A Far Look Ahead.* By Ismar Thiusen. New York: G. P. Putnam's Sons, 1883. In this disputed prototype of Edward Bellamy's utopia, law is the instrument for order and happiness. A republican form of government strictly enforces laws upon men who are generally considered weak and depraved. However, all have an opportunity to work and be properly educated. Private property is the rule. Science is important.

Man or Dollar, Which? By a Newspaperman. Chicago: Charles H. Kerr & Co., 1896. Farming is the national occupation in this society, which incorporates the reforms of the Populist party. The Senate is abolished after the revolution, and everyone, except professionals, becomes employees of the government. Economic equality is the prime goal.

Masquerier, Lewis. *Sociology; or, The Reconstruction of Society, Government and Property.* New York: The Author, 1877. In this society, everyone has an inalienable right to the product of his or her labor. The local community is the center of life; it legislates by common consent the few laws necessary for order. No landlords or middlemen are allowed. The church and state are separated in this very close approximation of an ideal Jeffersonian society.

Mendes, Henry Pereira. *Looking Ahead: Twentieth Century Happenings.* London: F. T. Neely, 1899. A book written by a Rabbi to advance the cause of a separate Jewish state as well as an ideal society in which all disputes and social life are regulated by a Board of Pastors, reminiscent of the role of elders in the Jewish community. Education is one of the highest values; government owns all land, and workers participate in the profits of business.

Merrill, Albert Adams. *The Great Awakening.* Boston: George Book Publishing Co., 1899. In this pure democracy, hard work is rewarded and laziness is punished. Sufficient money is equally distributed to all who work, but only personal property is owned. It is a classless society in which everyone is free to pursue his or her own talents or vocation. The race inevitably improves with selective breeding.

Moore, M. Louise. *Al-Modad; or, Life Sciences Beyond the Polar Circumflex.* By An Untrammeled Free Thinker. Shell Bank, Cameron Parish, La.: No Publisher, 1892. A scientific paradise in the Arctic ocean allows each member of this society to be a law unto himself. The state government is nonexistent since everyone possesses the kingdom of God within himself. Prices are determined by the usefulness of a thing, not by its cost of production. Much mechanical invention avoids the need for hard work.

Morison, George Shattuck. *The New Epoch As Developed by the Manufacture of Power.* Boston: Houghton Mifflin Co., 1903. In a series of lectures, this civil engineer predicts a future that will be unalterably changed by the ability of man to manufacture power. Cooperation will gradually replace old reliance on individualism.

Morris, Henry O. *Waiting for the Signal.* Chicago: Schulte Publishing Co., 1897. After the revolt of the proletariat a new constitution incorporating the principles of the Populist party is instituted. Ignatius Donnelly is elected the first president.

Noto, Cosimo. *The Ideal City.* New York: No publisher, 1904. Modeled after the wisdom of Solomon, Jesus, and Marx, this utopia is dedicated to the principles of science and socialism. Health is a matter of great importance in this doctor's work. Much effort is spent in regulating and beautifying the environment. Everyone must engage in visibly productive labor.

Olerich, Henry. *A Cityless and Countryless World: An Outline of Practical Co-Operative Individualism.* Holstein, Iowa: Gilmore & Olerich, 1893. An advanced state of evolution on Mars enables everyone to work. Public warehouses, labor checks, and the common use of land solve the problem of distribution. There is no government because it detracts from self-reliance, a central value in this land. All live as they please. Herbert Spencer is admired.

———. *Modern Paradise.* Omaha: Equality Publishing Co., 1915. A sequel to the above book; however, further emphasis is put upon cooperative living and equality for women. Mass production, visible wealth, and evolution are all praised.

Peck, Bradford. *The World A Department Store.* Boston: Bradford Peck, Publisher, 1900. The cooperative association of America is formed to unite producer and consumer for the sake of efficiency. Money is the incentive for all work and frequent bonuses are the rule. The entire country adopts this plan in which personal health and education are stressed. The author was a successful Maine businessman.

Persinger, Clark Edmund. *Letters From New America; or, An Attempt At Practical Socialism.* Chicago: Charles H. Kerr & Co., 1900. All activities except religion, newspapers, and education are run by the government and a large civil service. A president elected by the people heads the political system. Elaborately planned cities and public health hold an important place. Personal property is allowed.

Peterson, Ephraim. *An Ideal City For An Ideal People.* Independence, Mo.: The Author, 1905. This city is the city of heaven located in Missouri for those who have reached the state of Christian perfection. They are allowed by the theocratic government to hold their possessions in common. The Bible is the fundamental law. Material equality and chastity are the chief values.

Phelps, Corwin. *An Ideal Republic: or, A Way Out of the Fog.* Chicago: W. L. Reynolds, 1896. Economic equality and political democracy are the chief aims of this ideal land. A government department corresponds to each area of business. Production and wages are fixed by the government, and the profits are shared by the people, all of whom are stockholders.

[Phelps, George Hamilton]. *The New Columbia; or, The Re–United States.* By Patrick Quinn Tangent. Findlay, Ohio: New Columbia Publishing Co., 1909. An overriding faith in the democratic process combines with various reforms borrowed from Edward Bellamy, Henry George, and the Populists to produce greater economic equality. The government becomes one large, efficient business replacing the wasteful monopolies. John D. Rockefeller and Thomas A. Edison are praised.

Rehm, Warren S. *The Practical City.* By [Nemo Omen]. Lancaster, Pa.: The Lancaster County Magazine, 1898. The practical city is a combination of Puritan practicality and Greek beauty. Limited to five thousand inhabitants, the city is planned to the last doorknob. Hard work, physical culture, and the practical application of man's mind are extolled. Political democracy allows for universal suffrage. Land speculators are prohibited.

Roberts, Isaac. *Looking Forward.* Philadelphia: Roberts & Co., 1913. A detailed plan for a community modeled after certain English cooperative societies, including Rochedale. All share equally. Christianity provides the necessary values and cooperative spirit. Presented in the form of a series of lectures.

Rogers, Bessie Story. *As It May Be; A Story of the Future.* Boston: Richard G. Badger, The Gorham Press, 1905. A land in which the innocence of children is preserved throughout life. Science has conquered environmental problems including human disease. Universal kindness makes crime an anachronism. The story takes place in the year 2905. Thought transference is the primary means of communication.

Rosewater, Frank. *'96: A Romance of Utopia.* Omaha: Utopia Publishing Co., 1894. In this campaign document for the Free Labor Party in the election of 1896, the author creates an ideal state whose government is composed of the representatives of each industry. These, in turn, are elected by the workers. This single, efficient employer brings about an equitable distribution of wealth. Only personal property is owned.

―――. *The Making of a Millenium.* Omaha: Century Publishing Co., 1908. A continuation of Rosewater's previous utopia, this book advocates a system close to socialism called Centrism. Here, money is based on either trade or jobs and used exclusively by consumers. The system avoids all taint of capitalism such as interest, banks, high finance, and so forth.

Salisbury, Henry Bernard. *The Birth of Freedom; A Socialist Novel.* New York: Humbolt Publishing Co., 1890. All signs of capitalism are expunged from this socialist state in which labor certificates replace money, and all work for the government. Inventions abound. New York City is landscaped with broad avenues, trees, flowers, and parks. Originally written for the Nationalist magazine.

Schindler, Solomon. *Young West.* Boston: Arena Publishing Co., 1894. A sequel to Edward Bellamy's work in which Julian West carries on as president of the new republic. Bellamy's industrial plan is kept. There are a few innovations, including hypnotism to cure bellicose spirits, medical and sex education for all, a universal language, and restricted immigration.

Schuette, H. George. *Athonia; or, The Original Four Hundred.* Manitowoc, Wisc.: Lakeside Co., 1911. Equality is satirized in Athonia, a Greek colony, where it is thought that working for the public good is too weak an incentive for doing one's best. Self-interest and fair play are the most important values in this community. Physical fitness is required of everyone.

Simpson, William. *The Man From Mars.* San Francisco: Bacon & Co., 1891. Human sympathy and reason combine to provide beauty and equality in this single-tax state. Labor is evaluated and paid according to skill, strength, and activity. Only the most honorable and rational citizens are allowed in public office. Rural living, small businesses, control of environment, and selective breeding are emphasized.

Smith, Titus. *Altruria*. New York: Altruria Publishing Co., 1895. A cooperative community in which Christian love is the most imporant value. All work for each other, but he who does not work does not eat. Farming is the major occupation, yet people live in town, having the advantages of both. Machines do most of the work.

Spaulding, Wayland. *When Theodore Is King*. By Viter Strikeshoulder. New York: Chauncey Holt, 1909. An ideal society, set in Rome, is built around the reforms advocated by Theodore Roosevelt and Samuel Gompers. Wealth and wages are limited for everyone. The surplus is channeled into welfare and public improvement projects. Legislation deals with the problems of child labor, tariffs, stock manipulation, alcoholism, and leisure time. In the end, Theodore is made king in the manner of August Caesar.

Steere, C. A. *When Things Were Done*. Chicago: Charles H. Kerr & Co., 1908. In a land called Altruria, socialism reigns. Agriculture and cooperatives have prime importance in this simple society. The good of the common weal is the criterion for all laws. Political corruption is severely punished. Invention and mechanical wonders abound.

Stone, Mrs. C. H. *One of "Berrian's" Novels*. New York: Welch, Fracker & Co., 1890. An ideal society that presumes all the features of Edward Bellamy's *Looking Backward* with the addition of a psychic theory, called a "grandly developed Ego," that demands an integration of body and mind. Once developed, the boredom of Bellamy's society will disappear. Believes in hard work, but denounces competition.

Stump, D. L. *From World to World*. Asbury, Mo.: World to World Publishing Co., 1896. The government owns and operates everything. The fundamental principle is to provide for all the people's needs. A simple society with few laws and agriculture as its chief occupation. The home is central. All vote. Much invention.

Swift, Morrison I. *A League of Justice; or, Is It Right to Rob the Robbers?* Boston: Commonwealth Society, 1891. A profit-sharing plan whereby the hard-working laborer is equitably rewarded, and the lazy are treated as sick. Education is the prime instrument of social reform.

———. *The Monarch Billionaire*. New York: J. S. Ogilvie Publishing

Co., 1903. A billionaire takes control of the earth and organizes its resources to eliminate destructive competitions and create a world fraternity of capitalists who bring the earth and all its peoples to prodigious riches.

Sullivan, J. W. "A Modern Cooperative Colony." In *So The World Goes*, pp. 213–44. Chicago: Charles H. Kerr & Co., 1898. A group of dissatisfied city workers forms a cooperative enterprise in the suburbs in which the ideal life is ushered in through the elimination of the middleman and usurious banking practices. Productive labor and a strong independence characterize this colony's inhabitants.

Taylor, William Alexander. *Intermere*. Columbus, Ohio: Twentieth Century Publishing Co., 1901. A pure democracy in which everyone is equal in every way. A single-tax system enables the government to make improvements and maintain a simple country of farms, beautifully designed cities, and small manufactures. Reforms include no lawyers, few laws, no pay for officeholders, no police, no army, no envy, no vanity, no land speculation, and education for all. Electricity is revered.

Thomas, Chauncy. *The Crystal Button; or, The Adventures of Paul Prognosis in the Forty-Ninth Century*. Boston: Houghton Mifflin Co., 1891. Truth and honesty, the basis of this state instill a reverence into its citizens for its few laws. The government owns all land and rents it for use. It also runs the insurance business as well as transportation and communication systems. Wealth and social position are unnecessary in this socially homogeneous country.

Tibbles, T. H., and Beattie, Elia M. *The American Peasant*. Chicago: F. J. Schulte & Co., 1892. A Christian manuscript, which the survivors from the fall of Pompeii took with them, becomes the law of this land in the Arctic. Here, a man is of less importance to himself than he is to the state. Money is plentiful. Written by a leader of the Populist party.

Tincker, Mary Agnes. *San Salvador*. Boston: Houghton Mifflin Co., 1892. This secluded religious community trains its children in righteousness and virtue so that in adulthood few problems arise. Order and subjection to a leader are the rule. A benevolent despot is preferred to majority rule. The discovery of gold keeps them in material comfort.

Trammell, William Douglas. *Ca Ira*. New York: United States Publishing Co., 1874. Syndicalism is the model for this system of cooperative production in which every worker receives the whole value of that which he produces. No one is idle. An internationale regulates all production and distribution within an industry. The object is to destroy arbitrary power over the workers through a wage system

[Van Deusen, Alonzo]. *Rational Communism: The Present and Future Republic of North America.* By A Capitalist. New York: Social Science Publishing Co., 1885. The federal government manages all enterprises of a public nature through a warehouse system of distribution. This land, dedicated to the principle of unlimited effort, is elaborately and attractively planned for the comfort of its citizens. There are few laws, and the only punishment for violating them is expulsion from the land. Education is highly valued.

Veiby, John. *The Utopian Way.* South Bend, Ind.: No publisher, 1917. In this land, that which works is good. Individuals, the basic unit of society, are allowed to pursue their diverse ends and wishes. Although democracy and equality are valued, a natural aristocracy possesses all powers of rule. Middlemen are denounced.

Welcome, S. Byron. *From Earth's Center: A Polar Gateway Message.* Chicago: Charles H. Kerr & Co., 1894. The government of Centralia, a land in earth's center, relies upon the single tax to run all public business. However, autonomous local governments have the most power. Everyone is employed. Electricity is revered.

Wheeler, David H. *Our Industrial Utopia and Its Unhappy Citizens.* Chicago: A. C. McClurg & Co., 1895. The basic law of this state is that by having everyone pursue his or her own interests, the good of all is ensured. Pure competition is advocated. Supply and demand determine price. All workers are potential capitalists. The industrial virtues are stressed. The author praises Thomas More.

Woodridge, C. W. *Perfecting the Earth.* Cleveland: Utopia Publishing Co., 1902. The army of the unemployed is hired by the government to undertake vast reclamation projects in the West. They life in the utopian city of Ft. Goodwill where, when they are not harnessing the powers of nature, they live in cultured comfort. Education is provided for the children and social security for the aged. The army enlarges until everyone works for the government and the landscape looks like a beautiful garden.

[Worley, F. U.]. *Three Thousand Dollars A Year: Moving Forward; or, How We Got There.* Washington, D.C.: J. P. Wright, 1890. Told in the form of a history of the United States until the year 2000. The power of the federal government increases steadily until, in its most advanced stage, it operates all industry, provides free education and a welfare program, and subsidizes the arts. All places for living are well planned and healthy.

SECONDARY SOURCES

Adkins, N. F. "An Early American Utopian Fiction," *Colophon* n.s. 1 (Summer 1935), pp. 123–32.
Arms, George. "The Literary Background of Howell's Social Criticism," *American Literature* 14 (November 1942), pp. 260–76.
Bailey, J. O. *Pilgrims Through Space and Time: Trends and Patterns in Scientific and Utopian Fiction.* New York: Argus Books, Inc., 1947.
Becker, Carl L. *The Heavenly City of the Eighteenth-Century Philosophers.* New Haven: Yale University Press, 1932.
Bellamy, Edward. "Progress of Nationalism in the United States," *North American Review* 154 (May 1892), pp. 742–52.
Bentley, Wilder. *The Communication of Utopian Thought: Its History, Forms, and Use.* San Francisco: San Francisco State College Bookstore, 1959.
Berthoff, Rowland. "The American Social Order: A Conservative Hypothesis," *The American Historical Review* 65 (April 1960), pp. 495–514.
Bleiler, Everett F. *A Checklist of Fantastic Literature.* Chicago: Shasta Publishers, 1948.
Bowman, Sylvia E. *Edward Bellamy Abroad.* New York: Twayne Publishers, 1962.
Bredvold, Louis I. *The Brave New World of the Enlightenment.* Ann Arbor: The University of Michigan Press, 1961.
Bury, J. B. *The Idea of Progress.* New York: Dover Publications, 1932.
Crane, Verner W. "A Lost Utopia of the First American Frontier," *Sewanee Review* 27 (January 1919), pp. 48–61.
Davies, Wallace Evans. "A Collective Experiment Down East: Bradford Peck and the Cooperative Association of America," *The New England Quarterly* 20 (December 1947), pp. 471–91.
Davis, J. C. *Utopia and the Ideal Society: A Study of English Utopian Writing: 1516–1700.* New York: Cambridge University Press, 1981.
Dewey, John. "A Great American Prophet," *Common Sense* 3 (April 1934), pp. 6–7.
Dombrowski, James. *The Early Days of Christian Socialism in America.* New York: Columbia University Press, 1936.

Dorfman, Joseph. *The Economic Mind in American Civilization.* Vol. 3. New York: Viking Press, 1949.
Egbert, Donald, and Persons, Stow. *Socialism and American Life.* 2 vols. Princeton: Princeton University Press, 1952.
Engles, Frederick. *Socialism, Utopian and Scientific.* Translated by Edward Aveling. New York: New York Labor News Co., 1901.
Erasmus, Charles J. *In Search of the Common Good: Utopian Experiments, Past and Future.* New York: Free Press, 1977.
Fine, Sidney. *Laissez-Faire and the General Welfare State.* Ann Arbor: University of Michigan Press, 1956.
Flory, Claude. *Economic Criticism in American Fiction: 1792–1900.* Philadelphia: University of Pennsylvania Press, 1936.
Forbes, Allyn B. "Literary Quest for Utopia, 1880–1900," *Social Forces* 6 (December 1927) pp. 179–89.
Gallagher, Buell G. *A Preface to the Study of Utopias.* Yellow Springs, Ohio: The Antioch Press, 1960.
George, Henry. *Progress and Poverty.* New York: Robert Schalkenbach Foundation, 1940.
Gerber, Richard. *Utopian Fantasy.* London: Routledge & Keegan Paul, Ltd., 1955.
Hansot, Elisabeth. *Perfection and Progress: Two Modes of Utopian Thought.* Cambridge, Mass.: M.I.T. Press, 1974.
Hartz, Louis. *The Liberal Tradition in America.* New York: Harcourt, Brace & Co., 1955.
Hays, Samuel P. *The Response to Industrialism: 1885–1914.* Chicago: University of Chicago Press, 1957.
Hertzler, Joyce O. *The History of Utopian Thought.* New York: Macmillan Co., 1926.
Hicks, John D. *The Populist Revolt.* Minneapolis: University of Minnesota Press, 1931.
Hofstadter, Richard. *Social Darwinism in American Thought.* Rev. ed. Boston: Beacon Press, 1955.
Hopkins, Charles H. *The Rise of the Social Gospel in American Protestantism: 1865–1915.* New Haven: Yale University Press, 1940.
Hough, Robert L. *The Quiet Rebel: William Dean Howells As Social Commentator.* Lincoln: University of Nebraska Press, 1959.
Kasson, John F. *Civilizing the Machine: Technology and Republican Values in America; 1776–1900.* New York: Grossman, 1976.
Kazin, Alfred. *On Native Grounds.* New York: Doubleday & Co., 1956.
Keniston, Kenneth. "Alienation and the Decline of Utopia," *The American Scholar* 29 (Spring 1960), pp. 161–201.
Kirk, Clara M. *W. D. Howells, Traveler from Altruria: 1889–1894.* New Brunswick, N.J.: Rutgers University Press, 1962.

Lasky, Melvin J. *Utopia and Revolution.* Chicago: University of Chicago Press, 1976.

Lewis, Arthur Orcutt, Jr. Introductions to *Utopian Literature*, the Arno Press Collection. New York: Arno Press, 1971.

Library of Congress, Division of Bibliography. "List of References on Utopias," September 19, 1922; and Supplements, November 22, 1926, April 27, 1938, and January 31, 1940 (typewritten).

Lippman, Walter. "The White Passion," *The New Republic* 8 (October 23, 1916), pp. 293–95.

McCloskey, Robert G. *American Conservatism in the Age of Enterprise: 1865–1910.* Cambridge: Harvard University Press, 1951.

McNaught, Kenneth. "American Progressives and the Great Society," *The Journal of American History* 53 (December 1966) pp. 504–20.

Mannheim, Karl. *Ideology and Utopia.* Translated with an introduction by Louis Wirth and Edward Shils. New York: Harcourt, Brace & Co., 1936.

Manuel, Frank (ed.). *Utopias and Utopian Thought.* Boston: Houghton Mifflin Co., 1965.

Manuel, Frank E., and Manuel, Fritzie P. *Utopian Thought in the Western World.* Cambridge, Mass.: The Belknap Press, 1979.

Martin, Jay. "Paradise Regained." In *Harvests of Change, American Literature 1865–1914.* Englewood Cliffs, N.J.: Prentice-Hall, 1967, pp. 202–39.

Masso, Gildo. *Education in Utopias.* New York: Bureau of Publications, Teacher's College, Columbia University, 1927.

May, Henry F. *The End of American Innocence.* New York: Alfred A. Knopf, 1959.

Molnar, Thomas. *Utopia, The Perennial Heresy.* New York: Sheed & Ward, 1967.

More, Sir Thomas. *Utopia with the Dialogue of Comfort.* London: J. M. Dent & Sons, Ltd., 1942.

Morgan, Arthur E. *Nowhere Was Somewhere.* Chapel Hill: University of North Carolina Press, 1946.

Morgan, Howard W., ed. *The Gilded Age, A Reappraisal.* Syracuse, N.Y.: Syracuse University Press, 1963.

Mumford, Lewis. *Values for Survival.* New York: Harcourt, Brace & Co., 1946.

Negley, Glenn, and Patrick, J. Max. *The Quest for Utopia.* New York: Henry Schuman, 1952.

Negley, Glenn. *Utopian Literature, A Bibliography.* Lawrence, Kans.: Regents Press of Kansas, 1977.

Niebuhr, H. Richard. *The Kingdom of God in America.* New York: Harper & Bros., 1937.

Parrington, Vernon Louis, Jr. *American Dreams: A Study of American Utopias*. Providence: Brown University Press, 1947.
Pfaelzer, Jean. "American Utopian Fiction 1888–1896: The Political Origins of Form," *Minnesota Review*, n.s. 6 (Spring 1976), pp. 114–17.
Polak, Fredrik L. *The Image of the Future*. Translated by Elsie Boulding. 2 vols. New York: Oceana Publications, 1961.
Pratter, Frederick Earl. "The Uses of Utopia: An Analysis of American Speculative Fiction: 1880–1960." Ph.D. dissertation, University of Iowa, 1973.
Quint, Howard H. *The Forging of American Socialism: Origins of the Modern Movement*. Columbia, S.C.: University of South Carolina Press, 1953.
Ransom, Ellene. "Utopus Discovers America; or, Critical Realism in the American Utopian Novel: 1798–1900." Ph.D. dissertation, Vanderbilt University, 1947.
Rhodes, Harold V. *Utopia in American Political Thought*. Tucson, Ariz.: University of Arizona Press, 1967.
Rideout, Walter B. *The Radical Novel in America*. Cambridge: Harvard University Press, 1956.
Roemer, Kenneth, ed. *America As Utopia*. New York: Burt Franklin & Co., 1981.
Roemer, Kenneth M. *The Obsolete Necessity: America in Utopian Writings, 1888–1900*. Kent, Ohio: Kent State University Press, 1976.
Rose, Lisle A. "A Bibliographical Survey of Economic and Political Writings, 1865–1900," *American Literature* 15 (January 1944), pp. 381–410.
――――. Supplements to the above. 1 (April 28, 1944) and 2 (October 1, 1944), Houghton, Mich.; 3 (October 5, 1949) and 4 (1949–1951), Urbana, Ill. (1, 2, and 3, mimeographed; 4, handwritten notes.)
Russell, Francis T. *Touring Utopia, the Realm of Constructive Humanism*. New York: Dial Press, Inc., 1932.
Sadler, Elizabeth. "One Book's Influence: Edward Bellamy's *Looking Backward*," *The New England Quarterly* 17 (December 1944), pp. 531–55.
Sanford, Charles. *The Quest for Paradise*. Urbana: University of Illinois Press, 1961.
Sargent, Lyman T. "Authority and Utopia: Utopianism in Political Thought," *Polify* 14 (Summer 1982) pp. 565–84.
――――. *British and American Utopian Literature: 1516–1975*. An Annotated Bibliography. Boston: G. K. Hall, 1979.
Segal, Howard P. "American Visions of Technological Utopia, 1883–1933," *Markham Review* 7 (Summer 1978), pp. 65–76.

Shurter, Robert L. "The Utopian Novel in America, 1865–1900." Ph.D. dissertation, Western Reserve University, 1936.

Smith, Godwin. "Prophets of Unrest," *The Forum* 9 (August 1890), pp. 599–614.

Stupple, A. James. "Utopian Humanism in America, 1888–1900." Ph.D. dissertation, Northwestern University, 1971.

Taylor, Walter Fuller. *The Economic Novel in America*. Chapel Hill: University of North Carolina Press, 1942.

Thal-Larsen, Margaret W. "Political and Economic Ideas in American Utopian Fiction: 1868–1914." Ph.D. dissertation, University of California, 1941.

Tyler, Alice F. *Freedom's Ferment*. Minneapolis: University of Minnesota Press, 1944.

Walker, Robert H. *The Poet and the Gilded Age*. Philadelphia: University of Pennsylvania Press, 1963.

Walsh, Chad. *From Utopia to Nightmare*. New York: Harper & Row, 1962.

Wyllie, Irving. *The Self-Made Man in America*. New Brunswick, N.J.: Rutgers University Press, 1954.

Index

Adams, Frederick U., 115-16
Albertson, Ralph, 8, 26, 34, 104-105, 155
Alcoholism, 54, 69
Alexander, James B., 32, 110, 143, 149, 162
Allen, Henry Francis, 22, 28, 31
Armour, J. P., 22, 98, 99

Bachelder, John, 11, 32, 95-97, 156
Bartlett, J.M.D., 25, 108, 157, 163
Bassett, Edward B., 104
Bellamy, Edward, 7, 8-9, 11, 12, 14, 19, 50, 55, 57, 121-23, 142-43, 149, 161, 171, 173, 177
Bible, 30, 31; language of, 49, 64, 105, 147, 154. *See also* Christianity; Religion
Bird, Arthur, 97
Bishop, William, 11, 12, 66, 70, 71, 80, 105, 149, 151
Bond, Daniel, 32, 119
Brant, John Ira, 122, 156
Brinsmade, Herman H., 112
Brook Farm, 6
Brooks, Byron Alden, 11, 29, 48, 55, 75, 113, 143, 153, 154, 156

Call, Henry L., 30, 48, 50, 112, 114, 144, 149
Caryl, Charles W., 27, 56, 57, 60, 107, 109
Chambless, Edgar, 13, 32, 66, 76, 130-31
Chapman, Richard, 13, 127-29
Charity, 50, 52, 55, 123
Chavannes, Albert, 8, 35, 80, 116-17, 161
Child, William Stanley, 33, 49, 52, 57, 65-66, 118, 150
Christianity, 19, 24-27, 49, 80, 104-105, 110; anti-Christian values, 76; doctrine, 25, 31; duty, 147; ethics, 26, 113; love, 23, 26, 30, 35, 53, 100, 141, 153, 172; morality, 48-49; Sermon on the Mount, 27; service, 63; virtues, 175. *See also* Bible; Charity; Religion
City, 41, 65, 129-33
Cole, Cyrus, 123, 143, 150, 153, 157-58
Collens, Thomas, 104
Communism, 34, 105. *See also* Engles; Marx
Cooley, Winnifred H., 81, 118
Cowen, James, 25, 55, 58, 61,

Index

68, 100-102, 149, 154, 156, 161
Cridge, Alfred Denton, 109, 110
Crime, 54, 66-67. *See also* Environment; Problems
Crocker, Samuel, 61, 118

Dague, Robert A., 28, 29, 49-50, 56, 73, 124
Darwin, Charles, 7, 31, 94, 126, 159. *See also* Darwinism; Evolution
Darwinism, 19, 148, 172. *See also* Evolution
Debs, Eugene V., 32, 81
Declaration of Independence, 8, 142, 172
Deism, 23-24. *See also* Enlightenment
Democracy, 42, 59, 61. *See also* Problems, political
Devinne, Paul, 9, 22, 48, 62, 68, 71, 72, 122, 149, 158
Donnelly, Ignatius, 11, 50, 65, 67, 70, 118-19
Dowding, Henry W., 26, 67, 68, 70, 78, 111, 157
Dystopia, 4, 14

Edson, Milan C., 13, 27, 65, 66, 107-108, 156
Education, 22, 74-77
Efficiency, 56-58, 107
Emerson, Ralph Waldo, 8, 23, 94, 154, 159, 173
Engels, Friedrich, 3, 32. *See also* Communism; Marx
Enlightenment philosophy, 20-24, 75, 97, 99, 102, 171-72. *See also* Natural Rights philosophy
Environment, 63-69, 75, 111, 114, 125, 130-33

Equality: equal opportunity, 52, 53, 59, 134; principle of, 30, 60, 63, 74, 109-11, 115, 132, 141, 142-46, 174; social, 144-45
Everett, Henry L., 108
Evil: doctrine of man's fall, 27; problem of, 22; selfishness and greed, 52, 83
Evolution, 19, 27-31, 94, 173. *See also* Darwin, Darwinism

Fishbough, William, 21, 57, 108
Fiske, Amos K., 11, 97
Fitzpatrick, Ernest Hugh, 115
Forbush, Zebina, 33-34, 62, 79, 124, 158, 160, 162, 163
Fourier, Charles, 3, 8, 103, 104, 106, 177
Franklin, Benjamin, 8, 56, 94, 141
Free Enterprise, 58
Frisbie, Henry S., 26, 32, 48, 81
Fry, Lena J., 67, 107, 108
Fuller, Alverado M., 115

Galloway, James M., 123
Geissler, Ludwig A., 121
George, Henry, 7, 8, 9, 51, 112, 114, 177
Giles, Fayette S., 75, 80, 100, 158
Gillette, King Camp, 11, 107, 109
Gilman, Nicholas P., 7
Goodness, of man, 22-23, 36, 159
Griffin, C. S., 33, 121
Grimshaw, Robert, 106
Grigsby, Alcanoan O., 27, 70, 157
Gronlund, Laurence, 8, 123

Hale, Edward Everett, 11, 64, 79, 125, 162, 171
Harben, William, 130-31
Harris, William S., 12, 68, 78, 115
Hatfield, Frank, 127-29
Hatfield, Richard, 12, 32, 81, 127-29, 164
Health, 67-68, 98. *See also* Environment
Henry, Walter O., 11, 73, 128
Heywood, D. Herbert, 97, 98, 158
Holford, Costello N., 26, 81, 113, 149
Horner, Jacob N., 127
House, Edward M., 11, 25, 30, 34, 51, 54, 56, 59, 61, 77, 115, 148, 150
Howard, Albert W., 68, 78, 128
Howells, William Dean, 8, 11, 123
Human nature, 34, 60, 74; goodness of, 100
Hutchinson, Alfred, 25, 33, 53, 55, 63, 117, 145, 149, 160-61
Huxley, Aldous, 14
Huxley, Thomas, 27

Individualism, 28, 29, 32, 34, 59, 94-95, 98-102, 141, 145-46, 156, 159-65, 175; self-help, 55

Jefferson, Thomas, 8

Kirwin, Thomas, 22, 110, 147-48, 163

Labor, 54-59; theory of value, 106
Laissez-faire capitalism, 29, 33, 36, 59, 117, 154

Lane, Mary E., 23, 57, 67, 71, 81, 98, 99, 150
Law, 112; respect for, 115-16
Leggett, Mortimer D., 11, 21, 23, 30, 100-102, 153
Leisure, lack of, 54
Lippman, Walter, 13
London, Jack, 11, 49, 57, 124, 161
Longley, Alcander, 8, 11, 105
Love, 104
Lull, D., 100

McCoy, John, 118
McGrady, Thomas, 12, 123
Macnie, John, 8, 115
Mannheim, Karl, 4
Man or Dollar, Which?, 7, 33, 50, 118
Manuel, Frank, 4
Marx, Karl, 110
Marxism, 3, 31, 32, 103
Masquerier, Lewis, 8, 11, 104
Mendes, Henry Pereira, 12, 127, 128
Merrill, Albert Adams, 28, 33, 51, 54, 60, 74, 77, 117, 150
Middle class, 52
Middle man, 57
Monopoly, 42, 51, 116, 120
Moore, M. Louise, 101
Morality, 152-56; education of, 76
Morison, George Shattuck, 12, 106
Morris, Henry O., 118
Mumford, Lewis, 14

Natural Rights philosophy, 8, 15; natural law, 64
Niebuhr, Richard, 5
Noto, Cosimo, 23, 30, 32, 68, 77

Olerich, Henry, 12, 13, 28, 59, 60, 66, 110, 150
Orwell, George, 14
Owen, Robert, 3, 8, 103, 106, 176-77

Peck, Bradford, 48, 65, 81, 82, 108, 148
Persinger, Clark Edmund, 34, 124, 151, 156
Peterson, Ephraim, 80, 105, 151, 155
Phelps, Corwin, 6, 106
Phelps, George Hamilton, 21, 25, 64, 122, 156
Plutocracy, 28, 33, 42
Politics, problems of, 59-63
Populism, 117-20, 177; populists, 7, 177
Poverty, 52, 63
Problems described by utopian authors: education, 74-77; environment, 63-69; labor, 54-59; politics, 59-63; religion, 77-86; social, 69-73; summary of, 83-86; table of, 43-47; wealth, 42-53
Progress, idea of, 28, 156-59. See also Enlightenment
Protestant ethic, 141-42, 146, 151, 165, 174. See also Christianity; Religion
Public Works projects, 53
Puritans, 5, 24, 25, 131, 141

Rehm, Warren S., 13, 66, 130-32
Religion, 77-86; churches, 79-80; clergy, 79-80; sectarianism, 78, 108
Roberts, Isaac, 106
Roemer, Kenneth M., 15 n.5
Rogers, Bessie Story, 48, 98

Rosewater, Frank, 48, 50, 52, 79, 122

St. Simon, Claude-Henri, 3, 8, 177
Salisbury, Henry Bernard, 124
Schindler, Solomon, 8, 11, 68, 122, 149
Schuette, H. George, 29, 130-32
Science, 24, 30, 114; scientific utopia, 97-99
Simpson, William, 23-24, 51, 60, 64-65, 79, 150
Smith, Adam, 134
Smith, Titus, 105
Social classes, 145, 175
Social Gospel movement, 24, 78, 141, 172, 178
Socialism, 31-36, 120-21, 123-26, 173, 177
Spaulding, Wayland, 115, 116
Spencer, Herbert, 7-8, 27, 29, 31, 33, 59, 110, 126, 159, 173, 177
Steere, C. A., 52, 124, 144-45
Stone, C. H., 121
Stump, D. L., 110-11
Sullivan, J. W., 104
Swift, Morrison I., 106

Taxes, 53
Taylor, William Alexander, 48, 54, 76
Temperance, 69. See also Alcoholism
Thomas, Chauncy, 115
Tibbles, T. H., and Beattie, Elia M., 11, 70, 148
Tincker, Mary Agnes, 105-106
Tolstoi, Leo Nikolai, 8
Totalitarianism, 127-29. See also Plutocracy

Index   209

Trammell, William Douglas, 106

Unemployment, 55
Unions, 58
Utopian writings: annual frequency, 10; background of authors, 11-12; causes in late nineteenth-century America, 6-9; composite picture, 176; decline, 13; definition, 4, 15; foreign influences, 7-8; geographical distribution, 10-11; history of in America, 5-6; intellectual heritage, 8-9; motivation for writing, 12-13; novel, 19-20, 178; types of: cooperative, 102-11; ideal city, 129-33; individualist, 94-102; legal, 111-20; socialist, 120-26; totalitarian, 126-29; values, 141-42

Van Deusen, Alonzo, 12, 49, 57, 74, 124

Veiby, John, 12, 57, 69, 73, 78, 130-32

Wealth, 42-53, 149, 165; common property, 110; distribution of, 94, 101, 105, 113, 115, 119, 121, 125, 174; evils of, 42, 48, 49; imbalance of, 41; money supply, 52
Welcome, Byron, 22, 73, 113-14, 153
Wheeler, David H., 11, 28, 29, 34, 95-97, 154, 160, 163
Women, 54; role of, 69-72; marriage and divorce, 72; suffrage, 73
Woodridge, C. W., 29, 48, 82, 130, 132-33, 155, 162
Work: value of, 54, 107-108, 125, 146-52; working man, 55; work week, 55
Worley, F. U., 21, 60, 108, 109

About the Author

CHARLES J. ROONEY, JR., is Professor and Chairman of the English Department at Felician College, Lodi, New Jersey. He is the author of *Post-Civil War, Pre-Looking Backward Utopia: 1865-87* and a contributor to *America as Utopia* and the journal *American Literature*.